PEI MEI'S Chinese Cook Book

培梅食譜

傅培梅 著

CONTENTS

本 書 要 目

FOREWORD

Miss Fu Pei-Mei, Taiwan's celebrated television chef, has had about fifteen years' experience in demonstrating the art of Chinese cookery. Her association with ladies of many other countries, who have shown interest in her art, has encouraged her to present this most comprehensive book in English and Chinese.

She has skillfully compiled and up-dated recipes for more than one hundred traditional dishes which will appeal to both western and eastern tastes. Hopefully, the ease with which these dishes can be prepared will increase interest in Oriental cuisine and encourage further research by young and old cooks alike.

I congratulate Miss Fu and trust that her book will further advance the friendship and interest between the Chinese and American people.

Dorothy D McConaughy

The American Embassy to Republic of China
Mrs. W. P. McConaughy
（美國駐華大使馬康衛夫人序言）

1

前　言

　　人民是國家的根本，根本健全之後，國家始能富强，飲食是民生的基礎，基礎鞏固了，民族纔能强大；所以　國父在民生主義中提出食衣住行爲民生四大需要，而「食」卻爲四要之首，一日三餐直接關係人類的身心健康，間接影響個人的精神情緒，因此「食」在諸多人生要素中實已佔據特殊而最重要的地位。我國有五千年的悠久歷史，各方面之文化均優於其他各國，在食的方面早於春秋時代卽已知道如何運用刀法，講求火工，使各種食物發揮其最高效能達到爽心快口，健壯體魄的目的。烹飪原不是一件複雜的工作（只要將每種生的食物變成熟而能食卽是）但隨着時代進步人類口體之需也日漸提高，不但希望每一道菜色香味俱佳更要求符合經濟衛生與營養之條件。因此烹飪一事已形成一種專門學術，值得多加研究與創作。

　　一個初學烹飪者，首先必需明瞭正確之方法，再勤加實習由經驗中獲取心得，從失敗中探求成功之途。本人基於對烹飪之愛好，早在少女時期卽已下廚參與治饌工作，來臺後更爲興趣所驅曾先後從不同省藉之名廚多人（包括京、川、閩、粤、湘、浙等）學習中國烹飪數年並悉心鑽研探究頗有所得，旋於民國四十四年經友人催促而設班，公開將多年之所學所知與各種心得經驗，全部教授予同好此道前來就學之仕女們，十五年來數以千計，舉凡結業於本班者，莫不對烹飪有高度興趣與自信，均可做出理想之菜點以增進家庭幸福。民國五十二年臺灣電視開播後本人卽應邀擔任烹飪節目之製作兼主持事宜，至今已歷六年有餘，每於節目中示範或講解時本人莫不竭盡所能詳細述說個中要訣，務使觀衆明瞭，因此無數觀衆表示受益，本人也深感自慰。數年來曾有許多中外仕女希望購買本人之講義或食譜以便參照製做；尤其卽將出國或有親友在國外者更感迫切需要，許多在華外僑也一再催促希望獲得用英文所撰寫而極正確純粹之中菜食譜，在各方盛情催促下，更爲使留居國外之華僑得以重嘗祖國佳餚起見，終於利用授課之餘暇着手整理與編寫這本食譜。

　　在這本書中將中國菜用東南西北四大部門劃分編輯，東部以上海爲中心有江蘇浙江兩省菜式，南部包括福建廣東，西部指湖南與四川菜，北部卽以京菜爲主，當然若以中國地域之廣，菜式種類之繁多與每省每地所別具之特殊風味，而做如此劃分似嫌

2

太過攏統，但為使外國讀者能藉此對中國地域有所辨別並對各種菜式易做概念起見，除此別無善策。又本書限於篇幅每一地區之菜式僅選出二十五種，而該二十五種並非完全屬於大菜，亦非每一種均富特別風味或俱代表性者，但由整體而言其已保存着當地應有之風格，又以兼顧國外採購材料之困難及缺乏各種配料等情形而盡力挑選出屬於一般性之菜式。至於調味方面本人曾謹慎處理務求每一菜一湯均能突出而純正，保持其原來風味，唯本人希望讀者能注意調味料之份量，可不必硬性效仿，因本人所用之各種調味料與國外各地之品種成分或不相同，而口味之輕重又是因人而異，故其分量之多少可酌量增減調配之。

按中國菜除普通家常小吃菜與人口少時不用大型盤碗盛裝之外，通常宴客菜點均以一桌（十至十二人）為單位，故此書中每菜所列之材料分量也均為一大盤或一大碗為標準，每一桌正式之宴客菜數量均有十二至十四道之多（即冷盤四種，大菜四道，熱炒菜四道，點心兩種），但也可減少為八道（即大拼盤一個，大菜四道，熱炒菜兩種，點心一種）如在最後，加上一份炒飯或炒麵湯麵之類也無不可，為了避免烹飪者臨時過度忙碌也可將某些適宜冷吃或慢火功之菜點預先準備妥當或烹煮到某種程度放置，又按中國正式宴會所列出之各菜每一種不但材料不可重複，菜之色，與味也應避免相同，而烹飪方法更不得採取同樣手法，例如：蒸、炸、燴、燒、溜、炒、煎、爆等只能各用一次（在一種菜），但如係普通家常便餐或隨意小吃，則不必嚴守此則了。

中國烹飪素以刀工、火工見長，刀工（俗稱切菜）之精拙優劣不但直接關係菜之色與味，也將影響菜之觀瞻與火工之控制，而火工（又稱為火候）是中國烹飪中最難處理卻也是最重要的一項，凡一道菜之成功與否幾乎是全部決定在烹飪之火候如何，而該火候又多半是需憑烹調者之經驗去體會和加以熟練之運用，這是初學中國烹飪者最感到困惑之一點，卻正是中國烹飪藝術價值之所在。

本人研究中國烹飪將近廿年雖亦自信已能粗通此術，略俱經驗，但仍感學無止境，日新又新，尤以烹飪之道形形色色深奧無比，一切均待精益求精，當此中國傳統文化之烹飪術享譽全球備受讚賞之際，本人謹以此書獻給讀者，並願互事研究，共相推行，以期中國烹飪更得發揚宏遠，造福大眾。

著　者

中華民國五十八年四月　　於臺北

3

ABOUT THE AUTHOR

Miss Fu Pei-Mei (Mrs. S. K. Chen) is a Professional Chinese Cook with a most distinguished background. Born in Shantung, raised in Dairen Manchuria where she attended Japanese schools for girls. She completed her middle school and went to Peiping for futher study of her particular interest. Miss Fu has been interested in cooking since childhood. When she was a young girl she studied for several years with many famous cooks from all provinces of China. Through much practice, she has now perfected their recipes to keep pace with modern tastes.

About 15 years ago she was encouraged by friends to teach in her home. When Television was introduced to Taiwan (October 1963) she began classes (The Chinese Cooking Program) which continues to this day. Miss Fu has judged experienced chefs in consideration for jobs abroad and aboard ships. She was also sought by the Free Chinese Government to improve their Military Messes. Invitations from Japan and Hongkong to demonstrate Chinese Cuisine have been frequent and she has, on Taiwan, conducted taped radio programs to explain and popularize Chinese dishes.

Miss Fu has taught at the Chinese American Cultural and Recreational Association and Foreign Affairs Service Department thereby reaching hundreds of ladies from all lands who eagerly sought her classes. It is with their interest and encouragement that she has offered this completely authentic Chinese cookbook.

Introduction

Chinese cooking is an ancient art which dates from the Emperor Fu Hsi who introduced agricultural procedures and domestication of animals about 5,-000 years ago. With the development of culture and religion this art was absorbed into the Chinese social order. The two dominant philosophies of China, Taoism and Confusianism, soon prescribed kitchen customs and table etiquette. Chinese scholars, and indeed their leader Confucious, were gourmands who urged others to perfect this art, all the time encouraging and criticizing with wisdom.

To achieve this perfection we always use fresh, young, tender vegetables and meat. Frozen foods are never used. However, dehydrated vegetables such as mushrooms are often included in our recipes. Food must be washed and sorted carefully then cut in a variety of ways depending upon the use: sliced, chopped, shredded, diced, minced or mashed. We pay careful attention to the seasoning sauces and marinades because through them we develop taste and eliminate undesirable odors or taste. This cutting is done beforehand as the essence of Chinese cookery is tenderness achived through quick cooking. Flavor and color are retained more easily. All must be ready at hand, the seasoning sauces prepared and the proper items marinated. Our principal cooking procedures include cold mix, barbecuing, deep-frying, roasting, sauted dishes, shallow frying, simmering or braising, steaming, (steming) and stir-frying. Timing is important as is the selection of fine materials, proper heating facilities, blending and foremost, the harmonizing of color, taste and aroma. The experienced cook is an artist who uses his knowledge as any artist uses his tools. A Chinese proverb tells us to become a good cook one must first be a good matchmaker who understands harmony and marriage of flavors.

In the Chinese manner we use chopstcks instead of forks. Knives are not set on a Chinese table as all the cutting is done during preparation or before food is brought to the table. Experts with chopsticks, the Chinese use them as an extension of fingers to stir, mix, whip and sort food. They vary in length from 5 to 15 inches and are made from silver, ivory, wood, bamboo or plastic.

Looking at a map of mainland China one understands why each area soon developed its own style of cuisine. Easy transportation was unknown and the provinces made best use of its own products. Several main types evoled which include the famous Peking roast duck from the North, the Szechuan food also known as Honan or western style featuring highly peppered food and camphor-smoked duck. The Foochow and Cantonese style specializes in light tasting dishes often stir-fried to preserve texture and flavor. The eastern area around Shang-hai is noted for its oily food and wonderful special sauces.

One hundred popular recipes are collected in this book to give a cross section of the current trends in taste. These recipes are adaptations of the old, to fit the modern busy household schedule. Most of the ingredients in this cook book are widely available. The selected recipes are grouped into four principal schools:

1. Shanghai (Eastern Chinese style)
2. Canton (Foochow or Southern Chinese style)
3. Szechuan (Honan and western Chinese style)
4. Peking (Northern Chinese style)

Twenty-five recipes are offered in each group. Twenty additional recipes for snack and desserts are included.

As a rule of thumb, the following pointers should be kept in mind in planning a menu: the texture of each dish should be varied, each main ingredient should not appear twice in the same menu, color combination should be attractive, variation in taste of each dish should also be taken into consideration.

Family style meals: Several main dishes are placed in the center of the table for every one to help himself to a little of each. Rice is always served in individual bowls at each place setting.

Sample menu #1 Stewed Beef or Pork with Brown sauce.

    Deep Fry Fish (small whole). Egg with Dried Shrimp.

    Egg Plant with chili sauce. Spinach with Bean curd soup.

Sample menu #2 Spicy Fish Slices.

    Stuffed beancurd. Stir fry string beans.

    Double cooked pork. Tomato with egg soup.

Informal dinner: An informal dinner usually consists of six dishes and one soup. It can be served the same way as family style.

Sample menu #1 Stewed chicken or Duck with brown sauce.
Fish with chili sauce. Pork kidney with mushroom.
Scrambled eggs with shrimp. Mold san-sze soup.
Stir fry pork or beef string with green pepper. Cabbage with cream sauce.

Sample menu #2 Disced chicken with cashew nuts. Steamed fish.
Ma-Po's Beancurd.
Assorted dish with brown sauce.   Sweet and sour spareribs.
Deep fry shrimp balls.   Scallops with corn soup

Formal dinner: In general, the seat at the inner side of the room facing the entrance is for the guest of honor, while the seats on the serving side are for the host and hostess. The guest of honor is always seated facing the host.

A formal Chinese dinner for 10 to 12 people begins with four cold dishes or appetizers, following with four quick sauted dishes, and then four main courses, some times they served six main dishes, soup is always served later and desserts at last.

Sample menu #1

Appetizers (served simultaneously):
1. Wined chicken.   3. Spicy fish slices.
2. Steamed ham with honey.   4. Chicken and cucumber salad.

Four sauted dishes (served one at a time)
1. Shrimp with cashew nut.   3. Saute pork kidney.
2. Chicken with chili sauce.   4. Crab meat with cabbage.

Four main courses (served one at a time):
1. Shark's fin with chichen shreds. 3. Crispy duck home style
2. Stewed prown with tomato sauce.   4. Sweet and Sour whole Fish.

Soup: Assorted meat soup in winter melon.

Dessert (with one sweet soup):
Eight treasure rice pudding.   Sweet louts seeds soup.

Rice (optional, usually everybody is too full to touch it)

Sample menu #2

Appetizers (served simutaneously):

1. Jellied chicken, (or bon bon chicken)
2. Roast pork slices (or spiced pork)
3. Steamed ham (or sweet walnuts)
4. Pork kidney with peppercorn sauce (or chicken and bean sheet salad

Six main dishes (served one at a time):

1. Minced chicken with abalone (or shark's fin in brown sauce)
2. Saute lobster tail in tomato sauce (or saute sliced prown)
3. Cabbage rolls with cream sauce (or 4 kinds of braised vegetable)
4. Beef steak Chinese style (or mold pork in brown sauce)
5. Stewed duck with vegelable (or Roast duck)
6. Sweet sour whole fish (or steamed whole fish)

Soup: Flowered chicken soup (or steamed whole chicken soup)
Dessert (with one sweet soup)
Candied banana fritters (or sponge cake can-ton style)
Sweet walnut soup (or Almond Jelly with fruits soup.)

Many friends helped in many ways to make the publication of this cook book possible. While it is impossible to name them all here, the author sincerely wishes to thank them for their kind interest, ardent encouragement and generous assistance. Special thanks are offered to mrs. Yvonne Zeck, who helped me explain to American cooks how to prepare these dishes which are typical of my country.

Fu Pei-Mei

Taipei, Taiwan
Republic of China
May, 1969

8

東 部 菜

Dishes of **Eastern** China

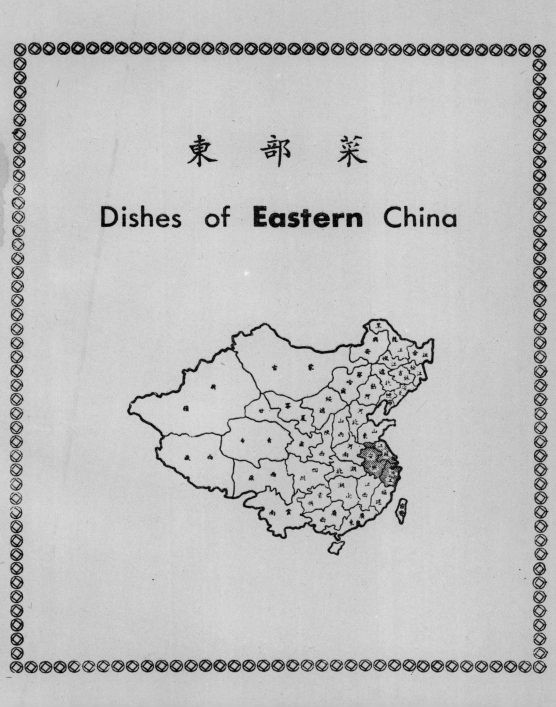

第一圖
中式銀質餐具排放格式

Picture No. 1
Formal Chinese Table Setting in Silver

第二圖

中式餐具個人份按排圖

Picture No. 2

The Chinese Individual Place Setting

第四圖（下）
胡桃炸鷄片
（做法參照第18頁）

Picture No. 4
Deep Fried Chicken with Walnuts
(See Recipe Page 19)

第三圖（上）
菠蘿燒嫩鷄
（做法參照第十六頁）

Picture No. 3
Stewed Chicken with Pineapple Sauce
(See Recipe Page 17)

第五圖（右）
醬 肉
（做法參照第22頁）

Picture No. 5
Spiced Pork
(See Recipe Page 23)

第六圖（左）
走油扣肉
（做法參照第24頁）

Picture No. 6
Mould Pork in Brown Sauce
(See Recipe Page 25)

第七圖

松鼠黃魚 （做法參照第36頁）

Picture No. 7
Sweet and Sour Fish
(See Recipe Page 26)

第八圖（上）

蜜汁火腿 （做法參照第28頁）

Picture No. 8

Honey Dew Ham

(See Recipe Page 29)

第九圖（上）

醋溜魚捲 （做法參照第38頁）

Picture No. 9

Fish Rolls in
Sour Sauce

(See Recipe Page 39)

第十圖（左）

炸蝦球

（做法參照第40頁）

Picture No. 10

Deep Fried Shrimp
Balls

(See Recipe Page 41)

第十一圖 **蟹黃菜心**
（做法參照第46頁）
Picture No. 11
Crab meat with Green Cabbage
(See Recipe page 47)

第十二圖 **紅扒鵪蛋**
（做法參照第52頁）
Picture No. 12
Quail Eggs in Brown Sauce
(See Recipe Page 53)

第十三圖（右）　三絲魚翅羹

（做法參照第50頁）

Picture No. 13

Shark's Fin with Shredded Chicken

(See Recipe Page 51)

第十四圖（下）　全家福

（做法參照第51頁）

Picture No. 14

Assorted dish with Brown Sauce

(See Recipe Page 52)

東部菜目錄　　　Contents of Eastern

9

醉　鷄

材料：

嫩鷄	一隻（約二斤左右）
鹽	二湯匙
酒	二杯（紹興酒或清酒，日本酒皆可）

做法：

1. 將一隻除淨內臟，斬下頭腳之光鷄，先用水冲洗後擦乾水份，再將鹽平均撒下用手指揉搓在鷄身四週和鷄腹中，放置醃約六小時左右。

2. 將鷄放在一只大碗或小盆內，置入水已沸滾之蒸鍋中，用大火蒸熟（水需大滾，約二十五分鐘左右即可致熟）

3. 已蒸熟之鷄，由大碗中取出，待其冷却後分切成四大塊或六大塊，再整齊的放進一只深鉢或大碗中。

4. 將蒸鷄所出之鷄汁倒入鷄塊中（需過濾一次，勿使雜質進入）並將酒也傾下，略為搖動使鷄汁與酒混合，覆上蓋子，放進冰箱中燜浸一天（約半天後可將鷄塊上下加以調動一次務使每塊鷄均能浸到酒湯）。

5. 食時將鷄塊取出一或兩塊，斬切成細窄條狀之長方塊，排列在菜盤內並澆上一湯匙泡汁即可供食（如欲美觀可配飾香荽或生菜蕃茄片等）

註：泡鷄之汁可以久放，也可做浸泡第二隻鷄所用，但每次浸泡時間最好不要超過四天，以免酒味太重。

10

Wined Chicken

Ingredients:

    1 *whole Chicken* (*about 2-1/2 lbs.*)
    2 *T. Salt*
    2 *C. Wine* (*Sherry or Chinese Shao-Shing Wine or Japanese wine*)

Procedure:

1. Clean and dry chicken. Rub the chicken with salt. both inside and outside. Let stand from 4-6 hours.

2. Put chicken in a bowl, steam it over high heat about 25 minutes.

3. Remove chicken from bowl, let cool, then cut in 4 or. 6 large pieces, lay in a deep bowl.

4. Pour the chicken broth from the steamed bowl through a strainer into the deep bowl. Add wine and mix by shaking the bowl, cover and keep in refrigerator about one day. Turn once after 6 hours.

5. Remove 1 or 2 pieces chicken at a time, cut into pieces 1″ wide 2″ long. Lay on a serving plate and sprinkle with 1 T. wine brine. Decorate with tomato slices or pickles if desired.

NOTE:

    The wine brine can be saved and used again. It is advisable not to soak the chicken any longer than 4 days, otherwise the flavor might get too strong.

水　晶　鷄

材料：

嫩鷄	半隻（約一斤）	鹽	一茶匙半
熟火腿	一兩	酒	一湯匙
香菜葉	十數枚	味精	半茶匙
洋菜	1/6兩（或膠粉一包）	生菜葉	六枚（或煮熟碗豆半杯）

做法：

1. 鷄洗淨放進開水中（水中應加入葱、薑少許）用小火煮二十分鐘將鷄取出，待稍冷後折除鷄骨，再將所有鷄肉連皮切成一寸長方塊（鷄肉較厚處可先批開再切）。

2. 洋菜用溫水泡軟後擠乾水份，放進小鍋內，加入一杯半煮鷄之湯用小火煮七、八分鐘，然後倒在一只中型碗內（或小盆），再將鷄肉放入並加鹽，酒及味精，上鍋蒸半小時左右。

3. 熟火腿切成三角形或葉子形薄片，整齊排入一只中型碗內使成爲花朵狀再飾排香菜葉，然後將已蒸過之鷄肉先選取比較整齊之數塊將鷄皮朝下舖排在火腿上（卽碗之底層），再續排下所有之鷄肉，最後將蒸鷄之汁也倒入。待其冷却之後便移進冰箱內冷凍一小時以上。

4. 食時將鷄由冰箱中取出，覆扣在一只菜盤中，輕輕揭去原碗而在盤邊可將生菜葉切絲，或用碗豆圍飾便成。此菜宜於夏季食用，做爲酒席上之冷盤也可。

Jellied Chicken

Ingredients:

1/2 Chicken (about 1-1/2 lbs.)
2 oz. Cooked ham
10 Parsley leaves
1/6 oz. Agar-agar (or 1 envelope unflavored gelatin)

1-1/2 t. Salt
1 T. Wine
1/2 t. M.S.G.
6 Lettuce leaves (or 1/2 cup green peas)

Procedure:

1. Place the chicken, 1 green onion and 2 slices ginger in boiling water, cook for about 20 minutes. Remove only the chicken from the pan and let cool, then remove all the bones. Cut into 1″ wide 1½″ long pieces (with skin).

2. Soak the agar-agar about 10 minutes, squeeze and cook with 1¼ cup chicken soup remaining from #1 about 8 minutes (low heat). Stock will be reduced to 1 cup. Pour in a bowl, add chicken meat, salt, wine and M.S.G. Steam for 1/2 hour.

3. Slice the ham and cut into small leaf shape or triangles. Lay in the bottom of bowl attractively, and place parsley leaves, then add steamed chicken meat. Add the stock. When it's cool place in refrigerator until firm. This will take more than 1 hour.

4. Turn the bowl on a plate, remove the bowl, decorate with shredded lettuce leaves or cooked green peas around the plate, serve.

紙 包 鶏

材料：

鷄胸肉（或大鷄腿三支）	十兩	醬油	三湯匙
熟火腿	一兩	鹽	半茶匙
香茹（一寸直徑大小）	三個	糖	一茶匙
香菜葉	十四枚	酒	一湯匙
玻璃紙	十四小張	胡椒粉	1/4茶匙
花生油	六杯	麻油	二湯匙

做法：

1. 鷄肉連皮切成一寸半寬兩寸長之大斜薄片（共廿四片）全部放在碗裏，加入醬油、糖、鹽、酒、胡椒拌醃十五分鐘。

2. 香菇用溫水泡軟之後去蒂，每只切兩個交叉（即四刀），使每只變成八片尖角小塊。

3. 熟火腿（也可用西洋火腿）切成同香菇相仿大小之尖角小片留用。

4. 將玻璃紙（約五寸四方大小）在中央先刷上麻油少許，放進一片香菜葉，再在其左右各放一片火腿及一片香菇然後覆上一片鷄肉（皮向下）包裹成長方形小包狀，（餘下之紙端折向內部夾住）。

5. 將油燒滾後，待稍冷却（至八成熱度），即投下紙包，需正面朝下投入用小火慢炸，以免玻璃紙炸焦，約三分鐘，至鷄肉已變白而够熱時撈出，瀝乾油漬，排入盤內（盤邊可用蔬菜裝飾）。

14

Paper Wrapped Chicken

Ingredients:

3/4 lb Chicken breast meat
  (or 3 Chicken legs)
.2 oz. Ham (Chinese ham or any
  cooked ham)
3 Black mushrooms
1 1 Parsley leaves
1 4 Squares of cellophane paper
  (5" x 5")

3 T. Soysauce
1/2 t. Salt
1 T. Wine
1 t. Sugar
1/4 t. Black pepper
2 T. Sesame oil
6 C. Peanut oil

Procedure:

1. Cut the chicken meat (with skin) into 1½" wide, 2½" long cross wise slices, lay in bowl and marinate with soysauce, sugar, salt, wine and black pepper about 15 minutes.
2. Soak mushrooms in warm water and remove stems. Cut each in 8 small triangular pieces.
3. Slice the ham and cut the same size as mushrooms.
4. Using 1 sheet of paper brush it with some sesame oil, with corner facing you, place in the middle 1 parsley leaf with face down, on one side place mushroom slice and on other side ham slice, lay on top of this 1 slice of chicken meat. Fold up the corner nearest you to edge of chicken, fold the left and then right corners over the chicken to make a package. Tuck the remaining corner inside to make a neat rectangular package. The parsley, mushroom and ham side is the topside
5. Heat oil in fry pan about 300° C., drop the packages into oil, fry about 1½ minutes each side, remove the package and lay on platter and serve.

NOTE:

1. Decorate platter with flower shaped fresh vegetables.
2. Use fingers to open package but use chopsticks in eating.

菠蘿燒嫩雞

材料：

嫩雞	一隻（約二斤重）	醬油	五湯匙
鳳梨	五片（切成小塊）	酒	一湯匙
洋葱	一個（小型）	清水	二杯半
葡萄乾	二湯匙（可免）	太白粉	一湯匙
鳳梨汁	半杯	麻油	半湯匙
香菜	數支	花生油	五杯

做法：

1. 將雞洗淨拭乾水份後，用錐子（或削尖之竹筷）將雞胸，雞腿等處肉較厚實之部份挿刺數遍，然後放在大碗中加入醬油，酒醃泡（需時加翻轉），約半小時之後，投入爛熟之花生油中將雞全身炸黃。

2. 雞撈起後，倒出鍋中之油，僅留三湯匙在其中爆炒切成小方丁之洋葱，炒至洋葱之香氣已透出後，便將醃雞之醬油汁與鳳梨汁傾下煮滾，再放雞入鍋同煮一分鐘（兩面）隨後注入清水先用大火煮滾隨後改用小火燜約半小時左右至湯汁僅餘下一半為止。

3. 將雞由鍋中撈出，而在鍋中湯汁內加入鳳梨小塊及葡萄乾續用小火煮約五分鐘，便淋下太白粉（用水調溶後）見湯汁煮成黏稠時再淋入麻油即成。

4. 用利刀將雞（趁熱）斬切成適當之大小塊狀，再按原隻雞形排列在菜盤內並將鍋中煮成之湯汁澆在面上便可（香菜置上面做為點綴）。

※請參考照片第三號。

16

Stewed Chicken with Pineapple Sauce

Ingredients;

1 whole Chicken (about 2-1/2 lbs.)

5 slices Pineapple (diced)

1 Small onion (diced)

2 T. Raisins (Optional)

1/2 C. Pineapple juice

5 Parsley leaves

5 T. Soy souce

1 T. Wine

2-1/2 C. Cold water

1 T. Cornstarch   (make paste)

1 T. Cold water   "

1/2 T. Sesame oil

5 C. Peanut oil

Procedure:

1. Clean the chicken. Soak with soysauce and wine for about half an hour. Deep fry in the hot peanut oil, until it becomes golden brown.

2. Remove the chicken and drain off oil from frying pan. Put back only 3 T. oil in pan and stir fry the onion. Add the remaining soaked sauce and Pineapp e juice. Place the chicken in, then add cold water, cover with lid. Stew at low heat about half an hour, until the chicken is done; when only half of liquid is left.

3. Remove the chicken and cut into small pieces, then lay on a platter in a chicken shape.

4. Add pineapple and raisins in pan, cook with the chicken liquid for 5 minutes (low heat). Add cornstarch paste and sesame oil, stir well. Pour the sauce over the chicken, with parsley leaves on the top for decoration.

---

* Refer to Picture No. 3.

17

胡 桃 炸 鷄 片

材料：

鷄胸肉	半斤	鹽	一茶匙
胡桃仁（或花生仁）三兩		太白粉	二湯匙
鷄蛋白	一個	花生油	六杯
酒	半湯匙	五香花椒鹽	一茶匙

做法：

1. 鷄肉去皮除筋後，用薄而鋒利之菜刀片切成一寸半寬兩寸多長之大薄片，然後全部用蛋白，太白粉，鹽及酒拌醃約十五分鐘。

2. 將胡桃仁（已剝去皮之桃仁）在開水中川燙一下（約半分鐘）撈出後吹乾，斬切成小粒狀，盛在一只盤內備用。

3. 將鷄片，一片片在胡桃粒上沾滿（兩面）然後投入已燒至八成熱之油中以慢火炸黃（約一分半鐘）

4. 撈出胡桃鷄片排置菜盤中，在盤之兩端各放少許五香花椒鹽上桌以供蘸用。

註：五香花椒鹽係將花椒炒香（乾鍋小火炒），加入同量細鹽再略炒，盛出後待冷，研磨成粉狀加入少許五香粉拌勻便是。

※請參考照片第 4 號。

18

Deep Fried Chicken with Walnuts

Ingredients:

3/4 lb. Chicken breasts

1/4 lb. Walnuts

1 Egg white

1/2 T. Wine

1 t. Salt

2 T. Cornstarch

6 C. Peanut oil

1 t. Flavored pepper salt

Procedure:

1. Remove the skin and membrane from chicken meat, slice into 1½" wide, 2" long, 1/8" thick pieces, and place in a bowl to marinate with egg white, salt, wine and cornstarch. Set aside about 15 minutes.

2. Boil the walnuts in boiling water about half minute, remove skins and let cool, then chop in small pieces the size of rice.

3. Dredge the chicken pieces on all sides with chopped walnuts, then deep fry over low heat about 1½ minutes or until golden brown.

4. Remove chicken from frying pan, lay on plate, served with flavored pepper salt.

NOTE:

Flavored pepper-salt: 1 T. Brown pepper corn

1 T. salt

Stir and mix over low heat in a dry frying pan about 1 minute, when salt is brown and pepper corn is dark and smells good. Let cool, then grind very, very fine and sift with a very fine sieve. This keeps well in a tightly covered bottle and is used in fried and roasted dishes.

---

* Refer to Picture No. 4.

紅燒鴨

材料：

肥鴨一隻	（約三斤重）	冰糖	二兩
葱	四支	鹽	三茶匙
薑	三片	麻油	二茶匙
八角	一顆	花生油	八杯
醬油	六湯匙	清水	五杯
酒	二湯匙		

做法

1. 將整隻鴨挖除內臟，斬棄鴨掌後，洗淨擦乾水份，用醬油塗抹全身並醃泡（務使鴨皮每一處均能着上醬油色）約半小時。

2. 將油全部燒熱（十分熱）投下鴨子，以大火炸至金黃色，需用鏟勺將油不斷澆淋鴨身以使顏色相同，取出後將油倒出並將泡鴨之醬油傾入鍋中，再加放葱支、薑片、八角、酒等同時注入清水五杯，放進鴨去同燒。（需蓋嚴）

3. 先用大火燒滾後改用中火煮約一小時，然後加入鹽及冰糖再繼續燒煮至湯汁僅餘下半杯時為止。

4. 將鴨裝盤（用鏟子撳壓使呈扁平狀），再澆上鍋中之原汁（需先淋下麻油），並飾香荽數支在鴨腹上即成。

註：1. 可將青荽炒熟，放在盤底或週圍以做裝飾增加色調。

　　2. 如將鴨放冷後斬切成小塊（祇用四分之一隻或小半隻）裝盤可做為冷盤菜。

Stewed Whole Duck in Brown Sauce

Ingredients:

1 whole Duck or Chicken (about 4 lbs.)

4 Green onions

3 slice Ginger

1 Star anise (optional)

6 T. Soysauce

2 T. Wine

3 oz. Crystal sugar or 3 T. sugar

2 t, Salt

2 t. Sesame oil

8 C. Peanut oil

1/2 lb. Green vegetable (optional)

Procedure:

1. Clean duck, brush and soak with soysauce about 1/2 hour, reserve the soy sauce.

2. Deep fry the duck until it looks brown and the skin is crispy. Remove duck from frying pan and drain oil; which may be used in other recipes

3. Put the duck in stew pot or the same fry pan, add green onions, ginger, anise, wine, the above remaining soysauce, and 5 cups boiling water (to barely cover duck) cover with lid and stew about 2½ hours. Add sugar and 1 t. salt after 1 hour.

4. When the sauce is reduced to 2/3 cup, and splash sesame oil place duck on a platter and pour sauce on top.

5. Stir-fry green vegetable (or spinach) with 3 T. oil and 1 t. salt, 1/2 t. sugar, and place around duck, serve. Lettuce and parsley may be used, but do not stir fry.

醬 肉

材料：

猪肉	一斤	冰糖	一兩半
甜麵醬	二湯匙	八角	一顆
醬油	三湯匙	桂皮	一塊
紹興酒	一湯匙		

做法．

1. 購買較瘦之連皮前腿猪肉一方塊或蹄膀（即肘子）一個，先洗淨擦乾水份後用甜醬塗抹在肉之四週，並用力揉搓，放置並醃約二、三小時。

2. 在深底小鍋內，放入醬油、酒、八角、桂皮等煮滾，再將猪肉落鍋同煮一下，隨後加入滾水兩杯，改用小火慢慢燜燒，約半小時後加入冰糖再繼續小火煨熹一小時左右，（需時時加以翻面）。

3. 煨熹至鍋中湯汁僅剩下小半杯•而此汁已非常黏稠時，離火，待肉冷透後取出用利刀切成大薄片排盤，（原汁澆在上面供食）。

※請參考照片第5號。

Spiced Pork

Ingredients:

1-1/4 lbs. Boneless pork
or fresh ham
2 T. Soy bean paste
3 T. Soysauce

1 T. Wine
2 oz. Crystal sugar (or sugar)
1 pcs. Star anise (optional)

Procedure:

1. Wipe the pork and rub all sides with soy bean paste, soak about 2-3 hours.

2. Put soysauce, wine, star anise in deep pot and boil, then add pork and 2 C. boiling water, bring to boil over high heat, reduce heat to about half, stew for 1/2 hour. Then add sugar, continuing to stew 1 more hour. Turn meat often while stewing.

3. When the sauce is reduced to 1/2 cup and is rather thick, remove from fire and let cool in pot.

4. Slice the pork and lay on plate attrac vely and pour the sauce on top. Serve.

* Refer to Picture No. 5.

走 油 扣 肉

材料:

猪肉(五花肉)	十二兩	糖	二茶匙
葱段	四支	酒	一湯匙
薑片	二片	鹽	一茶匙
八角	一顆	太白粉	二茶匙
花生油	五杯	麻油	一茶匙
醬油	五湯匙	青菜(豆苗或菠菜、菜心)	六兩

做法:

1. 購買比較瘦肉多而皮薄之五花肉一方塊,洗淨放入鍋中,加清水(能淹沒肉爲度)用大火煮熟(約三○分鐘)。撈出後待稍冷並拭乾水份再浸泡在醬油中(肉皮部份需要泡得長久些),至肉四週均已着上醬油色之後,投入已燒熱之花生油中炸黃(約三分鐘,須要用鍋蓋先蓋一下,以免油爆到身上)。

2. 將已炸好之肉塊取出馬上泡在冷水裏(皮向下)約半小時,見肉皮起了趨紋與小泡而回軟爲止。

3. 用利刀,將已泡過之肉塊切成大薄片,全部排列在一只中型蒸碗中(碗底一層要整齊而如梯子形)然後加入糖、酒、葱段、薑片、八角及泡肉之醬油,將碗放入蒸鍋內用大火隔水蒸約一小時半至肉軟而酥爛爲止。

4. 將蒸爛之扣肉端出,先傾出碗中之湯汁到炒鍋中煮滾,用濕太白粉鈎茨,並淋下少許麻油即可澆到已扣覆在菜盤中之扣肉上。

5. 青菜用油炒熟(加鹽調味)盛在盤之兩端或四週便上桌供食。

※請參考照片第6號。

Mold Pork in Brown Sauce

Ingredients:

1 lb. Lean pork with marbled fat and skin

1 Green onion (cut into 1 inch segments)

2 slices Ginger

1 Star anise (optional)

5 T. Soysauce

1 T. Wine

1 t. Sugar

1 t. Salt

2 t. Cornstarch   (make paste)

1 T. Cold water   "

5 C. Peanut oil

1 t. Sesame oil

1/2 lb. Green vegetable (spinach or green pepper)

Procedure:

1. Cut pork into one cubic pieces and cook it with water. Bring to a rolling boil for about 30 minutes, then take the pork out and let it drain dry, then marinate it with soysauce until it becomes brown. Save the soysauce. Next, deep fry in very hot oil about 3 minutes until skin is very dark.

2. Soak the fried pieces of pork in cold water (skin side down) for about 1/2 hour until the skin becomes wrinkled and soft again.

3. Cut the soaked piece into large thin slices. Arrange the slices in a soup plate. Add sugar, wine, green onion, ginger, star anise and soysauce saved from marinating. Steam over high heat for 1½ hours until tender.

4. Pour the liquid mixture from the steamed meat into a saucepan. Bring to boil. Thicken it with cornstarch paste. Add a few drops of sesame oil. Put a serving plate upside down over the soup plate with steamed meat in. Turn the whole thing over so that the meat is on the serving plate. Pour the cooked gravy over the meat.

5. Saute the green vegetable and season to taste. Arrange in a ring along the rim of the meat plate.

---

* Refer to Picture No. 6.

糖 醋 排 骨

材料：

猪小排骨	一斤	鎮江醋	三湯匙
葱	三支	太白粉	二茶匙
醬油	五湯匙	清水	三湯匙
酒	半湯匙	麻油	一茶匙
糖	四湯匙	花生油	六杯

做法：

1. 選購肥肉少而大小均勻之小排骨，按肋條骨節分切開後再斬成一寸長之小塊，全部裝在大碗內，加入酒，醬油拌勻，醃漬半小時至一小時。葱洗淨切斜絲留用。

2. 將花生油燒熱後，投下醃漬過之小排骨，用中火炸約兩分鐘，至肉已熟透時即行撈出。

3. 再將鍋內之油重行燒熱，放下炸過之小排骨，用大火另炸一次（約半分鐘），撈出後，將鍋中之油倒出。

4. 在泡過小排骨之醬油汁內，加入糖、醋、水及太白粉、麻油和葱絲調妥備用。

5. 另在炒鍋內僅燒熱一湯匙油，然後倒下上項已調備之綜合味料用大火炒煮至滾，見其變黏稠時，即將排骨倒下速加拌勻裝盤。

註：糖醋排骨之做法有很多種，此篇係普通之上海式做法。

Sweet and Sour Spareribs

Ingredients:

1-1/4 lbs. Pork spareribs

3 Green onions

5 T. Soysauce

4 T. Sugar

3 T. Brown Vinegar

3 T. Cold water

1/2 T. Wine

2 t. Cornstarch

1 t. Sesame oil

6 C. Peanut oil

Procedure:

1. Cut the spareribs into 1" square pieces, then marinate with wine and soysauce for 30 minutes. Reserve soysauce in bowl.

2. Deep fry the spareribs for about 2 minutes, take out and heat oil again, then fry once more until spareribs turn very brown (about 1/2 minute). Remove spareribs and drain off oil from frying pan.

3. Add sugar, vinegar, water and cornstarch, sesame oil and shredded green onion to the bowl, used for marinating spareribs. This is the seasoning sauce.

4. Heat one tablespoon oil in frying pan, pour in the seasoning sauce, boil and stir until thickened and heated thoroughly, add spareribs and stir well before serving.

NOTE:

In China there are many versions of this. You may add green pepper and water chestnuts for color.

蜜 汁 火 腿

料料：

中段火腿（或家鄉肉）	一斤
熱水	半杯
碎冰糖	五兩
乾蓮子（或栗子）	一兩
酒	一湯匙
桂花醬	半茶匙

做法：

1. 火腿削除黑污部份用熱水泡軟（約半小時）再行刷洗乾淨，整塊放在一只盤或碗裏上鍋蒸熟（約半小時）。

2. 將蒸熟之火腿橫面切成一寸寬，兩寸多長之薄片排列在碗裏（底面一層務必排得整齊美觀較差部份放在內裏），加入冰糖（約三兩），酒並注入熱水（約半杯，與火腿面平），放入鍋中蒸二十分鐘。

3. 將碗中蒸出之火腿油連湯倒出（可留下少許在碗內）另加進泡軟之蓮子（或栗子）並放剩下之碎冰糖（約二兩）續上鍋蒸半小時以上（至蓮子酥爛為止）

4. 將蒸好之火腿由鍋中端出並將汁倒在小鍋內，用小火熬羹成稠汁加入桂花醬，澆到扣在盤內之火腿上便成。

註：如用罐頭或已羹熟之蓮子，栗子等墊底，則第二次蒸之時間可以縮短。另外也可用鮮藕或荔枝，甜酒釀等物代用。

※請參考照片第 8 號

Honey Dew Ham

Ingredients:

1-1/4 lbs. Chinese Virginia ham
1/2 C. Hot water
6 oz. Crystal sugar (or sugar)

2 oz. Dry lotus seeds or chestunts
1 T. Wine
1/2 t. Kuei-hua juice (optional)

Procedure:

1. Trim off the black surface of the ham. Soak the ham with hot water about 1/2 hour, then wash it. Put the ham in a plate. Steam for about 1/2 hour.

2. Cut the ham crosswise into 1″ wide, 2″ long, thin slices. Arrange the ham slices attractively on the bottom of a bowl or deep plate. Put the odd sized pieces in the center. Add half rock crystal (3 oz), wine and hot water. (to cover the ham). Steam for about 20 minutes.

3. Drain off the liquid from the steamed ham bowl. Add soaked lotus seeds (or chest nuts) and other half (3 oz.) rock crystal. Steam for another 1/2 hour until the lotus seeds are tender.

4. To prepare sauce, pour the liquid from the steamed ham bowl into a small saucepan. Add Kuei hua juice. Simmer and stir until thickened. Turn ham from bowl to plate and pour sauce over it and serve.

NOTE:

1. Kuei-hua is a popular Chinese flavoring, but there is no substitute for it in the States.

2. The canned lotus seeds or chestnuts will be used.

* Refer to Picture No. 8.

29

扣 三 絲

材料：

鷄胸	一個（約六兩）	葱			二支
火腿	四兩	薑			三片
鷄蛋	二個	鹽			一茶匙
笋	二支	清湯（即煑鷄之湯）			六杯
香菇	一個	鷄油			半湯匙

做法：

1. 在鍋內燒滾八杯清水後，放下洗淨之鷄胸與火腿，並加進葱薑，先用大火煮滾後，改以小火煑約二十分鐘，取出鷄肉與火腿，原湯（約六杯）留用（挾出葱薑不要）

2. 將鷄胸去骨取肉後用手撕成細絲（或切成絲也可）火腿亦切成細絲。

3. 笋去皮用水煑熟（約十分鐘），切細絲。冬菇泡軟去蒂整只留用。

4. 鷄蛋打散，在鍋中煎成薄蛋皮（分煎兩張）然後切成細絲留用。

5. 在一只中型碗裏，先放下冬菇在中央（正面向下平放）再將鷄肉絲火腿絲及蛋皮絲分三方面整齊而直絲排列在碗底，最後空隙處填裝笋絲，並撒上鹽及少許味精注入半杯清湯，置蒸鍋內大火蒸約二十分鐘。

6. 上桌時將蒸好之材料扣在一只大湯碗內，並注入沸滾之鷄湯（需另外加鹽調味），然後揭下蒸碗，最後淋下鷄油便可送席。

註：此菜所用三種絲料只要顏色明顯，任何肉類，蔬菜類皆可配用。

30

Mold San-Sze Soup

Ingredients:

6 oz. Chicken meat (or lean pork)

5 oz. Ham (or Canadian bacon)

2 Eggs (or shredded snow peas)

2 Bamboo shoots (or turnip)

1 Black dried mushroom

2 Green onions

3 slices Ginger

2-1/2 t. Salt

1/2 t. M.S.G.

6 C. Soup stock

1/2 T. Chicken grease

Procedure:

1. Boil the chicken and ham in 8 cups of boiling water with green orion, and ginger about 20 minutes. Remove the chicken and ham, let cool. Save the soup stock (about 6 cups) for later use.

2. Tear the cold chicken into shreds, cut the cold ham into thin strips.

3. Peel and boil whole bamboo shoots about 10 minutes cut into thin strips. Soak mushroom in warm water and remove the stem.

4. Using a frying pan make two thin pancakes, with the beaten eggs. Cut into thin strips.

5. In a medium size bowl put the mushroom upside down in the center. Arrange the shredded chicken, ham, egg attractively in the bottom of bowl. Add bamboo strips in center, Sprinkle some salt and 1/2 C. soup stock. Steam for 20 minutes.

6. Turn the steamed dish into a large soup bowl. Bring the soup stock to a boil and season to taste. (Add salt chicken grease and M.S.G.). Pour it around the steamed bowl. Remove the steamed bowl and serve.

NOTE:

The three ingredients are very colorful. Substitutes may be used too.

蘇 式 燻 魚

材料：

靑魚（或鯇魚）	中段一斤	鹽	半茶匙
葱	三支	糖	四湯匙
薑	五片	五香粉	一茶匙
醬油	五湯匙	花生油	五杯
酒	一湯匙		

做法：

1. 將魚洗淨瀝乾，由背部片切對開成爲兩大塊後，再直切成大斜片，（共可切得十六片）。

2. 葱與薑拍碎後放在大碗內加入醬油、酒、鹽拌調均勻，再將魚片放進醃泡四小時左右，（須上下翻動兩次以便平均入味）

3. 花生油燒熱後將魚片分兩批落鍋炸酥（每批約炸四分鐘左右）撈出後瀝乾油漬，旋即趁熱泡入糖水中（一杯開水溶化四湯匙糖後加入五香粉調勻）浸泡四分鐘左右。

4. 當第二批魚炸好時，即可將第一批泡在糖水中之魚片夾出留用，續泡第二批魚片。

5. 將炸魚之花生油倒出，鍋中傾下原來泡魚之醬油汁，並加入少許蔴油煑滾後熄火，將泡過糖水之魚片落入鍋中翻覆兩面沾裹一下即可裝盤，待冷後供食。

註：此種燻魚，係蘇州做法，較其他燻魚甜味略重。

Spicy Fish Slices

Ingredients:

1-1/4 lbs. Fish meat
  (any white fish meat)
3 Green onions
5 slices Ginger
5 T. Soysauce
1 T. Wine

1/2 t. Salt
4 T. Sugar
1-1/2 C. Boiling water
1 t. Five spice powder
  (Wu hsiang fen)
5 C. Peanut oil

Procedure:

1. Slice the fish meat in 1½″ wide and 2½″ long ½″ thick slices (about 16 slices).

2. Crush green onion and ginger. Put in bowl with soysauce, wine and salt. Marinate the fish slices with this mixture for about 3-4 hours.

3. Mix sugar and five spice powder in a bowl add boiling water to mix well.

4. Heat oil very hot in frying pan, fry the fish until very dark (about 4 minutes). Remove the fish from pan and put in sugar mixture immediately, soak about 3-4 minutes.

5. Remove the fish from sugar mixture and lay on platter. Let cool before serving.

NOTE:

A substitude for Five Spice Powder may be allspice.

西湖醋魚

材料：

活青魚（或草魚，鯉魚）一條（約一斤多）		鹽	二茶匙
嫩薑絲	半杯	鎮江醋	四湯匙
葱支	二支	醬色	二茶匙
薑片	二片	藕粉（或太白粉）三湯匙	
醬油	二湯匙	蔴油	一湯匙
糖	三湯匙	猪油	四湯匙
酒	一湯匙	味精	半茶匙

做法：

1. 將活魚剖殺刮洗乾淨後，從腹下切開，使魚成為背部仍相連之一大片，用刀斬斷中間大骨數處。

2. 在大鍋內燒滾開水（加入葱支薑片同燒），將魚背面朝上投入川燙，待再沸滾後改用小火煮約三分鐘左右，見魚之眼球變白而突出時，速予熄火或撈出裝在長盤內。

3. 嫩薑絲用冷開水泡一下後，搾乾，撒在盤中魚之身上。

4. 將猪油三湯匙燒熱淋下酒爆香，隨即加入清湯二杯半（可利用川魚之水）並放醬油、糖、醋、鹽、醬色，味精等，待再沸滾時淋下已調水溶解之藕粉（或太白粉）鈎芡使汁變黏稠狀，最後澆下另一湯匙熱猪油及蔴油便可全部傾淋在盤內魚面趁熱上桌。

註：此菜必需用活殺之魚才夠鮮嫩。也可以用大火蒸熟，而不必川燙。

34

West Lake Fish

Ingredients:

1 Live fish (carp or any fresh
 water fish)
1/2 C. Shredded young ginger
2 Green onions
2 T. Soysauce
3 T. Sugar
1 T. Wine
1/2 t. M.S.G.

2 t. Salt
4 T. Brown vinegar
2 t. Brown food color (optional)
3 T. Lotus root starch or cornstarch
 paste
1 T. Sesame oil
4 T. Lard (or cooking oil)
2 C. Soup stock

Procedure:

1. Kill fish by striking a blow to the head (do not remove head). Scale and
   clean. Split it lengthwise from gills down without cutting through the back.
   Chop the large bones into sections.

2. Put the fish in boiling water with some green onion and ginger, cook about
   3 minutes over medium fire until the fish is done (when the eyes puff out).
   Remove the fish from pan and place onto a platter.

3. Sprinkle the young shredded ginger on the fish.

4. Splash wine in the 3T. heated oil, add soup stock immediately. Add
   soysauce, sugar, vinegar, salt and food color. When the soup is boiling
   add lotus root starch or cornstarch (mix with 5 T. cold water) cook until
   thickened. Sprinkle 1 T. lard (or hot cooking oil) and sesame oil into the
   the fish. Serve immediately.
   sauce, pour over the fish. Serve immediately.

松鼠黃魚

材料：

大黃魚（或青魚）	一條（約一斤四兩）	醬油	半湯匙
香菇	小四個	酒	一湯匙
洋葱	小一個	糖	四湯匙
蕃茄	小一個	白醋	四湯匙
青豆	二湯匙	蕃茄醬	四湯匙
葡萄乾	二湯匙（可免）	清水	四湯匙
鹽	一茶匙	太白粉	一湯匙
酒	一湯匙	鹽	一茶匙
雞蛋	二個	麻油	一茶匙
麵粉	六湯匙	花生油	六杯
太白粉	三湯匙		
冷水	五湯匙		

（鹽、酒 為醃魚用料；雞蛋、麵粉、太白粉、冷水 為麵糊用料；右列 為綜合調味料）

做法：

1. 將魚頭切下，由嘴巴底對剖成一大片後撒鹽少許留用，魚身部份剔除大骨取下兩面魚肉後在魚肉上（內面）斜刀劃切刀紋，先直切三長刀，再橫面劃切（每隔半寸切一刀）唯不可切破魚皮，兩塊魚肉均切妥後，撒下鹽及酒醃十數分鐘。

2. 香菇泡軟後切一公分小丁，蕃茄去皮同洋葱亦切小丁狀留用。葡萄乾用冷水泡十分鐘留用。

3. 將麵糊用料及綜合調味料分別在兩只碗內調勻備用。

4. 將花生油燒熱後投下沾裹了麵糊料之魚肉用大火炸熟（約三、四分鐘），至十分酥脆時撈出排置大盤中，另將魚頭也裹上麵糊炸好放置在盤之一端。

5. 在鍋內燒熱三湯匙油炒香洋葱丁，再放進冬菇丁，蕃茄丁及青豆與綜合調味料煮滾（用大火）最後淋下一湯匙熱花生油便可，迅速澆到盤中之魚上即成。

註：松鼠魚分為去骨與帶骨兩種，切花紋之方法，及課味法亦有許多種類，此頁所介紹者係較適合一般人口味。

※請參考照片第 7 號。

36

Sweet and Sour Boneless Fish

Ingredients:

1 Whole fish (about 1-1/2 lbs.)		1/2 T. Soysauce	(seasoning sauce)
4 Dried mushroom		1 T. Wine	"
1 Onion	(small)	4 T. Sugar	"
1 Tomato	"	4 T. Vinegar	"
2 T. Green peas (or fresh soybeans)		4 T. Ketchup	"
2 Eggs	(flour batter)	4 T. Water	"
5 T. Flour	"	2 t. Cornstarch	"
3 T. Cornstarch	"	1 t. Salt	"
5 T. Water	"	1 t. Sesame oil	"
1 t. Salt	(to marinate fish)	6 C. Peanut oil	
1. T. Wine	"		

Procedure:

1. Cut the head off the cleaned fish. Split the fish length wise but do not cut through the back. Open the two halves to form the shape of a butterfly. Remove the bones. On the inside of the fish cut three 1/4" deep slashes lengthwise on each side and slash the same way crosswise 1/2" apart. Marinate the fish with salt and wine for 10 minutes.
2. Soften the mushrooms with warm water. Cut into cubes. Peel tomato and onion then cut into cubes.
3. Make batter with egg, flour, cornstarch and water.
4. Mix the seasoning sauce in a bowl.
5. Heat the oil. Dip the fish head in the batter. Fry until golden brown. Dip the two pieces fish and fry for 2 minutes. Take out, wait until the oil is heated up again. Turn and fry for another minute. Arrange the fried pieces on a large platter with the head.
6. Heat 3T. oil, saute onion, mushroom, tomato cubes and peas. Stir in seasoning sauce mixture until thickened and cooked through. Pour it over the fish and serve.

NOTE:

The fish can be either boned or not boned. There are several ways of cutting and seasoning. Most of our foreign friends prefer this way.

* Refer to Picture No. 7.

醋溜魚捲

材料：

中段草魚（或桂魚、鱠魚）	一斤	
熟火腿	一兩	
熟冬茹	二個	
葱	一支	
薑	五片	
洋葱	半個	
紅辣椒	一支	
青豆	一湯匙	
鹽	一茶匙	} 醃魚用
酒	一湯匙	
花生油	六杯	

鷄蛋	二個	麵糊用料
麵粉	半杯	
發泡粉	一茶匙	
水（大約）	半杯	
糖	四湯匙	綜合調味料
鎮江醋	四湯匙	
清水	三湯匙	
蕃茄醬	三湯匙	
鹽	一茶匙	
太白粉	一茶匙	
麻油	一茶匙	

做法：

1. 將魚除骨去皮後切成一寸半四方之薄片（約廿四片），全部放在大碗內，加入鹽一茶匙，酒一湯匙拌醃十分鐘左右。

2. 將熟火腿及熟冬菇（係先泡軟後蒸過）與葱薑，分別切成細絲，洋葱及紅辣椒則切成指甲片大小備用。

3. 將醃過之魚片，平舖在菜板或盤子上撒下少許乾太白粉然後將火腿絲，冬菇絲及葱薑絲各放進兩三支由手邊捲裹成筒狀。

4. 鷄蛋打散加入麵粉，發泡粉和水，調成糊漿，沾裹魚捲，隨即投入燒熱之花生油中炸熟（約兩分鐘），先撈出一次修整一下再重炸半分鐘至酥脆爲止。

5. 另用三湯匙油炒香洋葱丁後放下紅椒丁及青豆，並倒下綜合調味料用大火煮滾，隨即熄火後，速將魚捲落鍋拌和迅即裝盤上桌。（可撒下葱絲或香茭點綴）。

※請參考照片第9號。

38

Fish Rolls in Sour Sauce

Ingredients:

1-1/4 lbs. Fish (firm white meat)	2 Eggs	(flour batter)
3 Black mushrooms	1/2 C. Flour	"
(soaked and shredded)	1 t. Baking powder	"
2 oz. Ham (cooked and shredded)	1/2 C. Cold water	"
1 T. Shredded green onion	4 T. Vinegar	(seasoning sauce)
1 T. Shredded ginger	3 T. Sugar	"
2 T. Diced red pepper (or shredded)	3 T. Catsup	"
3 T. Diced onion "	3 T. Water	"
2 T. Green peas (optional)	1 t. Salt	"
1/2 T. Wine (to soak fish)	1 T. Cornstarch	"
1 t. Salt "	1 t. Sesame oil	
6 C. Peanut oil		

Procedure:

1. Removing all bones and skin, cut fish crosswise 1/4″ thick and 2″ long, 1½″ wide, then soak with wine and salt about 10 minutes.

2. On a flat slice of fish sprinkle a little bit of cornstarch. Lay a few pieces of shredded green onion, ginger, ham, mushroom on the fish and roll up.

3. Coat fish rolls with flour batter and deep fry it until brown, about 3 minutes, (take out once after 2 minutes, then heat oil again, and fry one more minute), remove fish rolls and drain off oil from fry pan.

4. Put back into frying pan 2T. of peanut oil to stir fry the diced onions, red peppers and seasoning sauce, stir until starchy. Then add green peas and fried fish rolls, mix well. Sprinkle a few drops of heated oil on the top before serving. (Decorate with shredded green onion).

* Refer to Picture No. 9.

炸　蝦　球

材料：

蝦仁	十二兩	蛋白	一個
肥豬肉	三兩	太白粉	三湯匙
葱	二支	淸水	三湯匙
薑	五片	花生油	八杯
鹽	一茶匙半	花椒鹽	二茶匙
酒	一湯匙		

做法：

1. 將蝦仁用鹽抓洗略冲淨並瀝乾後用刀面全部壓碎，再仔細斬剁使成爲極細爛之蝦泥狀，盛入大碗內，再將肥豬肉也剁爛合入蝦泥中。

2. 葱用刀拍碎，薑也拍碎，放入一只小碗內，加入淸水三湯匙浸泡（約十分鐘）。

3. 加入鹽與酒在大碗蝦泥中調拌，再將用葱薑所泡過之水陸續分三次加進（每加一湯匙即需加以調拌均勻）。

4. 將蛋白在別碗內打鬆後倒進蝦泥中調拌，並再放太白粉，仔細拌勻即可。（需向同一方向攪拌）。

5. 在炒鍋內燒熱花生油後（或豬油），暫時改爲小火，用左手抓一把蝦泥，撥弄大姆指揑擠使成圓型蝦球，而用右手執湯匙（需先沾過冷水）掐取蝦球投入油中，待全部做完投下之後，即用普通火候慢炸，約三分鐘，見蝦球已全部浮起始用筷子分開相黏者，待炸至，已微黃而熟透時，即行撈出裝盤，在盤邊置少許花椒鹽馬上供食。

※請參考照片第10號。

40

Deep Fried Shrimp Balls

Ingredients:

1 lb. Small shrimp   1 ½ t. Salt
    (without shell)   1 T. Wine
3 oz. Pork fat   3 T. Water
2 Green onions   3 T. Cornstarch (or flour)
3 slices Ginger   8 C. Peanut oil
1 Egg white   1 t. Pepper salt

Procedure:

1. Clean and chop the shrimp and pork very fine. Put in a bowl. Add salt and wine, mix well.
2. Crush the green onion and ginger with blade of knife. Put in a bowl, soak with 3 T. water about 10 minutes.
3. Add juice from #2 to shrimp and pork mixture, 1 T. at a time, mix well after each addition.
4. In another bowl beat egg white until dry and add to shrimp-pork mixture. Add cornstarch and mix well.
5. Heat peanut oil in frying pan. Wet left hand, place 2 or 3T. mix in palm of left hand. Close fingers. An amount about the size of a walnut will spurt from the top of the fist. With a wet spoon remove the ball and drop in hot oil right hand Separate the balls as they rise to the top and become crispy and golden. Keep oil at 270°C and fry 3 to 4 minutes.
6. Drain and remove to platter, serve immediately with peppercorn salt.

NOTE:

The shrimp-pork mixture may be kept in refrigerator for 1 day before frying.

* Refer to Picture No. 10.

蝦仁腰果

材料：

蝦仁	九兩	蛋白	半個	⎱醃蝦仁料
腰果	三兩	太白粉	一湯匙	
葱段（一寸長）	十支	鹽	半茶匙	
薑片	十小片	酒	一湯匙	⎱綜合料
豬油或花生油	三杯	鹽	1/4茶匙	
		麻油	一茶匙	

做法：

1. 蝦仁先放在盆裏用少許鹽抓拌，再用冷水冲洗後瀝乾並用乾布加以吸擦乾爽才放回大碗中，拌入醃蝦仁料（即蛋白、太白粉、鹽先在另碗內調勻）放入冰箱中約半小時以上。

2. 用燒至八成熱之油，炸黃腰果（慢火炸約三分鐘）然後撈出瀝去油漬，攤開在紙上晾冷。

3. 再將原鍋油燒熱（八成熱）傾下醃好之蝦仁泡炸，大火約半分鐘，見蝦仁已全部轉白時即行撈起，將鍋中之油也倒出。

4. 另燒熱兩湯匙油在鍋內先爆炒葱段及薑片約三秒鐘，便加入蝦仁與綜合料（預先調在小碗內）迅速拌炒，將火熄去後合入腰果拌勻即可起鍋裝盤。

註：炒蝦仁之配料可隨各自喜愛與方便採用筍丁、荸薺丁、青豆或豌豆苗等。

Shrimp with Cashew Nuts

Ingredients:

2/3 lb. Small fresh shrimp	1/2 Egg white (to marinate shrimp)
(without shell)	1 T. Cornstarch "
4 oz. Cashew nuts	1/2 t. Salt "
10 Green onions (1" long)	1 T Wine (seasoning sauce)
10 slices Ginger	1/4 t. Salt "
3 C. Peanut oil	1 t. Sesame oil "

Procedure:

1. Clean shrimp and pat dry, then mix with egg white, cornstarch, salt and soak for an hour at least.

2. Fry the cashewnuts in heated oil until brown, about 3 minutes over low heat. Remove, drain and set aside to cool.

3. Heat the same oil again, (about 320°C) pour in shrimp and fry for half minute, remove shrimp and drain oil from pan.

4. With another 2 T. oil fry the green onion and ginger slices, add shrimp and seasoning sauce quickly, then stir until thoroughly mixed over heigh heat. Trun off fire add the cashew nuts and serve.

NOTE:

You can use green peas or diceed bamboo shoot or water chestnut as a sunstitute for cashew nuts

茄汁明蝦

材料：

明蝦（中型）	十二隻（約一斤半）		
甜酒釀（可免）	二湯匙	酒	一湯匙
葱屑	二湯匙	清湯（或清水）	一杯半
薑屑	二湯匙	蕃茄醬	四湯匙
鹽	二茶匙	太白粉	一湯匙
糖	二茶匙	花生油	十湯匙

做法：

1. 明蝦首先剪除頭尖部份（蝦眼連前一段），再剪去尾尖部份與腳，並剖開蝦背，抽出腸筋（即砂囊）然後洗淨瀝乾。

2. 在炒鍋內先燒熱六湯匙油後，放下全部明蝦（入鍋時要將每隻蝦彎曲放下）將鍋傾斜轉動務使每隻明蝦均能被油煎到，待一面呈紅色後便翻轉一面再煎。

3. 見明蝦全部煎紅後，淋下料酒並放鹽、糖及清湯，用大火燒煮三分鐘，至明蝦已熟透，即可連湯全部盛出。

4. 另在原炒鍋內燒熱三湯匙油，放下葱屑、薑屑爆香並加入甜酒釀（需先攪碎）同炒，再放蕃茄醬炒拌，煮數滾（約半分鐘）然後將明蝦連湯傾入拌勻，再煮半分鐘便淋下調水之太白粉提起鍋子搖轉鈎芡使汁黏稠，澆上另一湯匙熱油即可裝盤。（盤底可用生荣葉舖飾）。

44

Prawns with Tomato Sauce

Ingredients:

12 Fresh prawns (about 2 lbs.)
2 T. Green onion chopped
1 T. Ginger chopped
2 t. Salt
2 t. Sugar
1 T. Wine

1-1/2 C. Soup stock (or water)
4 T. Tomato catsup
1 T. Cornstarch   (make paste)
1 T. Cold water,   "
10 T. Peaunt oil

Procedure:

1. Cut each prawn down the back and remove black vein. Do not remove shells, clean.

2. Heat 6 T. peanut oil in frying pan, cook the prawns until red (fry each side one minute).

3. Sprinkle wine and add salt, sugar and soup stock, cook about 3 minutes. Remove all from frying pan.

4. In the same fry pan heat another 3 T. peanut oil to fry shredded green onion and ginger then add tomato catsup stir-fry about half minute. Pour into the prawn and sauce mixture, cook another half minute, add cornstarch paste, stir and fry until thickened Spinkle 1T. hot cooking oil last and serve. Lay lettuce leaves on platter for garnish.

蟹 黃 菜 心

材料：

熟蟹肉	二兩（約半杯）	鹽	二茶匙
熟蟹黃	一兩（約1/3杯）	酒	一湯匙
青荣心	二十小棵	太白粉	1½湯匙
鷄蛋白	一個	清湯	三杯
葱屑	一湯匙	猪油或花生油	六湯匙
薑屑	一湯匙		

做法：

1. 將青荣心用開水燙兩分鐘（大火），撈出後用冷水漂洗一次再用油兩湯匙炒過，並加入一茶匙鹽及味精少許清湯一杯養約一分鐘即全部連湯倒在盆裏保暖留用。

2. 將三湯匙猪油燒熱，先放下葱屑及薑屑爆香，再將蟹肉落鍋略炒，並淋下酒，注入二杯清湯當湯養滾後加入鹽一茶匙，並淋下調水之太白粉鈎芡。

3. 將熟蟹黃略切碎放入鍋中與前項材料拌合，並淋下打散之蛋白，迅速攪勻，澆下另一湯匙熱油後即可倒在荣盤中青荣心上供食。（青荣心由盆中揀出後需濾乾湯汁盛在大荣盤內）。

註：此荣也可將青荣心改爲白荣心或蘆筍，豆腐草菇等。

※請參考照片第11號。

Crab Meat with Green Cabbage

Ingredients:

1/2 C. Cooked crab meat (or
      1/2 can crab meat)
1/3 C. Hard cooked crab roe
20 pcs. Small green cabbage
1 Egg white
1 T. Ginger Chopped
1 T. Green onion Chopped

1/2 t. Salt
1 T. Wine
1-1/2 T. Cornstarch   (make paste)
1/2 T. Cold water   "
3 C. Soup stock
6 T. Peanut oil

Procedure:

1. Boil cabbage in boiling water about 2 minutes over high heat, discard water, remove cabbage and soak in cold water, then stir fry with 2T. heated oil and add one cup soup stock, 1/2 t. salt. Cook 1 minute, place all into a bowl.

2. Heat 3T. oil in fry pan, fry green onion and ginger a few seconds, add the crab meat and splash with wine, stir-fry, add 2 C. soup stock, 1 t. salt, and cornstarch paste, boil until thickened.

3. Now add the crab roe (chopped well), and splash beaten egg white carefully. Stir until blended, drop one more table spoon heated oil; pour this on top of green cabbage, which has been removed from its warm bowl and placed on a platter. You do not use this cabbage soup stock.

NOTE:

Chinese cabbage, cauliflower, cucumber or asparagus may be used in place of green cabbage if you prefer.

* Refer to Picture No. 11.

全 家 福

材料：

鷄肉	四兩	酒	一湯匙
絞豬肉	半斤	醬油	四湯匙
火腿	四兩	太白粉	三湯匙
冬菇	五個	鹽	三茶匙
筍	一支	魷魚	半條
海參	一斤	清湯	三杯
豌豆夾	十二片	麻油	一茶匙
鷄蛋	二個	花生油	六湯匙

做法：

1. 鷄蛋一只打散加入半茶匙鹽，半茶匙太白粉及半湯匙水調勻，煎成一張蛋皮留用，（煎蛋皮時應用乾淨鍋，祗塗抹少許熱油攤煎）。

2. 絞豬肉再仔細斬剁一下後加入鹽半茶匙太白粉二茶匙酒一茶匙及一只鷄蛋慢慢向同一方向攪拌成泥狀，先將一半平塗在蛋皮上捲成筒狀放菜盤內上鍋蒸熟，另一半做成梭子狀小丸子置菜盤中亦上鍋蒸熟（各約十分鐘，可同放一只盤內去蒸）。

3. 鷄肉與火腿先整塊煮熟後分別切成大薄片（煮過之湯可當清湯用）。

4. 冬菇用熱水泡軟，筍煮熟均各切片，魷魚（已發泡過之）在光面切交叉細刀花紋後分割成寸半長段用開水燙熟。

5. 海參切成二寸半長之大斜片後，先用水（加葱薑少許）煮十分鐘然後撈出，用油（約二湯匙）爆炒一下加醬油二湯匙煮約二分鐘後撈出，鍋中之汁倒棄（因有腥味）。

6. 另燒熱三湯匙油在鍋中先炒冬菇、筍、鷄肉及豌豆夾加入清湯及醬油二湯匙，鹽一茶匙半，同煮一分鐘然後放進海參魷魚及火腿再煮數秒卽用調水之太白粉鈎芡，淋下麻油裝入大盤內，蒸熟之肉丸及蛋捲（需切成片狀）預先放在大菜盤中不必下鍋再煮。

註：此菜所用材料不做硬性規定，其種類及份量均可加多或減少。

※請參考照片第14號。

48

Assorted Dish with Brown Sauce

Ingredients:

6 oz. Chicken meat
10 oz. Ground pork
1/4 lb Ham or squid (soaked)
1-1/4 lbs. Sea cucumber
5 Dried mushrooms
1 Bamboo shoot
12 Snow pea pods
2 Eggs

1 T. Wine
4 T. Soysauce
3 T. Cornstarch   (make paste)
3 T. Cold water   "
3 t. Salt
3 C. Soup stock
1 t. Sesame oil
6 T. Peanut oil

Procedure:

1. Beat 1 egg, add ½t. salt, ½t. cornstarch, and ½T. water, mix well. Using frying pan make 1 large thin pancake with the mixture.
2. Add ½t. salt, 2t. cornstarch, 1t. wine and 1 egg to ground pork, mix well. Put half of the mixture on the pancake, roll into a tube. Make small meat balls with the other half of the mixture, steam the meat roll and balls for about 10 minutes or until done.
3. Cook ham and chicken with water, let cool, save the stock. Slice the ham, chicken, and squid.
4. Peel and boil whole bamboo shoot about 15 minutes, let cool and slice. Soak dried mushroom in warm water and remove stem, then slice.
5. Cut sea cucumber crosswise about 2½" long, boil with some extra green onion and ginger about 10 minutes. Fry the sea cucumber in 2T. heated oil, add 2T. soysauce, cook about 3 minutes. Drain and discard the juice.
6. Heat 3T. oil. Fry the chicken meat, sliced bamboo shoots, mushrooms and pea pods, then add soup stock, 2T. soysauce, 1½t. salt, cook for 1 minute. Add sea cucumber and ham, continuing to cook a while. Stir in cornstarch paste until thickened and heated through, sprinkle sesame oil, arrange the meat balls and sliced meat roll on a large platter. Pour the thickened mixture on the platter and serve.

NOTE:

A variation of the ingredients may be optional.

* Refer to picture No. 14.

三絲魚翅羹

材料：

水發散魚翅	一斤	酒	兩湯匙
熟鷄肉	四兩	醬油	三湯匙
多菇	五個	鹽	二茶匙
筍	兩支	糖	半茶匙
熟火腿絲	二湯匙	清湯	八杯
葱	二支	太白粉	六湯匙
薑	四片	猪油（或花生油）	四湯匙
香荽	數支	胡椒粉	少許

做法：

1. 將熟鷄肉（已羹過）切成一寸多長之細絲，多菇泡軟後去蒂也切絲，筍去簿後整個羹熟然後切成細絲留用。

2. 將已發好之散翅（荣市場有售）放在鍋內加入葱一支（拍碎）薑兩片酒一湯匙及冷水四杯，用小火羹十數分鐘，以去腥味，撈出魚翅後倒棄鍋中之水，另加入兩杯清湯再放進魚翅重又羹十分鐘（小火）。

3. 在炒鍋內燒熱四湯匙油後放下一支葱，兩片薑爆香，淋下一湯匙酒隨即加入六杯清湯並將鷄絲，多菇絲筍絲及魚翅也放下用大火羹滾，再將各調味料（醬油、鹽、糖）加入拌匀然後淋下太白粉（已加水六湯匙調溶）慢慢鈎芡至成稠糊狀便離火。

4. 盛入一只細瓷大湯碗內，在上面撒下火腿絲及胡椒粉中央放置香荽點綴便成。（如有鷄油淋下少許更佳）。

註：如用乾魚翅自行發泡，大約三兩散翅（或翅餅）即够。先用冷水浸泡兩小時再羹半小時離火後，待水冷却再換清水重複一次同樣過程便可使用。

※請參考照片第13號。

50

Shark's Fin with Shredded Chicken

Ingredients:

1-1/4 lbs. Short shark's fin
    (soaked)
1 C. Cooked chicken meat
    (shredded)
1/3 C. Dried black mushroom
    (soaked and shredded)
1 C. Bamboo shoots
    (cooked and shredded)
2 T. Cooked ham (shredded)
2 Green onions
4 Slices ginger

A few Parsey leaves
2 T. Wine
3 T. Soysauce
2 t. salt
2/1 t. sugar
9 C. soup stock
6 T. Cornstarch   (make paste)
6 T. Cold water
4 T. Lard or peanut oil
1/4 t. Black pepper

Procedure:

1. To improve the flavor of the shark's fin place it in a pan, add 3C. cold water, 1 piece green onion, 2 slices ginger, 2T. wine and cook for 10 minutes over low heat, drain and discard this water.

2. Add 3 C. soup stock to the same pan, cook another 10 minutes over low heat. Remove the shark's fin and discard this soup stock.

3. Heat 3 T. oil in frying pan, stir fry 1 green onion and 2 slices ginger. Sprinkle in 1T. wine and add 6 C. soup stock quickly. Add shredded chicken, black mushrooms, bamboo shoots and shark's fin. Let boil, season with soysauce, salt and sugar, then thicken with cornstarch paste.

4. Pour in big soup bowl, sprinkle with ham shreds and black pepper. Place parsley leaves on top for decoration.

NOTE:

    To soften dried shark's fin place in 6C. cold water, let remain 2 hours, boil about 1/2 hour over low heat. Let cool. Discard water, add fresh 6C. cold water and repeat procedure. 1/4 lb. dried = 1-1/4 lbs. softened shark's fin.

---

* Refer to picture No. 13.

紅扒鵪蛋

材料：

鵪蛋	二打	糖	一茶匙
洋菇（或小型香菇）	二十粒	鹽	一茶匙
青荣心	十二棵	麵粉	二湯匙
胡蘿蔔	半支	太白粉	半茶匙
醬油	二湯匙	清湯	半杯
花生油	四杯	麻油	一茶匙

做法：

1. 青荣心用開水炙熟（大火一分半鐘），再放在冷水中浸過，擰乾備用。胡蘿蔔炙熟切小花片。

2. 將鵪蛋放入碗中，加入清水浸泡，再用大火蒸十分鐘即行撈出，泡在冷水中片刻之後剝去外殻，放碗內加入二湯匙醬油醃泡約兩分鐘（需不斷加以搖動）然後再沾滿麵粉旋即投入已燒熱之四杯油中炸黃，撈出後備用。

3. 將糖、鹽、麻油各一茶匙及清湯加入在泡鵪蛋所餘下之醬油中調勻備用。

4. 鍋中放油三湯匙，待油熱後，落青荣心下鍋，並淋下上項調味料之一半，炒約一分鐘後盛出，排飾盤邊。

5. 另在鍋中放入二湯匙油，落下洋菇及葫蘿蔔片爆炒，隨後淋下所餘之一半調味料（需加入太白粉）慢慢拌勻再加入炸黃之鵪蛋將火熄去，稍加拌合後，即可盛在盤中荣心上趁熱送席。

※請參考照片第13號。

Quail Eggs in Brown Sauce

Ingredients:

2 dozen Quail eggs	1 t. Sugar
20 Canned mushrooms	1 t. Salt
12 Tender hearts of green	1 T. Cornstarch (make paste)
vegetable (or snow peas or	1 T.Cold water "
Chinese brocecli)	1/2 C. Soup stock
1/2 Carrot	1 t. Seame oil
2 T. Soysauce	4 C. Peanut oil
2 T. Flour	

Procedure:

1. Put the quail eggs in a bowl. Cover the eggs with cold water. Place into steamer and steam about 10 minutes. Put the eggs in cold water. After 5 minutes remove the shell. Marinate the shelled eggs with soysauce for about 2 minutes, turn the eggs frequently, coat with flour. Deep fry the eggs until golden brown.

2. Cook the green vegetable in boiling water. Plunge into cold water immediately and squeeze dry. Boil the carrot until tender and cut into slices.

3. Add sugar, salt, sesame oil, cornstarch and soup stock in the bowl used for marinating quail eggs. This is the seasoning sauce.

4. Heat 3T. oil, saute the green vegetable, add half of seasoning sauce, cook about one minute. Remove to plate.

5. Heat another 2T. oil in frying pan, stir fry the mushrooms, and carrots. Add the remaining seasoning sauce mix thoroughly. Add quail eggs and stir well, pour in plate. Serve.

* Refer to picture No. 12.

奶油白菜

材料：

大白菜	一斤半	太白粉	一湯匙
牛奶水	三湯匙	清湯	一杯
鹽	二茶匙半	花生油	六湯匙
糖	一茶匙		

做法：

1. 大白菜一瓣一瓣剝下後洗淨先切成兩寸半長之段，再順紋切半寸寬之條狀，（葉子可切得寬一些）

2. 在炒菜鍋內燒熱四湯匙油後，放下全部白菜拌炒，先放菜莖部份略炒片刻後加放葉子，以大火炒至菜莖變軟，加入鹽二茶匙及糖，味精調味，然後鏟出，瀝乾菜汁（盛在漏勺中）。

3. 將炒鍋洗淨重行燒熱後放下一湯油及一杯清湯，待湯再煑沸時加入鹽，並用調水之太白粉鈎芡使成爲糊狀，隨即再淋下牛奶水攪勻並澆下一湯匙熱油即可先盛出其中之一半在小碗內。

4. 將白菜傾入鍋中同奶油汁拌勻，盛到菜盤上，然後將另一半預先盛出之奶油淋澆在上面便成。

註： 此菜也可加入蝦米或是干貝之類鮮味品同炒，裝上盤後如撒少許火腿屑則可增加美觀。

54

Cabbage with Cream Sauce

Ingredients:

1-1/4 lbs. Chinese cabbage	1 T. Cornstarch (make paste)
4 T. Milk	1-1/2 T. Cold water "
2½ t. Salt	1 C. Soup stock
1 t. Sugar	6 T. Peanut oil

Procedure:

1. Remove cabbage leaves, wash and cut in 2½" crosswise slices then slice in ½" wide strips (leaf portions may be cut in wider pieces)

2. Heat 4T. oil in frying pan, add all of the cabbage and stir-fry with high heat, about 3 minutes, until cabbage is soft; then add salt, sugar, and M.S.G.. Place in a strainer and let cabbage drain.

3. Heat the frying pan and add 1T. oil with soup stock. When the soup stock boils, add salt and cornstarch paste to make it starchy. Add milk and another 1 T. oil. Stir well. Remove half of this sauce and reserve. Add cabbage to remaining sauce, mix thoroughly.

4. Lay the cabbage on platter, then pour the reserved sauce on top.

NOTE:

To this dish we may add 1/3 cup shrimp or scallops or ham cut in small pieces.

什景素燴

材料：

洋山芋（即馬鈴薯）	一個（約六兩）	清湯	二杯
白蘿蔔	一條（約八兩）	鹽	三茶匙
胡蘿蔔	一條（約三兩）	糖	半茶匙
小黃瓜	二條（約四兩）	太白粉	一湯匙半
洋菇（罐頭）	十個	花生油	五湯匙
腐竹	一支	鷄油	半湯匙
乾通心粉	1/3杯		

做法：

1. 洋山芋及胡蘿蔔削去皮後，雕成花樣，然後切片，全部用開水羹熟（先放胡蘿蔔羹三分鐘後，才加入洋芋再同羹三分鐘即可）。

2. 黃瓜洗淨不必去皮分成三面切下，中間之瓜芯不要，再將每面切成斜角塊（菱形），也用開水燙熟（水滾後放下約羹一分鐘大火不可蓋鍋）。

3. 白蘿蔔用挖球器挖成圓球狀（或用刀削修成橄欖形也可），用開水羹七、八分鐘至透明爲止，撈到冷水中浸泡。

4. 洋菇或草菇，每個直切爲二，腐竹用溫水泡十五分鐘後，切成小段（約一寸長）留用。

5. 通心粉放入開水內煮七分鐘撈出後，用冷水冲淋一下留用。

6. 將油燒熱放進各料同炒（除通心粉及腐竹之外）並加入清湯及鹽煮兩分鐘，傾下通心粉及腐竹後再淋下調水之太白粉鈎芡，卽可裝入盤中，然後滴下鷄油便可上桌。

註：1. 各種用開水燙過之蔬菜，撈出後均需泡入冷水中以保持原色。

2. 此菜如在最後加入牛奶三湯匙拌勻卽成爲奶油素燴，味道特別也非常可口。

56

Sauteed Mixed Vegetables

Ingredients:

1 Potato (large)
1 Turnip
2 Cucumbers (small)
1 Carrot (small)
10 Mushrooms
1 Beancurd sheet
1/3 C. Macaroni
3 t. Salt

1/2 t. Sugar
1½ T. Cornstarch   (make Paste)
1½ T Cold water   "
5 T. Peanut oil
2 C. Soup stock
1/2 T. Chicken grease
1/2 t. M.S.G.

Procedure:

1. After peeling and slicing the potato and carrot into flower shape, boil them with boiling water, (put carrot in first, boil 3 minutes, then add potato and continue to boil another 2 or 3 minutes).

2. Trimming tip off, (do not peel) slice the cucumbers, then boil with water about 2 minutes, remove and soak in cold water.

3. Cut the turnip in balls, and boil with boiling water until soft (about 7 or 8 minutes). Remove and soak in cold water.

4. Slice each mushroom in two. Soften the beancurd sheet with warm water and cut it into dice shape.

5. Boil the macaroni in boiling water about 7 minutes, then remove and rinse in cold water.

6. Heat the peanut oil, fry potato, turnip, cucumber, carrot, and mushroom together. Then pour in soup, and add salt, sugar, M.S.G. When it is boiling, add macaroni and beancurd sheet dices. Add cornstarch paste stirring until it is starchy. Splash on the chicken grease before serving.

NOTE:

1. All cooked vegetable should be soaked in cold water to keep their color.
2. To make a richer sauce, add 3T. milk to sauce mixture just before serving.

干貝蘿蔔球

材料：

干貝	一兩	酒	一湯匙
白蘿蔔	二支（約一斤半）	太白粉	一湯匙半
薑	一片	猪油	五湯匙
鹽	三茶匙	清湯	一杯半

做法：

1. 將干貝用溫水略洗，即用半杯熱清湯（或開水）浸泡（需蓋嚴）約兩三小時後放入鍋內再加以蒸軟（蒸半小時左右即够），取出待稍冷後用手撕成粗條留用。

2. 將白蘿蔔用挖球器挖出三、四十粒小球（或者用刀削切成荸薺般大小之圓球狀也可）全部投入開水中煮十分鐘左右，使成為透明狀而已熟爛即行撈出，浸泡在冷水中留用。

3. 將油（四湯匙）燒熱後放下薑片爆過，再將干貝下鍋略炒續將蘿蔔球落鍋同炒，並加入酒及泡干貝之汁與另外一杯清湯，放下鹽調味滾一分鐘（小火），隨後將太白粉淋下使汁變成稠糊狀。最後再淋下一湯匙熱油（或鷄油也可）便裝入深盤中上桌。

Scallops with Turnip Balls

Ingredients:

2 oz. Dried scallops

2 Turnips (about 2 lbs.) or
   30 small round radishes

1 slice Ginger

3 t. Salt

1 T. Wine

1 ½ T. Cornstarch   (make paste)

1 ½ T. Cold water   "

5 T. Peanut oil

1 1/2 C. Soup stock

Procedure:

1. Soak the scallops in 1/2 C. boiling hot soup stock (or water) and cover, about 2-3 hours, then steam another 1/2 hour. When soft, shred the scallops with fingers. Save the stock. (use in #3).

2. Cut turnips into 30 small balls with a melon ball scoop. Boil in water about 10 minutes, drain and soak in cold water.

3. Heat 4T. oil in frying pan, add ginger and scallops. Stir fry for a few seconds, then add turnip balls, wine and all soup stock. Cook about 1 minute over low heat. Add salt and stir in cornstarch paste, until thickened and blended. Sprinkle 1T. hot cooking oil or chicken grease and serve.

59

著者應邀赴港擔任全港烹飪比賽評審

The author judging the annual Hong Kong Amateur cooking contest

←著者爲參加出國甄選考試之廚師評分

The author judging Taiwan annual cooking contest for cook's going abroad

著者參加海鮮烹飪比賽獲取冠軍領獎紀念

The author acclaimed champion in 1965 Sea food Cooking contest.

南 部 菜

Dishes of **Southern** China

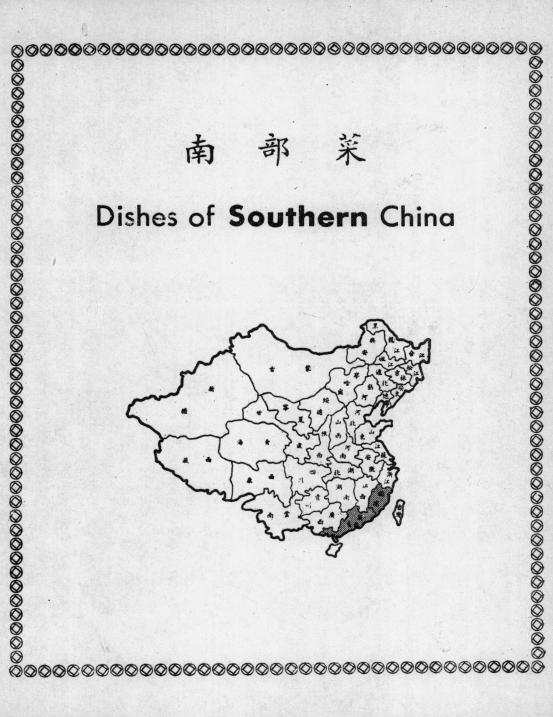

第十五圖（下）金華玉樹鷄
ing-Hua Chicken
(See Recipe page 67)
（做法參照第66頁）
Picture No. 15

第十六圖 八珍扒鴨
（做法參照第74頁）
Picture No. 16
Stewed Duck with Vegetable
(See Recipe Page 75)

第十七圖（左）
生菜鴿鬆
（做法參照第76頁）

Picture No. 17
Minced Pigeon
(See Recipe Page 77)

第十八圖（右）**菠蘿肫球**
（做法參照第72頁）

Picture No. 18 **Saute Gizzard with Pineapple** (See Recipe Page 73)

第十九圖（上）**滾筒肉**
（做法參照第78頁）

Picture No. 19 **Stewed Pork Rolls** (See Recipe Page 79)

第二十圖（左）
咕嚕肉
（做法參照第80頁）

Picture No. 20
Sweet and Sour Pork

(See Recipe Page 81)

第廿一圖（右）

糖醋荔枝肉

（做法參照第82頁）

Picture No. 21

Sweet Sour Pork
Litchi Style

(See Recipe Page 83)

第廿三圖(下) **茄汁魚片** （做法參照第92頁）

Picture No. 23 **Fish with Tomato Sauce**

(See Recipe Page 93)

第廿二圖（上）

中式牛排

（做法參照第88頁）

Picture No. 22

Beef Steak Chinese Style

(See Recipe Page 89)

第廿四圖
茄汁龍蝦片
（做法參照第96頁）

Picture No. 24
Saute Lobster Tail in Tomato Sauce
(See Recipe Page 97)

第廿六圖（下）**什錦冬瓜盅**
（做法參照第110頁）
Picture No. 26
Assorted Meat Soup in Winter Mellon
(See Recipe Page 111)

第廿五圖（上）　**客家釀豆腐**
（做法參照第104頁）
Picture No. 25
Cantonese Stuffed Bean Curd
(See Recipe Page 105)

南部菜目錄　　　Contents of Southern

61

葱　油　雞

材料：

嫩雞	一隻（約二斤左右）	酒	一湯匙半
葱	二支	葱絲	半杯
薑	三片	嫩薑絲	半杯
鹽	一湯匙	花生油	五湯匙

做法：

1. 葱二支用刀面在菜板上拍碎，薑三片也略拍扁同鹽、酒共放在一只盆或盤中加以調拌。

2. 將雞洗淨後用乾布擦拭水份，放在盆中，用前項葱薑鹽酒之混合料加以搓擦，抹遍雞身裏、外，醃約半小時以上（兩小時以內）。

3. 將醃過之雞連同容器（即盆或盤）上鍋用大火蒸熟（需待鍋中之水沸滾後始放進蒸，約十分鐘即可，將火熄去，再停候十分鐘才揭開鍋蓋，如此雞可自然收縮）。

4. 用快刀將雞斬切成適當之長方塊，仍按照原來雞形排列在一只菜盤內，並將葱、薑絲分別撒蓋在雞肉上。

5. 將花生油在炒鍋內燒熱，用小湯勺掐油向葱薑絲上面澆淋，待油已全部澆完後，再將菜盤傾斜使盤中之油慢慢流回鍋中再重複一次澆淋工作，則葱薑絲已呈半熟狀而雞肉也香嫩可食。

註：此菜也可將雞不用蒸，改為在鹽水滷內燙煮至熟，其他做法則相同。

Steamed Chicken with Green Onion

Ingredients:

1 whole Chicken (about 2-1/2   1-1/2 T. Wine   "
    lbs.)

2 Green onions   (to marinate   1/2 C. Shredded green onion

3 slices Ginger   chicken)   1/2 C. Shredded young ginger

1 T. Salt   "   5 T. Peanut oil

Procedure:

1. Crush green onion and ginger with blade of knife, put in bowl with wine and salt, mix well.

2. Clean and rub the chicken with # 1 ingredients (outside and inside) soak about 1/2 hour, but not over 2 hours.

3. Place the bowl of chicken and marinade in boiling steamer to steam over high heat for 10 to 15 minutes.

4. Turn off heat and remove the chicken after 15 minutes. Cut the chicken into 1" wide, 2" long pieces, lay on platter in a chicken shape. Sprinkle the shredded green onion and ginger on top.

5. Heat oil in frying pan, with a large cooking spoon scoop up all heated oil and splash over chicken dish. Drain this oil back into pan and reheat. Repeat process a second time but do not drain from dish, serve.

63

脆 皮 肥 鷄

材料：

嫩光鷄	一隻（約二斤重）	麥芽糖（或蜂蜜）	二湯匙	淋
花椒	一茶匙	白醋	二湯匙	鷄
八角	二顆	太白粉	二茶匙	用
桂皮	一段（約一寸）	開水	一杯	料
鹽	二茶匙	花生油	六杯	
檸檬	半個	花椒鹽	一茶匙	

做法：

1. 在鍋內煮滾八杯開水放進花椒、八角、桂皮及鹽續煮五分鐘，然後將已洗淨之鷄整隻放下鍋中，用大火燙煮成半熟狀態（不必蓋，燙約八分鐘，需翻面數次）

2. 將鷄由鍋中提出，擦乾水份後，用淋鷄用料（需預先在一只小盆內調備妥當）澆淋（或用小刷子塗擦）在鷄身各處（重複澆淋許多次），然後用一條繩子扎住鷄頸，吊掛在當風處吹乾（約六小時左右）。

3. 在鍋內燒熱花生油後，將鷄用漏勺托住，放進油中炸熟（用小火慢炸，約需炸五分鐘以上）炸時應將油不斷用鏟勺澆淋在鷄身上，以保持顏色一致。

4. 將炸熟之鷄瀝乾油後，迅速斬剁成半寸多寬之長方形，並按鷄之原形整齊排列在菜盤中，盤之兩端附上切開之檸檬塊及少許五香花椒鹽一起上桌（檸檬為擠汁淋在鷄肉上用，五香花椒鹽可為蘸食之用）。

註：此菜係著名粵菜之一，首先需注意選購嫩而較肥之鷄，又必需吹至鷄皮十分乾硬始能炸脆而歷久不軟，斬切時動作要快速才好。

Crispy Chiken

Ingredients:

1 whole Chicken (about 2 lbs.)	2 T. Syrup or honey (basting sauce)
1 t. Brown peppercorn	2 T. Vinegar "
2 Star anise (pa chiao)	2 t. Cornstarch "
1 Cinnamon stick (1" long)	1 C. Boil water "
2 t. Salt	6 C. Peanut oil
1/2 Lemon (sliced)	1 t. Pepper salt

Procedure:

1. Add peppercorn, star anise, cinnamon and salt to 8C. boiling water. Boil 5 minutes. Put the whole chicken in, continue to boil until half cooked (about 8 minutes.) without cover.

2. Take the chicken out, wipe dry. Baste chicken with basting sauce thoroughly many times. Tie a string around the chicken neck. Hang it up in a drafty place to wind dry for about 6 hours.

3. Deep fry over low fire. Baste the chicken with oil constantly so that it will be evenly brown.

4. Take out the chicken and blot the oil. Chop into 1" wide 1¼" long pieces. Serve with peppercorn salt and lemon slices.

NOTE:

This is a well known Cantonese dish. The chicken should be tender and fat. Make sure the skin is thoroughly wind dried to insure the crispness. Chop quickly in order to serve it piping hot.

金華玉樹鷄

材料：

光嫩鷄	一隻（約一斤半左右）	薑	三片
熟火腿	六兩	鹽	半茶匙
芥蘭菜（或其他靑菜）	半斤	太白粉	三茶匙
葱	二支	鷄湯	1-2/3杯

做料：

1. 在鍋內煮滾八杯開水（加入葱薑同煮）放下整隻鷄（最好連頭）蓋好鍋蓋，用大火煮五分鐘，然後將鷄翻一次身，再煮三分鐘，即將爐火關閉（或將鍋端離也可）約過十五分鐘之後，才揭開鍋蓋將鷄由鍋中取出瀝乾水份。

2. 將鷄拆除全部骨頭（要按鷄胸肉、鷄腿等順序先分開後拆骨，而盡量要保持鷄肉之完整），然後將鷄肉斜刀切成一寸寬兩寸長之片狀，再按原樣（鷄形）排列在大菜盤中。

3. 將火腿切成同鷄肉一樣大小（或稍小一點）之薄片，夾放在每兩片鷄肉之間（即一片鷄肉，一片火腿相間隔排列）。

4. 將原來煮鷄之湯燒滾，取一杯澆在大盤內用着浸泡鷄肉與火腿，約浸五分鐘後倒出

5. 另將三分之二杯鷄湯在炒鍋內煮滾，並加入鹽調味，再用太白粉（加水調溶）鈎芡，然後澆淋在盤中鷄與火腿上。

6. 盤邊可放用油炒過之綠色靑菜（需加少許鹽調味）伴飾即成。（如用芥蘭菜則需先在開水中燙熟再炒，並淋酒少許加糖鹽各少量調味之）。

註：「金華」是我國盛產火腿之地方，而品質優良之火腿均慣用金華二字以徵信用。

※請參考照片第15號。

King-Hua Chicken

Ingredients:

1 Chicken (about 1-1/2 lbs.)	1/2 t. Salt
6 oz. Chinese Virginia ham	3 t. Cornstarch (make paste)
1/2 lb. Green cabbage	3 t. Cold water "
2 Green onion	1-2/3 C. Soup stock
3 slices Ginger	

Procedure:

1. Clean the ham and put in a plate. Steam for about 20 minutes.
2. Put 8 cups of water in the pan and boil, add green onions, ginger and whole chicken. Cover and cook for 3 minutes, turn chicken once then cook another 3 minutes, turn off the fire. Take the chicken out after 15 minutes. Reserve the water that is the soupstock.
3. Remove chicken bones, slice chicken meat 1″ wide and 2″ long, arrange on the platter. Between every two pieces of chicken meat, put one piece of the ham, that was cut into equal size as chicken.
4. Soak the chicken and ham with 1 C. boiling soup for 5 minutes to make it hot, then carefully discard. With remaining 2/3 cup of soup boil with salt and thicken with cornstarch paste. Then pour over chicken and ham on the platter.
5. Arrange the cooked green cabbage (seasoned with added salt) around the platter before serving.

NOTE:

"King-Hua" is a city of China, which produces the best hams in the country.

* Refer to Picture No. 15.

桃仁鷄丁

材料：

光鷄	一隻（約一斤半	蛋白	半個	醃
	或淨鷄肉十二兩）	醬油	一湯匙	鷄用料
靑辣椒	一個	太白粉	一湯匙	
紅辣椒	一個	醬油	二湯匙	綜
葱	一支	醋	半湯匙	合調味料
薑	三片	酒	一湯匙	
桃仁（或腰果）	2/3杯	太白粉	半湯匙	
花生油	六杯	鹽	半茶匙	
		糖	一茶匙	

做法：

1. 將鷄全身大小骨頭除淨，取用鷄肉，先將鷄肉有筋處輕輕斬剁數刀後，分別切成像桃仁般大小（即一寸四方丁狀）全部放進已調妥之蛋白，醬油與太白粉中（即醃鷄料）拌醃半小時左右。

2. 將靑、紅辣椒分別除籽後切成小方塊或滾刀塊留用。

3. 將油燒至八成熱，投下桃仁以慢火炸成金黃色，需不停鏟動約三分鐘，撈出後攤開在紙上待涼。

4. 將上列之綜合調味料在一只小碗內調妥備用。

5. 在炒鍋內燒熱花生油（不可太熱，約七、八成即可），傾下全部鷄肉用大火炸熟（約半分鐘）隨即撈出，瀝淨餘油（鍋中之油應全部倒出）。

6. 再另燒熱兩湯匙油在鍋內爆炒一下薑片、葱段（切成一寸長數段）然後放靑辣椒塊（如喜食辣味可先加入紅辣椒）同炒約半分鐘，續將鷄肉落鍋用大火拌炒，並將綜合調味料倒下拌炒至熟，將火關熄後迅速加進桃仁拌勻裝盤即成。

Diced Chicken with Walnuts

Ingredients:

1 Chicken (boned) or 1 lb. chicken breasts	2/3 C. Walnut halves (or cashewnuts)
1 Green onion	2 T. Soysauce (seasoning sauce)
1 Green pepper	1 T. Wine "
1 Red hot pepper	1/2 T. Brown vinegar "
3 Slices Ginger	1/2 T. Cornstarch "
1/2 Egg white (to marinate	1/2 t. Salt "
1 T. Cornstarch chicken)	1 t. Sugar "
1 T. Soysauce "	4 C. Peanut oil

Procedure:

1. Cut the boned chicken into pieces the size of a walnut half and mix thoroughly with marinade. Let stand for at least 30 minutes.
2. Cut green onion into 1/2″ long pieces. Cut green pepper, red pepper the same size as chicken (keep separate) and 2 slices of fresh ginger (or 1/4 t. powdered ginger). If fresh ginger is used, by far the best, the slices should be about the size of a quarter.
3. Now fry or crisp in oven 2/3 cup walnut halves. Set aside and prepare the seasoning sauce in a bowl.
4. Deep fry chicken in oil, that is not too hot, (about 300°C). If the chicken pieces stick to each other the oil is too hot, lower temperature slightly. Fry for 1/2 minute. Remove chicken and drain off oil from frying pan.
5. Put back only 2T. oil in pan and stir fry the ginger slices. Add onion, stir quickly, frying for only a few seconds, then add the green pepper. If you like a spicy hot taste. add the red pepper now then add chicken and seasoning sauce, stir until thickened and heat thoroughly turn off heat. Add the walnuts and red pepper if it is used only for color.

鷄茸粟米羹

材料：

鷄胸肉	四兩	鹽	二茶匙
粟米（二號罐頭）	一罐	太白粉	四或五湯匙
蛋白	二個	清湯	五杯
熟火腿屑	一湯匙		

做法：

1. 鷄胸肉，需先除淨皮與筋，然後切碎，再加以剁爛至成泥狀（無粒塊為止），放進碗裏加入一個蛋白慢慢調拌至勻滑，再將罐頭粟米加入仔細拌合使與鷄肉完全混合均勻為止。

2. 在鍋內燒滾清湯，（如無清湯可將猪油一湯匙燒熱，淋下數滴料酒注入清水加少許味精也可）倒進上項已調勻之鷄茸粟米（形如膏醬狀）急加調勻再煮至沸滾，並放鹽調味，煮滾後即改為小火，再將太白粉（用四湯匙水調溶）慢慢淋下，調攪成糊狀。

3. 將另一個蛋白在小碗內打散（不要打起泡沫）緩慢淋入鍋內（要將碗抬高淋下，才會細如絲狀）並需用湯勺速加攪拌便成。

4. 將煮成之粟米羹盛在細瓷湯碗內，並在面上撒下熟火腿屑即可端上桌供食。

註：1. 此菜也可將鷄茸改為蝦仁或干貝或鮑魚絲之類，任何各人所喜愛之海鮮品。

2. 此菜也可加入牛奶若干（在起鍋之前）則別有一番風味。

70

Minced Chicken with Corn Soup

Ingredients:

1/4 lb. Chicken breast	3 t. Salt
2 Egg white	6 C. Chicken broth
1 T. Chopped cooked ham	4 T. Cornstarch (make paste)
1 can Sweet corn (# 2 can)	4 T. Cold water "

Procedure:

1. Mince into fine slivers, 1/4 lb. chicken breast. Place in a bowl, add 1 egg white and cream style corn. Mix carefully, put aside. In another bowl, beat 1 egg white and set aside.

2. Bring to a boil 5 cups chicken broth or consomme. Add chicken with corn and salt, when it boils again, add cornstarch paste. Stir well and let boil until thickened. Reduce heat to low, add the beaten egg white carefully and stir until blended.

3. Pour into serving bowl and sprinkle 1T. chopped ham. Serve.

NOTE:

1. Instead of chicken meat, the scallops, abalone, or shrimp may be used.
2. To this soup we may add 1/3 C. milk just before serving.

菠蘿肫球

材料：

鴨肫（或雞肫十個）	六個	蕃茄醬	三湯匙	綜合調味料
菠蘿（卽鳳梨）	四片	清水	三湯匙	
靑辣椒	一個	糖	二湯匙	
紅辣椒	二支	白醋	二湯匙	
酸甜薑	十小片	太白粉	半湯匙	
葱（細支）	二支	鹽	一茶匙	
薑汁（或薑粉）	半茶匙	麻油	一茶匙	
酒	一湯匙	花生油	五杯	

做法：

1. 將鴨肫上之白筋與硬皮用刀削下，取用肫肉部份（卽紅色肉）再每一塊用刀在上面切劃十字交叉刀紋，（需割切深些以便炒時裂開）待全部切好之後（每一只鴨肫可分爲四小塊切，如用雞肫則分爲二塊）放在碗內加入酒及薑汁拌醃片刻。

2. 靑、紅辣椒剖開除籽後切成小塊（比肫塊小些）鳳梨每片切成六小塊（或八小塊）細葱切成斜小段（約半寸多長）備用。

3. 將綜合調味料在一只碗內調備妥當留用。

4. 將油燒至極熱，然後放下肫塊用大火炸約五秒鐘，隨卽撈起餘油倒出。

5. 另在鍋內放下三湯匙油，先炒甜薑片及靑紅椒，鳳梨等，約半分鐘後將炸過之肫塊落下，同時倒進綜合調味料以大火快加拌炒，至汁成爲黏稠狀便行裝盤，盤邊可用餛飩皮或麵包片炸脆圍飾也可就食。

※請參考照片第18號。

Sauteed Gizzard with Pineapple

Ingredients:

6 Duck gizzards (or 10 chicken gizzards)

4 slices Pineapple

1 Green pepper

2 Red hot peppers

10 slices Sweet ginger

2 Green onions

1 t. Ginger juice   (to marinate
1 T. Wine   gizzards)

3 T. Tomato catsup (seasoning sauce)

3 T. Cold water   "

2 T. Sugar   "

2 T. Vinegar   "

1 T. Cornstarch   "

: t. Salt   "

1 t. Sesame oil   ₊

5 C. Peanut oil

Procedure:

1. Score the gizzards after removing hard skins. Divide each into 4 pieces. Put them in a large bowl and soak with wine and ginger juice about 10 minutes.

2. Cut each piece of pineapple into 6 cubes. Dice green pepper and red pepper. Cut green onion into 1″ long pieces.

3. Mix all ingredients of seasoning sauce in a bowl.

4. When the peanut oil in the pan is heated, fry gizzards for 5 seconds and remove immediately. Drain oil from frying pan.

5. Heat another 3T. oil, fry green onion, sweet ginger, pineapple and green pepper, red pepper, then add gizzards and fry for 1/2 minute. Pour in the seasoning sauce and stir briskly until thoroughly heated.

NOTE:

Make some crispy bread or Hun-Tung skins to decorate plate, and eat.

* Refer to Picture No. 18.

73

八 珍 扒 鴨

材料：

光肥鴨	一隻（約三斤）	八角	一顆
鴨肫	一個	醬油	六湯匙
鴨肝	一付	酒	一湯匙
筍	一支	糖	半湯匙
冬菇	三個（或木耳數朵）	太白粉	一湯匙
胡蘿蔔	半支	麻油	一茶匙
豌豆夾	十個	花生油	六杯
葱	二支		

做法：

1. 將鴨洗淨，擦乾水份後，由腹部中間直刀切開，使成為背部互連之一大片原形鴨狀，放在一只盆或大盤內（鴨皮朝上）再淋下醬油六湯匙塗抹着色，泡約十數分鐘，使鴨皮一面均呈醬油色（應用顏色較深之醬油）

2. 將六杯花生油在炒鍋內燒得極熱之後，將鴨放下油鍋（鴨皮面朝下）用大火炸黃（約兩分鐘）將鴨撈出瀝淨油後，鍋中之油全部倒出。

3. 用一只深底鍋（或原鍋也可）先倒下泡過鴨之醬油，並加入酒、葱、八角、糖煮滾，將鴨入鍋，再注入開水六杯（至與鴨面平）用小火燒煮，至鴨酥爛而汁僅剩下一杯為止（約需二小時半）

4. 鴨肫與鴨肝剔除白筋後，分別切成薄片，筍與胡蘿蔔先煮熟，同泡軟之冬菇各分別切成薄片狀留用。

5. 將已煮爛之鴨由鍋內取出平放在大菜盤內（並略拆去大骨）再放下各種切片之材料（包括豌豆夾）到鍋內所餘之汁中（需先將汁中之葱，八角等雜物揀出），用大火煮滾，即可淋下太白粉（先用水調好）將汁鈎芡，滴下少許麻油便可全部澆在鴨面上送桌供席。

※請參考照片第16號。

74

Stewed Duck with Vegetables

Ingredients:

1 Whole Duck (about 4 lbs.)	1 Star anise (optional)
1 Duck gizzard	6 T. Soysauce (dark colored)
1 Duck liver	1 T. Wine
1 Bamboo shoot	1/2 T. Sugar
3 Dried mushrooms	1 T. Cornstarch (make paste)
1/2 Carrot	1 T. Cold water "
10 Pea pods (snowpeas)	1 t. Sesame oil
2 Green onions	6 C. Peanut oil

Procedure:

1. Cut the duck through the breast lengthwise. Open the breast and lay the duck flat on a big round plate with skin side up. Sprinkle and rub the duck with soysauce. Let stand 10 minutes.

2. Deep fry the duck until golden brown. Drain.

3. In a Dutch oven (or deep pot) mix soysauce from # 1, wine, sugar, star anise, green onion. Bring to a boil. Put the duck in and cover it with boiling water (about 6 C.). Stew at low heat until the duck is tender when only 1 C. of liquid is left (about 2½ hour).

4. Remove the ligament of the gizzard. Slice the gizzard and liver. Slice and cook the bamboo shoots and carrots. Soften and slice the mushrooms.

5. Lay the duck on a platter with large bone removed. Remove the crumbs and spices from the stewed sauce. Add sliced ingredients from # 4. Stir until cooked through. Thicken the sauce with cornstarch paste. Sprinkle some sesame oil and pour it over the duck. Serve. Instead of duck the Chicken may be used.

* Refer to Picture No. 16.

生菜鴿鬆

材料：

鴿子	一隻（或鷄肉四兩）	醬油	半湯匙	醃肉用料
豬肉	五兩（瘦肉）	鹽	一茶匙	
鷄肝	二付	蛋黃	一個	
洋葱	一個（小型）	太白粉	二茶匙	
冬菇	四個	糖	半茶匙	
荸薺	八個（或筍一支）	醬油	一湯匙	綜合調味料
青豆	三湯匙（或青辣椒一只）	清湯	一湯匙	
生菜葉	二十四張	太白粉、鹽麻油	各一茶匙	
乾米粉	二兩	胡椒粉	1/4茶匙	
花生油	五杯			

做法：

1. 將鴿子剔淨骨頭後，取全部鴿肉（或用小鷄一隻代替也可，如用鷄肉，可省却剔骨之麻煩）然後同豬肉、鷄肝分別仔細切成小粒，（愈細小愈好）。
2. 將切好之各項材料裝在碗內，加入醃肉用料調拌，放置十分鐘以上。將冬菇先用熱水泡軟去蒂後連同洋葱，荸薺分別切碎留用。
3. 將油全部倒在鍋裏燒得極熱，放下米粉炸成鬆黃後隨即撈出（需兩面各炸三秒鐘）將油瀝淨，裝在大菜盤中，稍涼後用手撳壓成細碎狀。
4. 用三湯匙油將第二項之肉類炒熟，至十分乾鬆後（約三分鐘）盛出。
5. 另在炒鍋內燒熱三湯匙油先炒香洋葱，再加入冬菇，荸薺同炒，然後倒下已炒過之肉類及煑熟之青豆（或青椒）並加入綜合調味料大火急炒拌勻，盛放在米粉上。
6. 將生菜葉洗淨拭乾水份，切成三吋直徑之圓片狀，裝在另外小碟中與大盤鴿鬆同時上桌，由食者自行包食。（也可用單餅代替生菜葉包食之，或用單餅及生菜葉各一張也可）

※請參考照片第17號。

Minced Pigeon

Ingredients:

1 Pigeon (or 6 oz. chicken meat)	1/2 T. Soysauce (to marinate meat)
5 oz. Pork, lean	1 t. Salt "
2 Chicken livers	1 Egg yolk "
1 Onion (small)	2 t. Cornstarch "
4 Dried mushrooms	1/2 t. Sugar "
8 Water chestnuts	1 T. Soysauce (Seasoning sauce)
(or 1 bamboo shoot)	1 T. Soupstock "
3 T. Green peas	1 t. Cornstarch "
24 Lettuce leaves	1 t. Salt "
3 oz. Rice noodles	1 t. Sesame oil "
5 C. Peanut oil	1/4 t. Black pepper "

Procedure:

1. Remove all bones from the pigeon, cut pigeon meat, pork and chicken liver in small cubes, put in bowl, marinate with soysauce, salt, egg yolk, cornstarch, and sugar. Let stand for 10 minutes.

2. Soak dried mushrooms in warm water, discard stem, chop into small cubes. Chop onion and water chestnuts inso small pieces.

3. Heat oil very hot, deep fry the rice noodles until puffed and golden (only 3 seconds each side).

4. Use 3 T. heated oil to fry the pigeon, pork and chicken liver mixture until well done. (about 3 minutes). Remove to bowl.

5. Heat another 3 T. oil in fry pan, add chopped onion, fry one minute, add mushrooms and water chestnuts, stir fry another minute over heigh heat. Then add meat mixture, green peas and seasoning sauce. Stir until mixed thoroughly. Pour over the fried noodles. Serve with lettuce leaves cut into 2½" round pieces, which will be used to wrap around the meat and noodle mixture

NOTE:

Instead of lettuce leaves, spring roll skins or wheat tortilla may be used.

* Refer to picture No. 17.

滾 筒 肉

材料：

豬肉（大排骨肉）	十二兩	酒	一湯匙
筍	一支	糖	三湯匙
冬菇	二個	鎮江醋	三湯匙
葱（細小）	三支	開水	三杯
青蒜（或牙籤十四支）	一支	麻油	半湯匙
醬油	五湯匙	花生油	五杯

做法：

1. 將筍羹熟冷後切成一寸半長之粗條十四支，冬菇泡軟也切粗條（十四條），另將葱三支切成一寸半長（十四支）留用。

2. 青蒜放在開水中燙軟，並將蒜葉分別剝下，每支蒜葉再撕開成爲三或四條留用。

3. 將豬肉用利刀切成十四薄片，每片均經過刀面拍敲數下，以使肉質鬆嫩，再在每一片肉中間，橫放筍、冬菇、葱，各一支，然後由手邊捲成筒狀，用上項之青蒜一條捆紮並結好（或用牙籤別住）。

4. 全部做好結紮妥當之肉捲，放在一只大碗內，加入醬油浸泡，約泡二十分鐘，再投入已燒熱之油中，以大火炸約一分鐘即可，油便倒出。

5. 將炸過之肉捲重放回鍋中（或改用平底鍋也可），並倒下曾經浸肉之醬油，再加放糖，酒與醋便注入開水三杯（可與肉面平），用中火燒羹半小時，至湯汁僅剩餘小半杯時止，淋下麻油即可裝盤。

※請參考照片第19號

78

Stewed Pork Rolls

Ingredients:

- 1 lb. Pork loin
- 1 Bamboo shoot
- 2 Dried Black Mushrooms
- 3 Green onions (young)
- 1 Green garlic
- 5 T. Soysauve (to marinate pork)
- 1 T. Wine

- 3 T. Sugar
- 3 T. Brown vinegar
- 1-1/2 t. Sesame oil
- 3 C. Boiling water
- 5 C. Peanut oil

Procedure:

1. Boil the bamboo shoot and cut it into 1½" long pieces. Soak dried mushrooms, discard stems and cut in 14 pieces, cut green onion into 1½" long pieces.
2. Drop and soak the green garlic in boiling water and remove each leaf and separate it into 3 or 4 strands.
3. Cut the pork into 14 slices pound each slice with wood mallet or the back of knife a few times. Place on each one a mushroom, bamboo shoot and green onion, then roll it well, and each pork roll should be wrapped with green garlic strand or fastened with a toothpick.
4. Soak the pork rolls in soysauce and wine for about 20 minutes.
5. Deep fry the pork rolls in hot peanut oil about 1 minute, until brown, remove and drain the oil from pan.
6. Stew the fried pork rolls with remaining marinade sauce, add sugar vinegar and boiling water, cook about 30 minutes, or until done.
7. When the sauce is reduced to half a cup, add sesame oil and it is ready to serve.

* Refer to Picture No. 19.

咕嚕肉

材料：

猪肉（大排骨肉）	十二兩		糖	四湯匙	綜
青辣椒	二個		白醋	四湯匙	合
酸果（即廣東泡菜）	一杯		水	四湯匙	調
（或用四片鳳梨）			蕃茄醬	四湯匙	味
鹽	半茶匙	醃	鹽	一茶匙	料
醬油（淡色）	半湯匙	肉	太白粉	三茶匙	
濕太白粉	一湯匙	用	麻油	一茶匙	
蛋黃	一個	料	太白粉	半杯	
			花生油	六杯	

做法：

1. 將猪肉用刀背敲鬆，然後切成一寸四方之小塊，在碗裏先將蛋黃，鹽、醬油與濕太白粉（即太白粉一湯匙加一湯匙水調成膏狀）拌匀再放進肉塊調拌醃漬半小時以上。

2. 青辣椒剖開去籽後切一寸四方塊（或小滾刀塊也可）。如用鳳梨代替酸果時，鳳梨也切成小塊（一片切做六小塊爲宜）。

3. 用一只小碗，將綜合調味料全部調安備用。

4. 在鍋內將油燒熱，然後投入已沾裹過乾太白粉之猪肉塊，用大火炸上二分多鐘，用漏匀全部撈出一次，重將油燒至滾熱，然後再投入肉塊續炸一分鐘（第一次炸爲使肉塊熟透，第二次再炸可使肉塊外皮酥脆金黃）。

5. 將炸肉之油倒出僅留兩湯匙在鍋內，用大火炒青椒與酸果（或鳳梨塊），約炒數秒鐘即倒下綜合調味料煮滾，隨後將火熄去將炸過之肉塊放下鍋拌合一下，馬上裝盤送席。

註：酸果之做法係將白蘿蔔，胡蘿蔔及小黃瓜等切成小滾刀塊後用鹽拌醃（一斤菜需用一兩鹽）約六小時之後，擠乾鹽水再放入糖醋汁中（糖，白醋及冷開水各一杯調匀）浸泡六小時之後便可取食之。

※請參考照片第20號。

80

Sweet and Sour Pork

Ingredients:

1 lb. Pork tenderloin

2 Green peppers

4 slices Pineapple (or 1 C.
           Cantonese pickles)

1/2 t. Salt   (to marinate pork)

1/2 T. Soy sauce   "

1 T. Cornstarch   "

1 T. Cold water   "

1 Egg yolk   "

6 C. Peanut oil

3 T. Vineger   (Seasoning sauce)

4 T. Sugar   "

4 T. Tomato catsup   "

4 T. Cold water   "

3 t. Cornstarch   "

1 t. Salt   "

1 t. Sesame oil   "

1/2 C. Cornstarch

Procedure:

1. Pound pork with the back of a cleaver (this is to tenderize the pork), then cut into 1 inch squares. Soak with marinade for at least 1/2 hour.

2. Cut green pepper into halves, remove seeds and membrane, and cut into 1" squares. Next cut 4 slices of pineapple into the same size squares. Set aside.

3. Heat 6 cups oil. While oil is heating, coat each piece of pork in 1/2 cup cornstarch. When oil is ready, fry pork until brown and done (about 2 minutes), take out, reheat oil then fry once more until crispy. Remove pork and drain off oil from frying pan.

4. Put back into frying pan 2 T. oil, fry the green pepper and pineapple, stirring constantly. Add the seasoning sauce continuing to stir fry, until thickened. Turn off the heat. Add the pork, mix well and serve immediately.

---

* Refer to picture No. 20.

糖 醋 荔 枝 肉

材料：

猪肉（大排骨肉）	十二兩	醬油（淡色）	一湯匙	
靑辣椒	兩個	白醋	三湯匙	
荸薺	六個	糖	三湯匙	綜合調味料
葱	一支	水	三湯匙	
大蒜屑	半湯匙	太白粉	半湯匙	
醬油（淡色）	一湯匙	麻油	一茶匙	
太白粉	一茶匙	花生油	六杯	
酒	一茶匙			
鹽	半茶匙			
紅粉	少許			

（醬油至紅粉為醃肉用料）

做法：

1. 將猪肉整塊，洗淨後，剔除筋與肥肉，再橫面順肉紋切成大薄片（約半公分厚）然後每片肉切入交叉細刀紋，並切開成每兩寸一段，放在碗裏加入醃肉用料，仔細拌勻醃約十分鐘。

2. 將荸薺切片，靑辣椒去籽，切小方塊或滾刀塊，葱切半寸長小段留用。

3. 將醃過之猪肉，弄成筒狀，如一粒荔枝形放置菜盤中。

4. 將花生油在鍋內燒熱，投下荔枝形肉筒用大火炸熱，約一分鐘即行撈出。

5. 在炒鍋內只留兩湯匙油燒熱，先爆炒蒜屑及葱段，再加入荸薺及靑椒，大火拌炒數秒鐘，隨將綜合調味料（預先在一只小碗內調合），倒下迅速炒拌並煮滾再將荔枝肉落鍋鏟合隨即裝盤便可。

※請參考照片第21號。

Sweet Sour Pork Litchi style

Ingredients:

1 lb. Pork tenderloin

2 Green peppers

6 Water chestnuts

1 Green onion

1/2 T. Garlic (chopped)

1 T. Soysauce (to marinate pork)

1 t. Cornstarch   "

1 t. Wine   "

1/2 t. Salt   "

1/4 t. Red food color

1 T. Soysauce   (Seasoning sauce)

3 T. Sugar   "

2 T. Vinegar   "

3 T. Water   "

1/2 T. Cornstarch   "

1/2 T. Salt   "

1 t. Sesame oil   "

6 C. Peanut oil

Procedure:

1. Cut pork into 1" x 2", 1/4" thick slices, along the grain. Score each slice horizontally and vertically. Marinate with soysauce, cornstarch, wine, salt and red food color for 10 minutes.

2. Sliced water chestnut and green pepper, chop the garlic and cut green onion into 1/2" sections.

3. Roll pork slices into cylinder style, then deep fry about 1/2 minute or until done.

4. Heat 2 T. oil to saute garlic and green onion, then add water chestnut and green pepper, finally stirring in the seasoning sauce until cooked through. Add the pork in the sauce and mix well. Serve.

* Refer to picture No. 21.

掛爐叉燒肉

材料：

豬肉（大排骨肉或腿肉）	一斤	糖	二湯匙
葱	二支	海鮮醬	一湯匙
薑	五片	紅粉	1/3茶匙
醬油（淡色）	五湯匙	麻油（或鷄油）	一湯匙
酒	二湯匙		

做法：

1. 選購有肥肉及帶筋之大排骨肉（即靠上端部份），切成一寸寬五寸長之粗長條（約可切得六條），並在每條肉上劃切數刀斜紋。全部放在大碗內加入葱段（拍碎），薑片及酒、醬油、海鮮醬、糖、紅粉等（要預先調好在大碗內）拌和，醃約二小時至四小時。

2. 將肉條用S形小鐵絲鈎子吊起，掛進特製之鐵皮桶形爐內，並加蓋蓋嚴，用炭火燒烤（需將木炭燒至紅透無烟時始可使用）約八分鐘，全部取出一次調換一頭掛鈎位置再掛入爐中續烤七分鐘共計十五分鐘便成（如無此種掛爐，也可用普通烤箱或鐵絲笆子置炭火上烘烤肉條，唯普通烤箱則需將肉先橫置烤盤內，再放進烤箱，故時間也需加倍）。

3. 將烤熟之叉燒肉由鈎子上取下，並刷上鷄油或麻油（可加糖水少許同刷）便成。

註：叉燒肉除可做冷盤之外，適爲炒飯、炒麵或炒蛋，炒什錦，放入火鍋內或做烹調任何菜之配料，係爲粵菜中用途極廣之食物。

Cantones Roast Pork

Ingredients:

1-1/4 lbs. Pork (lean loin)
2 t. Sesame oil
1/2 T. Sugar (or syrup)
1/2 T. Hot water

2 Green onions (to marinate pork)
5 slices Gngeri "
5 T. Soysauce "
2 T. Wine "
2 T. Sugar "
1 T. Hoisin sauce "
1/3 t. Red food color "

Procedure:

1. Cut pork into strips 6″ long and 1″ around, Score each side in at least 4 slashes about 1/4″ deep. Soak with marinade for at least 3 hours but not more than 6 hours.

2. Hang pork strips on hooks and place in charcoal oven. Cover and roast for 8 min. Baste with marinade sauce, place hooks on opposite end and roast for 7 more minutes.

3. Remove from oven and brush with syrup made from 1/2 T. sugar, 1/2 T. hot water and 2 t. sesame oil.

NOTE:

1. This may be hung from the top rack of an oven but the flavor is improved when roasted over charcoal. If using an oven the roasting time should be doubled.

2. This is good sliced and served cold. It may also be added to fried rice, or noodles or many different egg and vegetable dishes.

蠔 油 牛 肉

材料：

嫩牛肉（全瘦腿肉）	十二兩	蠔油	二湯匙	綜
葱段（一寸長）	八支	清水	一湯匙	合
熟油	二湯匙	糖	一茶匙	調
薑片	三片	太白粉	半茶匙	味
蘇打粉	半茶匙 （醃	麻油	半茶匙	料
糖	一茶匙 肉	花生油	四杯	
醬油	一湯匙 用	芥蘭菜	半斤	
太白粉	一湯匙 料	酒	一湯匙	
清水	一湯匙	糖	一茶匙	
		鹽	半茶匙	

做法：

1. 牛肉選購無筋而細紋之全瘦肉，用利刀橫面切成一寸四方大小之薄片，全部用醃肉料在碗內拌醃，約半小時以上（時間醃得久長些較嫩），至臨炒前加入熟油兩湯匙再行拌調均勻。

2. 芥蘭菜（摘用嫩心部份），先在開水中燙兩分鐘（大火）撈出後沖一次冷水再用油三湯匙燒熱在鍋中急炒並淋下酒放鹽、糖調味，盛在菜盤，做墊底或圍邊之用。

3. 在炒鍋內燒熱四杯花生油，倒下全部牛肉片，用大火速加拌鏟至肉色已轉白（約十秒鐘）即行撈出，瀝乾，餘油倒出。

4. 另在炒鍋內僅燒熱兩湯匙油爆炒葱段及薑片，隨後將牛肉落鍋，同時倒下綜合調味料迅速以大火拌炒至十分均勻便可盛入盤中上桌即成。

86

Beef with Oyster Sauce

Ingredients:

1 lb. Lean beef (flank steak)

8 Pcs. Green onions (1" long)

3 slices Ginger

1/2 t. Baking soda (to marinate beef)

1 t. Sugar   "

1 T. Cornstarch   "

1 T. Soysauce   "

1 T. Water   "

2 T. Cooked Peanut oil

2 T. Oyster sauce (Seasoning sauce.)

1 T. Water   "

1 t. Sugar   "

1/2 t. Cornstarch   "

1/2 t. Sesame oil   "

4 C. Peanut oil

1/2 lb. Green Vegetable

1 T. Wine

1/2 t. Salt

1 t. Sugar

Procedure:

1. Slice the beef into 1" squares, put in a bowl and marinate for ½ hour at least (longer is better). Then add in 2 T. cooked oil and mix well.

2. Boil the green vegetable in boiling water about 2 minutes. Remove from pan and stir fry with 2 T. oil seasoned with wine, salt and sugar, lay on plate.

3. Heat 4 cups of oil in fry pan (about 300°) Add beef and fry until it turns light (done) about 10 seconds. Remove beef and drain off oil from pan.

4. Use another 2 T. oil to fry green onions and ginger, add beef, stir quickly over high heat, next add the seasoning sauce. Stir until thickened and heated through. Pour over green vegetables and serve.

中式牛排

材料：

嫩牛肉（菲利，或外脊肉）一斤		醬油（淡色）	三湯匙		醃
小青梗菜	十二棵	（粟米粉）或太白粉	三湯匙		肉
鹽	一茶匙	清水	半杯		用
蕃茄醬	三湯匙	綜	鬆肉粉	一茶匙	料
辣醬油	一湯匙	合	蘇打粉	半茶匙	
酒	一湯匙	調	熱油	三湯匙	
糖	一湯匙	味	花生油	三杯	
清水	五湯匙	料			
太白粉	半湯匙				

做法：

1. 牛肉剔淨白筋，橫紋切成半寸厚兩寸半四方大塊後，用已調好在大碗中之醃肉料（除熱油之外）仔細拌攪，反覆攪動肉塊，以使佐料全部被肉所吸收，然後加入熱油再續調拌均勻，醃約四小時左右。

2. 將油燒熱，排列全部牛肉塊在鍋中煎炸二至三分鐘（需翻一次面），然後將肉塊取出，油也倒出，僅留二湯匙在鍋內。

3. 將綜合調味料倒下原炸牛肉之鍋中以大火煑滾，然後淋下太白粉（先加一湯匙水調溶）鈎芡，隨後將牛肉塊再落鍋略加拌合。

4. 將牛肉裝盤，綜合調味料汁澆在上面，在盤之週圍排列每棵切成對半而先燙熟又沙過之青梗菜伴邊即成。（燙煑法請參照江浙菜〝紅扒鶉蛋〞中之做法第一及第四項）。

※請參考照片第22號。

88

Beef Steak Chinese Style

Ingredients:

1-1/4 lbs. Beef tenderloin

3 T. Soysauce (to marinate beef)

3 T. Cornstarch   "

1/2 C. Cold water   "

1 t. Meat tenderizer   "

1/2 t. Baking soda   "

1 Egg white   "

3 T. Cooking oil   "

1 lb. Green cabbage (or Chinese
    broccoli)

1/2 t. M.S.G.

1 t. Salt

3 T. Tomato catsup (Seasoning sauce)

1 T. Worcestershire   "

1 T. Wine   "

1 T. Sugar   "

5 T. Cold water   "

1/2 T. Cornstarch paste

3 C. Peanut oil

Procedure:

1. Cut beef across the grain into $\frac{1}{2}$" thick $2\frac{1}{2}$" square pieces. place the beef in the marinating sauce. Turn the pieces so that every piece is thoroughly soaked with the sauce. Add cooking oil. Turn occasionally. Marinate for at least 4 hours.

2. Heat the peanut oil. Deep fry the steaks until done, turn once. Take the steaks out. Drain the oil.

3. Heat 2 T. oil in same frying pan, pour in the seasoning sauce and bring to a boil. Stir in the constarch paste until thickened. Put the steaks into the sauce and mix well.

4. Arrange the steaks on a platter, pour the gravy over the steaks.

5. Boil the green cabbage in boiling water about 1 minute, plunge into cold water and squeeze dry. Fry with 2 T. oil and season with salt, M.S.G. and 1/2 C. soup. After 2 minutes remove and drain dry, lay in platter around the beef.

Refer to Picture No. 22.

青椒牛肉絲

材料：

瘦牛肉	半斤	葱	一支
青辣椒	三個	薑	三片
醬油	二湯匙	糖	半茶匙
熟花生油	一湯匙	鹽	一茶匙
酒	半湯匙	花生油	一杯
太白粉	二茶匙		
鹽	半茶匙		

（醬油、熟花生油、酒、太白粉、鹽爲醃肉用料）

做法：

1. 將牛肉橫紋切薄片後，再切成一寸多長之細絲，放在碗裏用醃肉用料（卽醬油、熟花生油、太白粉、鹽）仔細拌匀，醃約一小時左右。

2. 青辣椒洗淨剖開後去蒂與籽，切成一寸多長之橫絲，葱及薑亦切成細絲備用。

3. 將一杯花生油在鍋中燒熱（約九成熱）傾下牛肉絲用大火迅速拌炒，見牛肉變色（已熟）隨卽撈出瀝乾油漬，將此油僅留三湯匙再加燒熱。

4. 放葱薑絲及青辣椒絲在炒鍋裏，爆炒（大火），加入鹽，糖調味拌匀，再將炒過之牛肉絲重行落鍋，略加拌匀卽可裝盤供食。（如喜食辣味可加紅辣椒絲若干同炒）

90

Shredded Beef with Pepper

Ingredients:

10 oz. Tender beef

3 Green peppers

2 T. Soysauce (to marinate beef)

1 T. Cooked peanut oil "

1/2 T. Wine "

2 t. Cornstarch "

1/2 t. Salt "

1 Green onion

3 Slices ginger

1/2 t. Sugar

1 t. Salt

1 C. Peanut oil

Procedure:

1. Shred beef about 1 inch in length, mix with soy sauce, peanut oil, cornstarch, salt and soak for 1 hour.

2. Clean green pepper, remove seeds and membrane, cut in halves and shred crosswise.

3. Cut green onion and ginger into 1 inch lengths shred, heat peanut oil in pan, fry beef and stir briskly over high heat about 20 seconds, drain out.

4. Heat another 3 T. oil in pan. Stir fry ginger and green onion, then add

shredded green pepper salt, sugar and stir well. Add beef, blend thoroughly and serve.

茄汁魚片

材料：

新鮮白色魚肉	十二兩	糖	三湯匙
洋葱丁	半杯	白醋	三湯匙
冬菇丁	1/3杯	水	半杯
青豆	兩湯匙	蕃茄醬	三湯匙
蛋白	一個	酒	一湯匙
太白粉	一湯匙	太白粉	二茶匙
鹽	一茶匙	鹽	一茶匙
太白粉	半杯	麻油	一茶匙
花生油	六杯		

（第二欄標示「醃魚料」，第四欄標示「綜合調味料」）

做法：

1. 將魚皮及魚骨剔除乾淨之後，橫面切成約一寸半長二寸寬之長方形薄片（約1/4寸厚）。在碗內先打散蛋白加入太白粉，鹽調勻成糊狀再加入已切好之魚片仔細調拌，醃約半小時。

2. 將醃過之魚片，每片均在乾太白粉中（或麵粉）沾敷（兩面）隨即投入鍋內已燒熱之油中炸黃（大火炸約一分鐘），撈出魚片，將油倒出。

3. 另燒熱兩湯匙油，炒香洋葱丁，再放下冬菇丁同炒，隨後將綜合調味料傾入以大火煮滾（需不停加以攪動）放下青豆拌炒，隨手關熄爐火，繼將魚片落鍋略加拌合均勻即可裝盤上桌。

※請參考照片第23號。

Fish with Tomato Sauce

Ingredients:

1 lb. Fish, firm white meat

1/2 C. Diced onion

1/3 C. Diced dried mushroom

    (Soak in warm water first)

2 T. Green Peas, partially cooked

1 Egg white (to marinate fish)

1 T. Cornstarch   "

1 t. Salt   "

1/2 c. Cornstarch

3 T. Sugar   (Seasoning sauce)

3 T. Vinegar   "

1/2 C. Water   "

3 T. Tomato catsup   "

1 T. Wine   "

2 t. Cornstarch   "

1 t. Salt   "

1 t. Sesame oil   "

6 C. Peanut oil

Procedure:

1. Remove all bones and skin, cut fish meat crosswise 2" long, 1½" wide and 1/4" thick. Marinate with 1 egg white, 1 T. cornstarch, 1 t. salt, about 1/2 hour.

2. Prepare seasoning sauce in a bowl and set aside.

3. Coat each piece of sliced fish in cornstarch (1/2 cup.) and quickly drop in heated oil to deep fry about 1 minute until brown. Remove fish and drain off oil.

4. Heat 2 T. oil in frying pan, fry the onion, mushrooms and seasoning sauce, stir briskly until thickened. Add green peas and fried fish, turn off the fire and stir until blended. Serve immediately.

---

* Refer to Picture No. 23.

生炒魚球

材料：

石斑魚肉（或其他白魚肉）	一斤			
筍	一支	鹽	半茶匙	綜合調味料
多菇	三個	糖	半茶匙	
芥蘭菜心	半斤	酒	半湯匙	
葱白（半寸長）	十支	清湯	三湯匙	
薑片	五小片	醬油（淡色）	半湯匙	
蛋白	一個	太白粉	一茶匙	
鹽	半茶匙	麻油	一茶匙	
酒	半湯匙（醃魚料）	花生油	三杯	

做法：

1. 將魚肉除淨魚皮，魚骨後切成一寸寬三分之一寸厚之長方塊，全部拌入蛋白、鹽、酒（即醃魚料）醃約半小時左右。

2. 筍煮熟切成同魚肉相仿之大小片子，多菇泡軟也切片待用。

3. 芥蘭菜取用嫩心部份先燙熟（用開水燙約兩分鐘），再用兩湯匙油烹炒，加入酒、鹽、糖各一茶匙調味（未列在材料項內）起鍋裝在盤中做墊底用。

4. 將油在炒鍋內燒至八成熱後，傾入魚片，大火泡炸約十秒鐘，見魚片泛白即行撈出瀝淨，餘油全部倒出。

5. 另取兩湯匙油在炒鍋內燒熱，然後放下薑片葱段爆炒，並加入多菇片，筍片炒熟隨後將魚片落回鍋內，並將綜合調味料倒進（應預先調在一只小碗內）速加拌炒均勻，即刻起鍋裝盤。

94

Stir-fried Sliced Fish

Ingredients:

1-1/4 lbs. Fish firm white meat	1/2 t. Salt (seasonging sauce)
1 Bamboo shoot	1/2 t. Sugar "
3 Dried Black mushrooms	1/2 T. Wine "
1/2 lb. Green vegetable	3 T. Soup stock "
(Chinese broccoli)	1/2 T. Soy sauce "
10 pcs. Green onions cut 1" long	1 t. Cornstarch "
5 slices Ginger	1 t. Sesame oil "
1 Egg white (to marinate fish)	3 C. Peanut oil
1/2 t. Salt "	
1/2 T. Wine "	

Procedure:

1. After removing all bones and skin, cut fish crosswise 1" wide, 1½" long, 1/4" thick. Soak with 1 egg white, wine, and salt about 1/2 hour.

2. Cook bamboo shoot and slice into smaller size than fish. Soak mushrooms in warm water and remove stems, cut each into two or three pieces

3. Cook the green vegetable in boiling water about 2 minutes. Plunge into cold water immediately, then squeeze dry and fry with 2 T. oil, seasoned with added 1 t. wine, 1 t. salt and 1 t. sugar. Mix well and lay on the platter

4. Heat oil in frying pan, fry all the fish over high heat about 10 seconds. Remove the fish and drain oil from frying pan.

5. Heat the frying pan again, add 2 T. oil, fry green onion and ginger, add mushrooms and bamboo shoots. Stir fry a few seconds, add fish and seasoning sauce. Stir until thoroughly mixed. Serve.

茄汁龍蝦片

材料：

大龍蝦一隻或小型二隻		蕃茄醬	三湯匙
洋葱丁	半杯	清水	二湯匙
青豆（熟）	三湯匙	糖	一湯匙
蛋白	半個	醋	半湯匙
鹽	一茶匙	太白粉	二茶匙
太白粉	一湯匙	鹽	半茶匙
酒	半湯匙	花生油	三杯

中間：醃蝦肉料（蛋白、鹽、太白粉、酒）

右側：綜合調味料（蕃茄醬、清水、糖、醋、太白粉、鹽）

做法：

1. 將龍蝦頭與蝦身先用力扭轉使其分開後，再切開蝦腹取出蝦肉，全部橫切成薄片，放在碗裏加入蛋白，鹽，酒與太白粉拌勻醃約半小時以上。

2. 龍蝦頭與蝦身，放入蒸鍋內用大火蒸約二十分鐘，取出後刷上少許熱油，以增加亮光，排放在菜盤兩端備用。

3. 將綜合調味料盛在一只小碗內備用。

4. 在鍋內將油燒至八成熱後，傾入蝦肉泡炸，約十秒鐘見蝦肉轉白即可撈起，倒出鍋中之餘油。

5. 另在原鍋內燒熱三湯匙油，用大火爆炒洋葱丁，至透出香味後，倒下綜合調味料拌炒至沸滾而黏稠，放進青豆與蝦肉拌勻，迅速裝盤，（即已放有龍蝦頭及尾之橢圓形菜盤中）。

※請參考照片第24號。

Sauteed Lobster Tail in Tomato Sauce

Ingredients:

1 Large Lobster (about 3 lbs.) (or 2 Small Lobster)	3 T. Catsup (Seasoning sauce)
1/2 C. Diced onion	2 T. Water "
3 T. Green peas (cooked)	1 T. Sugar "
1/2 Egg white (to marinate lobster meat)	1/2 T. Vinegar "
	2 t. Cornstarch "
1 t. Salt "	1/2 t. Salt "
1 T. Cornstarch "	3 C. Peanut oil
1/2 T. Wine "	

Procedure:

1. Cut up the lobster tail and remove the meat from shell, slice the meat horizontally, (crosswise). Soak the lobster meat in marinade for 30 minutes at least.

2. Steam the head and tail of lobster about 20 minutes, remove from steamer and brush with some oil. Set on an oblong platter head at one end and tail at the other.

3. Measure into a small bowl catsup, water, sugar, vinegar, cornstarch and salt. as the seasoning sauce. Mix well.

4. Heat 3 C. oil in frying pan to 370°. When oil is hot add the lobster meat and stir fry about 10 seconds over high heat. Drain oil and place lobster in a bowl. Set aside.

5. Put in frying pan 3 T. oil, fry diced onions for a few seconds. Add the seasoning sauce and lastly the peas and lobster meat cook until thick. Pour on platter and serve.

* Refer to Picture No. 24.

97

酥 炸 生 蠔

材料：

大生蠔	十二兩
麵粉	2/3杯
太白粉	1/3杯
泡打粉	二茶匙
鹽	二茶匙
胡椒粉	少許
熟油	二湯匙
五香花椒鹽	二茶匙

（麵糊料用）

做法：

1. 生蠔先放在碗內，撒下少許鹽，用手指輕輕抓洗，並揀出細碎之蠔殼，再冲洗並用漏器瀝去水份（務必將黏液除淨）。

2. 在一鍋開水中，川燙一下生蠔（用大火）隨即撈出（不必等水再開）瀝乾水份備炸。

3. 將麵糊用料盛在一只碗內加入適量清水（約一杯）慢慢攪拌調勻，使成為稠度合適之酥炸糊料（粵人稱為脆漿）。

4. 在炒鍋內燒熱花生油（約九成熱，尚未冒油烟程度），即將生蠔先在麵糊中沾裹一下，旋即投入油中以普通火候炸至金黃色便可。

5. 將已炸成之生蠔裝盤，盤底與盤邊飾以生菜，蕃茄等，並附上少許五香花椒鹽在盤邊上桌供食即可。

98

Fried Oyster Chinese Style

Ingredients:

1 lb. Oyster (shelled)

2/3 C. Flour (flour batter)

1/3 C. Cornstarch   "

2 t. Baking powder   "

2 t. Salt   "

1/8 t. Pepper   "

2 T. Cooking oil   "

About 1 C. Water   "

2 t. pepper coru salt.

5 C. Peannt oil

Procedure:

1. Rub some coarse salt into the shelled oysters with fingers. Rinse with water until clear. Drain.

2. Dip the oysters in a pot full of boiling water only 5 secouds over high heat. Drain (Don't wait unil the water comes to boil again.)

3. Make flour batter stirring to a smooth pasty consistency.

4. Dip oyster in flour batter and deep fry over medium fire until golden brown.

5. Line the serving plate with lettuce and tomato slices. Arrange the oyster on top and serve with seasoned peppercorn salt.

炒芙蓉蛋

材料：

鷄蛋	六個	葱絲	1/3杯
蟹肉或蝦仁	半杯	醬油（淡色）	一湯匙
鹹肉或叉燒肉	四兩	鹽	二茶匙
冬菇	三個	清湯	半杯
綠豆芽（約四兩）一杯 （或筍絲 半杯）		油	八湯匙

做法：

1. 將鷄蛋敲開在碗內打散，並加入鹽一茶匙及清湯（或冷水）調打均勻至無粒塊而起泡沫爲止。

2. 將肉切成細絲，冬菇泡軟後去蒂也切絲，同蟹肉（或蝦仁）綠豆芽、葱絲、薑屑等用六湯匙油在鍋內炒半分鐘（大火）並加醬油、鹽調味。

3. 再由鍋沿淋下另外兩湯匙油，隨卽將打好之蛋汁傾入，並輕輕翻炒，使兩面均呈金黃色爲止，卽可盛到盤中供食。

註：此菜係一在國外頗爲盛行之中菜，有時另做饘汁澆在面上同食。（饘汁係將一杯鷄湯加入一茶匙鹽，沸滾後用一湯匙太白粉鈎芡便成）。

100

Egg Fu Yung

Ingredients:

6 Eggs.

1/2 C. Canned crab meat or
    shrimp

4 oz. Chinese ham or
    barbecued pork (shredded)

3 Dry black mushrooms
    (soaked and shredded)

1 C. Bean sprouts or
    shredded bamboo shoots

1/3 C. Green onion shredded

1 T. Soysauce

2 t. Salt

1/2 C. Soupstock

8 T. Peanut oil

Procedure:

1. Beat eggs until the consistency of shampoo foam, add 1 t. salt and soupstock (or cold water), mix again.

2. Heat 6T. oil in frying pan, stir fry crab (or shrimp) ham (or pork), mushrooms, bean sprouts (or bamboo shoots) and green onion. Add soysauce and salt. Stir fry about 1/2 minute over high heat.

3. Splash 2T. oil down side of pan and add No. 1 egg mixture. Fry on both sides until golden, remove to plate and serve.

NOTE:

A sauce may be added. Prepare this from 1C. chicken stock, 1 t. slat and bring to a boil, thicken with 1T. Cornstarch paste. (1T. cold water mixed with 1T. cornstarch).

101

蠔油鮑脯

材料：

罐頭鮑魚	一罐	鹽	一茶匙
嫩生荣	十二兩	糖	半茶匙
蠔油	三湯匙	酒	一湯匙
醬油	半湯匙	清湯	二杯
豬油（或花生油）	六湯匙	太白粉	一湯匙
味精	一茶匙	麻油	一茶匙

做法：

1. 鍋中倒入一杯清湯，加入豬油三湯匙，鹽一茶匙及味精少許，待湯沸滾後，將已剝除老葉，洗淨並每棵直切爲兩瓣之生荣放入清湯中，燙約半分鐘即可撈出。瀝乾排列在荣盤中。

2. 罐頭鮑魚取出後，橫面切成大圓片（如銀圓大小）放進滾水中川燙一下（約五秒鐘）旋即撈出備用。

3. 取一乾淨鍋，鍋中放豬油兩湯匙燒熱，淋下一湯匙酒，隨即注入一杯清湯並加入蠔油、醬油、糖、味精等調味料，待湯沸滾時，將鮑魚片落鍋，燴煮一滾隨後淋下用水調溶之太白粉，（需加攪動），見湯汁呈濃稠狀，即可澆下一湯匙熱油及一茶匙麻油便成。

4. 將鮑魚片堆排在盤中生荣面上，再淋下湯汁便可上桌供食。

102

Abalone with Oyster Sauce

Ingredients:

1 can Abalone

1 lb. Leaf lettuce

3 T. Oyster sauce

1/2 T. Soysauce

1 T. Wine

1 t. Salt

1/2 t. Sugar

2 C. Soup stock

1 T. Cornstarch   (make paste)

1 T. Cold water   "

1 t. Sesame oil

1 t. M S.G.

5 T. Peanut oil or Lard

Procedure:

1. Cut each lettuce leaf in two halves lengthwise. Boil with 1 cup of soup stock add 3 T. oil and 1 t. salt, 1/2 t. M.S.G. cook about 10 seconds. Drain out to a platter. Discard soup.

2. Remove the abalone from can and slice into 1/4" thick round pieces. Boil in boiling water about 5 seconds.

3. Heat 2 T. oil in frying pan, pour in wine and add 1 C. soup stock immediately. Bring to a boil, add oyster sauce, soysauce, and sugar; when it boils again, add abalone and cornstarch paste slowly stirring constantly. When thick add 1 T. heated oil and sesame oil.

4. Place the abalone attractively over the lettuce leaves. Pour the remaining sauce over the top. Serve.

客家釀豆腐

材料：

兩寸四方豆腐	六塊	鹽	半茶匙	⎫ 調
豬肉（半肥瘦）	六兩	酒	一湯匙	⎬ 肉
魚肉	二兩	太白粉	二茶匙	⎬ 用
乾蝦米（或左口魚乾）	一湯匙	醬油（淡色）	一湯匙	⎭ 料
葱屑	一湯匙	清湯（或水）一杯半		
葱絲	一湯匙	醬油（或蠔油）二湯匙		
花生油	2/3杯	味精	半茶匙	
		太白粉	一湯匙	

做法：

1. 選購較厚而嫩之板豆腐，放在平盤內，上面壓一塊不十分重之木板或菜盤，約兩小時，使豆腐中多餘之水份得以排出。亦可將豆腐用鹽水（六杯清水加一茶匙鹽）煮兩分鐘，取出後稍涼卽可使用。將豆腐每塊對角交叉切兩刀，使每一塊變成四小塊三角形，共得廿四個小三角塊。

2. 將豬肉和魚肉（需去淨魚皮魚骨）分別剁爛裝在同一只碗內，加入已泡軟並切碎之蝦米及葱屑拌勻，同時需放鹽、酒、醬油及太白粉等，調肉料時應仔細拌合，如嫌太乾可將泡蝦米之水加入兩、三湯匙，拌至十分黏而韌滑爲止，分別塞入三角形豆腐中（將豆腐底面劃切一道縫口挖出少許豆腐而後裝塞肉料）。

3. 在炒鍋內燒熱油，將豆腐之肉面向下全部排進煎黃（約兩分鐘，需時常轉動鍋子），加入清湯一杯半（或開水也可）以中火燒煮三、四分鐘（需蓋嚴鍋蓋），然後用鏟子小心祇將豆腐全部盛出在菜盤內。

4. 在鍋中煮過豆腐之湯汁內加入醬油（蠔油）及味精，並淋下濕太白粉使湯汁變黏，再撒下葱絲卽可澆到盤中豆腐上趁熱供食。

※請參考照片第25號。

Cantonese Stuffed Bean Curd

Ingredients:

6 pieces 2-1/2" square bean
    curd
6 oz. Pork (chopped)
2 oz. Fish fillet (chopped)
1 T. Dried shrimp (soaked
    & chopped)
1 T. Green onion (chopped)
1 T. Green onion (shredded)
2/3 C. Peanut oil

1/2 t. Salt   (to marinate pork)
1 T. Wine   "
2 t. Cornstarch   "
1 T. Soysauce   "
    (light color)
1-1/2 C. Soup stock
2 T. Soysauce (or oyster sauce)
1/2 t. M.S.G.
1 T. Cornstarch   (make past)
1 T. Cold water   "

Procedure:

1. Squeeze out the excess water by weighing down the bean curd with a cutting board or flat platter for about 2 hours. If you are in a hurry boil the bean curd in salt water (6 c. water, 1 t. salt) for 2 minutes. Drain. Cut each piece crisscrossly, altogether 24 triangle pieces.

2. Mix the chopped pork, fish, shrimp, onion with marinade. If too dry add 2 or 3 T. water (from soaking shrimp) to mix to the right consistency. Cut a slit on each bean curd triangle. Stuff the slits with meat mixture.

3. Fry the stuffed bean curd with meat side down for about 2 minutes until golden brown, tipping the frying pan a little so that the bean curd will not stick to the pan. Add soup stock (water will do). Cover and simmer for 3-4 minutes. Dish out carefully with pancake turner.

4. Add soysauce, M.S.G, cornstarch paste to broth and cook until thickened, sprinkle shredded green onion and pour over bean curd. Decorate with shredded green onion strips. Serve.

* Refer to Picture No. 25.

李公什碎

材料：

瘦猪肉	二兩	綠豆芽	四兩
猪腰	半個	乾米粉	二兩
水發魷魚	一條	醬油	二湯匙
蝦仁	二兩	鹽	二茶匙
叉燒肉（或鹹肉）	二兩	糖	一茶匙
筍	一小支	蔴油	一茶匙
紅蘿蔔	一小支	胡椒粉	1/4茶匙
青椒	一個	味精	少許
韭黃	二兩	花生油	五杯

（醬油至味精：綜合調味料）

做法：

1. 將猪肉，猪腰、尤魚及叉燒肉，筍（煮過）、紅蘿蔔（煮過）青椒等分別切成細絲，韭黃切一寸長之段留用。

2. 將五杯花生油在炒鍋中燒熱（至冒烟程度）放下米粉，炸成鬆黃（兩面各三秒鐘）隨後撈出放置在荣盤內（稍壓碎）。

3. 將猪肉絲，猪腰絲、魷魚絲及蝦仁等，在前項之油中泡炸約半分鐘，隨即用漏勺濾出，餘油亦倒出。

4. 另在炒鍋內燒熱五湯匙油，先炒叉燒肉，筍絲，青椒絲及豆芽等（約半分鐘），然後將泡過油之各絲料合入，並將韭黃落鍋淋下綜合調味料（預先在小碗內調好）用大火迅速拌炒至十分均勻，便可起鍋盛在淬米粉上供食。

註：此荣所用之材料種類多少及分量若干並無限定，可按各人嗜好及容易買到之材料取用，唯豆芽及韭黃（或葱絲）必須要在稍後放下，拌炒時間也不可過長。

Chop Suey

Ingredients:

3 oz. Lean pork
1/2 Pork kidney
1 Soaked Squid (optional)
1/2 C. Small and shelled
   shrimp
3 oz. Barbecued pork or
   cooked ham
1 Bamboo shoot (cooked)
1 Carrot (cooked)
1 Green pepper
2 oz. Spring onion

5 oz. Bean sprout
2 oz. Rice noodles or Vermicelli
2 T. Soysauce   (seasoning sauc
2 t. Salt   "
1 t. Sugar   "
1 t. Sesame oil   "
1/4 t. Black pepper   "
5 C. Peanut oil

Procedure:

1. Cut all of ingredients in string shape except shrimp.

2. Heat oil very hot, fry the rice noodles until puffed and golden (only 3 seconds each side). Remove to platter and crush fine.

3. Use the same oil to fry pork, kidney, squid and shrimp about 1/2 minute, remove from pan and drain oil.

4. Heat 5T. oil in frying pan, stir fry barbecued pork, bamboo shoot, green pepper, and bean sprout, about 1 minute. Add the fried ingredients (pork, kidney, squid and shrimp) and spring onion; mix well, Add the seasoning sauce; stir fry thoroughly, pour over fried rice noodles. Serve hot.

NOTE.

1. Many of these ingredients are optional. Add what you wish.

2. Bean sprouts and spring onion, should not be fried too long, keep them crispy.

3. The correct name, in China, for this recipe is "Lee Gone Chop Suey" and is a Cantonese dish. It was first served to General Lee Hon Chung while he was in Japan about 74 years ago. It was too late in the evening to be served a regular meal. The chef combined all his left-overs in a stir fry concoction. This new taste pleased the General so much it was named for him and become a favorite of his.

奶油什錦菜捲

材料：

鷄肉（或猪肉）	四兩	洋白菜葉（即包心菜葉）	十四張
鷄肝	二付	鹽	二茶匙
蝦仁	二兩	太白粉	二茶匙
熟火腿	二兩	清湯	1½杯
冬菇	三個	牛奶水（罐頭淡奶）	三湯匙
筍	一支	濕太白粉	二湯匙
靑豆	二湯匙	猪油（或花生油）	五湯匙

做法：

1. 將鷄肉（或猪肉）仔細切成小粒，拌入一茶匙乾太白粉留用，（如用熟鷄肉則不需用太白粉拌），蝦仁洗淨擦乾水份後也切成小粒，裝碗內加入一茶匙太白粉拌勻。

2. 鷄肝整只先用滾水煑熟（約五分鐘）取出後切小粒。火腿也需切成小粒。冬菇用溫水泡軟，筍煑熟分別切小粒同靑豆（煑熟或用罐頭皆可）共置一碟備用。

3. 在炒鍋內燒熱四湯匙油後，先炒鷄肉與蝦仁，再加入冬菇、筍、火腿各丁同炒，並加鹽一茶匙及清湯半杯，煑半分鐘。

4. 將鷄肝與靑豆下鍋拌勻，同時淋下一湯匙濕太白粉鈎芡即全部盛出。

5. 將包心菜在開水內燙軟（先將底梗部分用刀尖割斷，整棵放入，待葉子一張張被燙軟了便剝下）然後切除少許葉梗，僅取用四寸見方之葉子來包裹第四項之材料（約一湯匙）使成一個如同春捲般筒形，沾少許濕太白粉封口即排列在一只菜盤內，上鍋用大火蒸二十分鐘左右。

6. 另在炒鍋內燒熱一湯匙油，並倒下清湯一杯，加鹽一茶匙煑滾，淋下一湯匙濕太白粉（或再多一點）鈎芡，最後加入牛奶水拌勻，便可澆到已蒸好之菜捲上即成。

108

Cabbage Rolls with Cream Sauce

Ingredients:

1/4 lb. Chicken meat or pork
2 Chicken livers
3 oz. Shrimp (shelled)
3 oz. Cooked ham
4 Dried mushrooms
1 Bamboo shoot (cooked or 1/2 c. canned)
2 T. Green peas

14 Round cabbage leaves
2 t. Salt
2 t. Cornstarch
1-1/2 C. Soup stock
5 T. Fresh milk (or 3 T. evaporated milk)
1-1/2 T. Cornstarch paste
5 T. Lard or peanut oil

Procedure:

1. Cut the chicken meat (or pork) in small cubes, mix with 1 t. cornstarch. In a separate bowl clean shrimp then cut in small cubes, add 1 t. cornstarch and mix well.

2. Boil the whole chicken liver in boiling water about 5 minutes, then cut in small cubes. Cut ham, and mushrooms in small cubes too (soaked in warm water first remove stems).

3. Heat 4 T. oil in frying pan. Fry chicken meat and shrimp, stir a few seconds, add mushrooms, bamboo shoots and ham. Then add 1 t. salt and 1/2 C. soup stock, bring to a boil.

4. Add chicken livers and green peas, add cornstarch paste, stir until starchy, remove from pan.

5. Remove and discard core of cabbage. Place cabbage in deep pot of boiling water and gently remove softened leaves. This is not to cook the cabbage. Cut hard spine from leaf, keeping leaf oval shaped. Place 1 T. # 4 mixture in center of leaf and roll-sealing edges with a little bit of cornstarch paste. Set on platter cut side down. Place platter in steamer and steam for 15 min.

6. For cream sauce: heat 1 T. oil add 1½ C. stock quickly, add 1 t. salt, when boiling add 1½ T. cornstarch paste, mix until smooth, add milk, pour over cabbage rolls and serve while hot.

NOTE:

If cooked chicken and shimp are used, don't mix with cornstarch.

十錦冬瓜盅

材料：

熟雞肉（或鴨肉）	三兩	干貝	二個
熟火腿	二兩	冬瓜	六斤（約八寸高）
雞肝	二付	薑	二片
雞肫	二個	鹽	二茶匙
冬菇	四個	酒	半湯匙
小蝦仁	二兩	清湯	五杯
筍	一支	雞油	一湯匙

做法：

1. 冬菇用溫水泡軟，筍去籜蒸熟，分別切成小丁，雞肉與熟火腿也切小丁。
2. 雞肝、雞肫剔除白筋後切成小粒，蝦仁如太大也切成小塊備用。
3. 將以上各種材料全部放在開水鍋中川燙一次，隨即瀝出，（川燙時需用大火，把握時間，不可燙過久，以致走味）。
4. 干貝用熱水泡過後，再蒸半小時至十分酥軟，然後用手撕成粗絲。
5. 冬瓜應選購圓正而不太大之前頭半段（即無蒂之一端）刷洗乾淨後挖除瓜瓤，在綠色瓜皮上可雕刻些許圖案或花樣，並在瓜緣上削切成齒輪狀之尖角一圈，裝入一只盆內（或粗磁大碗），上鍋蒸約半小時，至七成爛為止。
6. 將第三項各種川燙過之材料與干貝（連汁）全部傾入冬瓜內並加鹽、酒及薑片，注入清湯再上鍋續蒸十五分鐘，取出後淋些雞油便可連同蒸碗一起上桌（薑片應挾出）。

註：冬瓜盅內之材料種類多少可隨意，如要名貴些可放入鮑魚、蟹肉、鴿蛋之類。

※請參考照片第二六號。

Assorted Meat Soup in Winter Melon

Ingredients:

4 oz. Cooked chicken meat
(or pork, duck meat)
2 oz. Cooked ham
2 Chicken gizzards
2 Chicken livers
4 Dry mushrooms
2 oz. Shrimp (small)
1 Bamboo shoot

2 Dry scallops
7 lbs. Winter melon
(Use only 6" or 7" from lower part)
2 slices Ginger
2 t. Salt
1/2 T. Wine
5 C. Soup stock
1 T. Chicken oil

Procedure:

1. Soften the mushrooms in warm water. Boil the bamboo shoots in water. Dice the mushroom, bamboo shoots, chicken and ham.
2. Remove the ligament of chicken gizzard. Cut the gizzard and liver in small cubes. Cut shrimp into small pieces.
3. Soak the scallops in hot water, then steam for about 1/2 hour until tender. Tear into shreds with fingers.
4. Dip the above prepared ingredients (except scallop) in boiling water only 10 seconds then drain. The water should be at a rolling boil. Do not over cook.
5. Scrub the skin of a balanced, small ball shaped winter melon. Remove the seeds etc, from the inside. Carve the rim into zigzag pattern. If desired, carve a design on the skin. Put the melon into a big bowl. Steam for about 1/2 hour or until soft.
6. Put all the ingredients from # 4 plus the scallop with liquid into the melon bowl. Add salt, ginger, wine and soup stock. Steam 15 minutes. Sprinkle in some melted chicken oil and serve in the big bowl. (Remove the ginger slices before serving).

NOTE:

The ingredients inside the melon bowl can be flexible. Abalone, crab meat, pigeon eggs can be used too.

* Refer to Picture No. 26.

著者爲空軍饍勤人員講授烹飪課程

Miss Fu instructing servicemen on proper food preparation for the Free
Chinese Government

西 部 菜

Dishes of **Western** China

第廿七圖（左）

油淋子鷄
（做法參照第120頁）

Picture No. 27
Oil Dripped
Chicken

(See Recipe Page 121)

八圖（右）

宮保鷄丁
（做法參照第124頁）

ure No. 28　　(right)

chen with Dry
Pepper

Recipe Page 125)

第廿九圖（左）**樟茶鴨**
（做法參照第126頁）

Picture No. 29
Camphor and Tea Smoked Duck
(See Recipe Page 127)

第卅一圖（下）
魚香肉絲
（做法參照第134頁）

Picture No. 31 (down)
Stir-Fried Pork String with Hot Sauce
(See Recipe Page 135)

第三十圖（右）
Ⓐ**紅燜肉**
（做法參照第130頁）
Ⓑ**麻婆豆腐**
（做法參照第150頁）
Ⓒ**乾煸四季豆**
（做法參照第162頁）

Picture No. 30 (right)
(A) **Stewed Pork in Brown Sauce**
(See Recipe Page 131)
(B) **Ma-Po's Bean Curd**
(See Recipe Page 151)
(C) **Dry Cooked String Beans**
(See Recipe Page 163)

第卅二圖（右）
Ⓐ 乾煸牛肉絲
（做法參照第138頁）
Ⓑ 紅油腰片
（做法參照第140頁）

Picture No. 32(right)
Ⓐ) Shredded Beef Country
Style
(See Recipe Page 139)
Ⓑ) Kidney with Hot Sauce
(See Recipe Page 141)

第卅三圖
蝦仁鍋巴
（做法參照第148頁）

Picture No. 33
Popped Rice
with Shrimp
(See Recipe Page 149)

第卅四圖（左）

紙包魚

（做法參照第144頁）

Picture No. 34(left)
Paper-Warpped Fried Fish

(See Recipe Page 145)

第卅五圖（右下）

Ⓐ**粉蒸牛肉**
（做法參照第136頁）

Ⓑ**四川泡菜**
（做法參照第158頁）

Ⓒ**麻辣黃瓜**
（做法參照第160頁）

Picture No. 35
(A) **Steamed Beef with Spicy Rice Powder**
(See Recipe Page 137)

(B) **Sze-Chuan Pickle**
(See Recipe Page 159)

(C) **Sze-Chuan Cucumber Relish**
(See Recipe Page 161)

西部菜目錄　　Contents of Western

113

棒 棒 鷄

材料：

嫩鷄	半隻（約一斤）	芝麻醬	二湯匙	綜
粉皮（新鮮）	十張	醬油	三湯匙	合
萵苣筍（或小黃瓜）	一條	鎮江醋	一湯匙	調
鹽	半茶匙	麻油	一湯匙	味
薑屑	半湯匙	辣椒油	一湯匙	料
蒜屑	半湯匙	糖	二茶匙	
花椒粉	半茶匙	味精	半茶匙	
		花椒油（可免）	一茶匙	

做法：

1. 選購肥嫩子鷄半隻洗淨後放入鍋內加入開水用中火煑約十二分鐘（可放少許葱薑同煑）。撈出後瀝乾水份並使其冷却。

2. 萵苣筍或黃瓜切成斜而小之薄片後，用鹽半茶匙拌醃，約十分鐘後，擠乾水份舖在菜盤作底用。

3. 粉皮切成寬條用冷開水漂洗一下，撈出瀝乾放在盤內筍片上。（如用乾粉皮則需用熱水先泡軟後再切），

4. 將鷄之大骨剔除連皮切成一寸半長三分寬之細條狀，全部排列在盤中之粉皮上，並撒下薑，蒜及花椒粉。

5. 用一只小碗先放芝麻醬再慢慢加入醬油調開成稀稠汁並相繼加入麻油、醋、辣椒油、糖、味精等調拌均勻，待上桌前澆到鷄肉上，食時略加拌勻便可。

114

Bon Bon Chicken

Ingredients:

1/2 Young chicken (about 1-1/2 lbs.)	-2 T. Sesame seed Paste (seasoning sauce)
10 Small green bean sheets	3 T. Soysauce "
1 Green bamboo shoot (or cucumber)	1 T. Brown Vinegar "
1/2 T. Ginger (minced)	1 T. Sesame oil "
1/2 T. Garlic (minced)	1 T. Hot red Pepper oil "
1/2 t. Brown Peppercorn Powder	2 t. Sugar "
1/2 t. Salt	1/2 t. M.S.G. "
	1 t. Brown Pepper corn oil (optional)

Procedure:

1. Boil water in a large pot, add chicken and cook for 20 minutes. Take chicken out, let cool.

2. Slice the peeled green bamboo shoots or cucumber into small slices, soak with salt about 10 minutes, squeeze and lay on plate.

3. Cut bean sheets in ½" wide and soak in cold water a few minutes. Lay on top of # 2

4. Remove big chicken bones, then cut meat into pieces 1½" long and thickness of pencil, place on top of bean sheets and sprinkle with peppercorn powder, ginger and garlic.

5. Mix the sesame seed paste with soysauce, then add sesame oil, vinegar, hot oil, sugar and M.S.G. in a small bowl, serve with chicken (pour the seasoning sauce over the chicken and mix carefully before eating).

115

東 安 鷄

材料：

光鷄一隻	（約一斤半重）	醬油	二湯匙
葱	三支	鎭江醋	一湯匙
薑	十片	鹽	一茶匙
紅辣椒	三支	糖	一茶匙
花椒	半湯匙	太白粉	半湯匙
清湯	一杯	蔴油	少許
酒	一湯匙	花生油	五湯匙

做法：

1. 鷄洗淨放入鍋內加入清水（以蓋住鷄面爲量）並放一支葱和兩片薑，用大火煮滾然後改用中火續煮十分鐘。

2. 將鷄由鍋中取出待稍冷之後，剔除大骨（卽鷄背、鷄胸等架骨，大腿骨可不必取出）以利刀斬切成一寸寬二寸長之塊狀。

3. 將葱二支薑八片與紅辣椒分別切成細絲備用。

4. 在炒鍋內燒熱油後先爆香花椒，再放下葱薑絲及紅辣椒絲同炒（如不喜食辣味可留待最後加入），並將鷄塊落鍋，加入醬油、酒、鹽、糖調味，然後注入清湯煮約三分鐘，卽淋下醋。

5. 用太白粉（加同量水調溶）將汁鈎茨，最後淋下蔴油卽可裝盤。（也可不鈎茨）。

116

Tung-An Chicken

Ingredients:

1 Young chicken (about 2
   lbs.)
3 Green onions
10 Slices ginger
3 Red hot peppers
1/2 T. Brown peppercorn
1 C. Soup stock
1 T. Wine

2 T. Soysauce
1 T. Brown vinegar
2 t. Salt
1 t. Sugar
1/2 Cornstarch   (make paste)
1 T. cold water   "
1 t. Sesame oil
5 T. peanut oil

Procedure:

1. Clean the chicken and put it in the stew pot with one green onion and 2 slices ginger on medium fire—cook for 20 minutes.

2. Let the stewed chicken cool remove large bones, cut meat into pieces 1 " wide 2" long.

3. Cut green onion, ginger, red pepper into strings.

4. Fry brown peppercorn in hot oil until it smells good, add green onion, ginger and red pepper, then add the chicken, soysauce, wine, salt and sugar. Finally add soup stock, stewing for 3 minutes, then stir in the vinegar.

5. Add cornstarch paste, stir until thick, splash on some sesame oil before serving.

成都子鷄

材料：

嫩鷄半隻	（約一斤）	鹽	二茶匙
葱屑	二湯匙	糖	一茶匙
薑屑	半湯匙	鎮江醋	半湯匙
蒜屑	半湯匙	酒	一湯匙
芹菜屑	二湯匙	猪油（或花生油）半杯	
紅辣椒屑	一湯匙	辣豆瓣醬	二湯匙
花椒	一茶匙	太白粉	二茶匙

做法：

1. 將鷄連骨帶皮斬切成一寸四方之小塊留用。

2. 在炒菜鍋內，先將油半杯燒至極熱，然後傾入鷄塊大火拌炒，約兩分鐘見鷄肉已半熟時放進花椒粒再同炒並將紅辣椒與辣豆瓣醬，落鍋繼續拌炒兩分鐘。

3. 淋下料酒，並放下薑、蒜屑與糖、鹽、醋調味，注入清水（熱水）約一杯，然後蓋嚴鍋蓋再燜羹五分鐘左右至鷄塊熟透爲止。

4. 將太白粉用一湯匙清水調溶後慢慢淋下鍋裏並炒拌均勻，再將芹菜屑與葱屑撒下，略加鑵拌卽行裝盤。

註：此菜所用之紅辣椒應用取自泡菜滷中已泡過之紅辣椒爲宜。

118

Sauteed Chicken Cheng-Tu Style

Ingredients:

1/2 Chicken (about 1-1/2 lbs.)

2 T. Shredded green onion

1/2 T. Shredded ginger

1/2 T. Shredded garlic

2 T. Shredded celery

1 T. Shredded red hot pepper

1 t. Brown peppercorn

2 t. Salt

1 t. Sugar

1/2 T. Brown vinegar

1 T. Wine

2 T. Hot soybean paste

2 t. Cornstarch   (make paste)

2 t. Cold water peanut   "

1/2 C. Lard or peanut oil

Procedure:

1. Chop the chicken with bone and skin into 1" square pieces.

2. Heat the oil boiling hot.   Saute the chicken pieces for about 2 minutes, (only half cooked), add pepper corn, stir thoroughly. Add red pepper and hot soybean paste, stir 2 more. minutes

3. Add wine, ginger, garlic, sugar, vinegar, salt and 1 C. hot water.   Cover and simmer for 5 minutes.

4. Stir in the cornstarch paste until thickened. Add shredded celery and green onion. Mix well and serve.

NOTE:

Cheng-Tu is a big city in the western part of China.

油淋子鷄

材料：

嫩鷄一隻（約一斤半重）

葱	二支	⎫
薑	三片	⎬ 醃
八角	一顆	⎬ 鷄
醬油	五湯匙	⎬ 料
酒	一湯匙	⎭

葱屑	一湯匙
花椒粉	一茶匙
麻油	二湯匙
花生油	五杯

做法：

1. 購買肥而嫩之光鷄一隻（或是鷄腿四支亦可）洗淨擦乾水份由背部剖開，放大碗裏用醬油，酒及拍碎之薑葱，八角醃泡（約一小時。）

2. 將已醃過之鷄連碗上鍋，用大火蒸二十分鐘左右取出。

3. 在炒菜鍋內燒熱油後，放下蒸過之鷄並用大火炸三分鐘，至鷄皮變脆而呈紅褐色時即可提出。趁熱斬剁成長方形塊狀按原鷄形排列在菜盤內。

4. 將葱屑與炒過之花椒粉撒在鷄肉上，再在炒鍋內燒滾麻油迅速淋上便成。（可將蒸鷄之汁也澆上兩湯匙）。

註：1. 此菜也可將鷄骨拆除後醃泡、蒸炸，則適宜老幼或外藉人士食用，並稱謂「油淋去骨鷄」。

2. 將鷄蒸好要下油鍋炸之前，需將鷄眼用筷子插串使鷄眼中之水漬流出，以免炸時濺爆。

3. 油淋子鷄也可不必蒸而僅泡後生炸稱謂「生炸油淋鷄」。

※請參考照片第27號。

120

Oil Dripped Chicken

Ingredients:

1 Whole young chicken (about
  2 lbs.)

2 Green onions (to marinate
            chicken)

3 slices Ginger   "

1 Star anise   "

5 T. Soysauce   "

1 T. Wine   "

1 T. Shredded green onion

1 t. Brown Peppercorn Powder

2 T. Sesame oil

5 C. Peanut oil

Procedure:

1. Clean chicken, then halve the back but do not cut apart, marinate with soysauce, wine, green onion, ginger slices and star anise. Let stand for 1 hour at least.

2. Steam chicken with marinade for about 20 minutes, remove from steamer and then remove chicken. Save the juice.

3. Heat the peanut oil in frying pan, deep fry chicken for about 3 minutes, until the skin is crispy and the color is brown, take chicken out and cut in pieces 1 "wide 2" long. Lay the chicken on platter in a chicken shape.

4. Sprinkle shredded green onion and peppercorn powder on chicken, then pour heated sesame oil and 2 T. chicken juice over and serve.

NOTE:

  Irt this dish the bones may be removed before cooking.

---

* Refer to picture No. 27.

麻辣子雞

材料：

雞一隻（約一斤半）			醬油	二湯匙	
青辣椒	二個		酒	半湯匙	
紅辣椒	三支		鎮江醋	一湯匙	綜合調味料
大蒜	四粒		糖	一湯匙	
蛋白	半個	醃雞用料	麻油	一茶匙	
太白粉	一湯匙		太白粉	一茶匙	
醬油	一湯匙		鹽	半茶匙	
花生油	三杯				

做法：

1. 將雞全身之大小骨頭剔除，連皮切成八分四方大小（雞腿部份筋多，需用刀先輕剁數下再切）。全部切好後裝入盆內放進蛋白，醬油及太白粉等醃雞用料拌勻，放約半小時以上。

2. 青辣椒及紅辣椒洗淨除籽後切成與雞丁同樣大小之塊狀，大蒜切薄片留用。

3. 在炒鍋內燒熱花生油後將雞肉全部傾下油中泡炸，約半分鐘，見雞肉變色即行撈出並瀝去油漬，鍋內之油倒出。

4. 在原炒鍋內另燒熱兩湯匙油後先落蒜片爆香，再將青，紅椒下鍋同炒，隨即將雞肉與綜合調味料一起倒進鍋中迅加鏟拌，至十分均勻後便可即速裝盤上桌。

Chicken with Green Pepper

Ingredients:

1 Young chicken (about 2 lbs.)

2 Green peppers

3 Red peppers

4. Garlic bud

1/2 Egg white   (to marinate chicken)

1 T. Cornstarch   "

1 T. Soysauce   "

3 C. Pecnut oil

2 T. Soysauce   (seasoning sauce)

1 T. Brown vinegar   "

1/2 T. Wine   "

1 t. Cornstarch   "

1 t. Sesame oil   "

1 t. Sugar   "

1/2 t. Salt   "

Procedure:

1. Remove all bone from chicken, cut into 1" cube. Soak with 1 T. soysauce, 1 T. cornstarch, 1/2 egg white mixture 1/2 hour (at least).

2. Remove seeds and stem from green peppers and red peppers, cut into 1" squares, slice garlic

3. Heat 3 cups peanut oil to boiling point, fry chicken about 1/2 minutes until done, remove chicken from pan and drain oil.

4. Use 2 T. oil fry garlic a little while, then add red peppers and green peppers, quick stir-fry a few seconds. Add the chicken and seasoning sauce, stir it until thickens. Serve immediatly.

宮保鷄丁

材料：

嫩鷄一隻（約一斤半）		醬油	二湯匙	
乾紅辣椒	八支	酒	一湯匙	
生花生米	半杯（約二兩）	糖	一湯匙	綜合調味料
薑屑	一茶匙	鎮江醋	半湯匙	
醬油	一湯匙	太白粉	一茶匙	
太白粉	一湯匙半	麻油	一茶匙	
花生油	五杯	鹽	半茶匙	

（醬油、太白粉為醃鷄料）

做法：

1. 光鷄洗淨，先割下兩隻鷄腿，再剝下鷄胸與鷄翅部份之鷄肉，鷄腿之大骨也除淨，剔取全部鷄肉，用刀輕輕拍剁，筋較多之部份須用力拍以使筋皮鬆弛，再分別切成一寸四方塊狀，用醬油及太白粉拌醃（約半小時）。

2. 生花生米需冲下熱水燙泡（約五分鐘），然後粒粒剝淨澀衣，放進熱油中（約兩杯），以小火慢慢炸熟並吹涼留用，（也可買回已炸過之無皮花生米。）

3. 在炒菜鍋內燒熱花生油五杯後，倒下已醃過之鷄肉，用大火迅速炸熟，約半分鐘即可撈出（需用快動作）。

4. 另在炒菜鍋內燒熱兩湯匙花生油，先放下切成一寸長段之乾紅辣椒炸至褐黑，再加進薑屑及鷄肉，以旺火拌炒數下，隨後倒入備妥在小碗中之綜合調味料，續加炒勻，至全部黏稠時淋下少許熱油，即可將火關熄加入炸過之花生米拌勻，即行裝盤供食。

※請參考照片第28號

Chicken with Dry Red Pepper

Ingredients:

1 *Young chicken (about 2 lbs.)*	2 *T. Soysauce (Seasoning sauce)*
or a pound chicken breast.	1 *T. Wine* "
8 *pcs. Dry red pepper*	1/2 *T. Brown vinegar* "
1/2 *C. Peonuts (without skins)*	1 *T. Sugar* "
1 *t. Ginger chopped*	1 *t. Cornstarch* "
1 *T. Soysauce (to soak chicken)*	1/2 *t. Salt* " :
1-1/2 *T. Cornstarch* "	1 *t. Sesame oil* "
5 *C. Peanut oil*	

Proeedure:

1. Remove all bones from chicken, cut into 1" cubes, add 1 T. soysauce and 1¼ T. cornstarch, stir evenly in one direction and soak for half hour.

2. Wipe clean, remove tips and seeds of dry red pepper, cut into 1" long pieces. fry peanuts until golden, remove and let cool.

3. Fry chicken in boiling oil for a half minute. Remove chicken and drain off oil from frying pan.

4. Heat 2 T. spoonful oil to fry dry red pepper until it turns black, add ginger and chicken, stir quickly, next add the seasoning sauce, stir until thickened and heated thoroughly; turn off the fire. Add the peanuts mix well just before serving, (mix well).

---

* Refer to picture No. 28.

125

樟 茶 鴨

材料：

光鴨	一隻（約三斤）	木屑	二杯
鹽	三湯匙	紅茶葉	半杯
花椒	二湯匙	水果皮（可免）	少許
硝粉	二茶匙	花生油	八杯

做法：

1. 光鴨洗淨，擦乾水份後，用已在鍋內乾炒過之花椒與鹽（冷却後拌入硝粉）均勻而用力抹擦在鴨身內外，醃置六小時以上（一晝夜以內）。

2. 將已醃過之鴨，揩淨花椒粒，用繩紮住鴨子頸部，吊掛在通風處，以使鴨皮被風吹乾（約六小時左右）。

3. 在一口舊鐵鍋內，放下木屑，紅茶葉及水果皮等燻料，上面放置一枚鐵絲網，網上置放已吹乾之鴨子，合上鍋蓋，移在爐上，用小火燒燃，使鍋中之燻料起烟，約五分鐘後，揭蓋將鴨身翻轉一面，再合上鍋蓋續燻，至鴨身全部呈茶黃色時便可取出

4. 將燻鍋之鴨放入蒸籠中，用大火蒸約二小時，便可。

5. 燒熱花生油，將鴨放下，用大火炸至鴨身全面呈棕黃色，而鴨皮酥脆為止。撈出後趁熱斬切成一吋寬二吋長之塊狀，整齊排入盤中上桌供席。（盤邊需配上葱白數支及甜麵醬少許以便醮鴨肉而食）。

註：按此菜為川味中著名而特殊之一種，鴨皮香脆，鴨肉肥嫩洋溢茶香及烟味，係川菜酒席中不可或缺之佳餚。

※請參考照片第29號

126

Camphor and Tea Smoked Duck

Ingredients:

1 Duck (about 4 lbs.)

3 T. Salt

2 T. Brown peppercorn

2 t. Saltpeter

2 C. Wood chips (Camphor wood is best)

1/2 C. Black tea leaves

8 C. Peanut oil

a little fruit peel (orange or lemon)

Procedure:

1. Fry peppercorns and salt in dry pan over low heat about 1 minute, take out and let cool, then mix with saltpeter. Rub the duck in side and out side, let stand for 6 hours or overnight.

2. Use string to hang the duck by the neck and place in shade in a windy area until very dry (about 6 hours).

3. In heavy iron pot place the wood chips, black tea leaves and fruit peel (well mixed together). Add a rock over this and place the duck on it. Cover. Smoke this about 10 minutes over low heat. Turn the duck and smoke for 5 minutes more. Duck will be brown.

4. Remove duck put in steamer to steam for 2 hours. Remove and deep fry until skin is crispy and very dark. Cut in 1″ wide 2″ long pieces, lay on platter. May be served with green onion and sweet bean paste.

* Refer to Picture 29.

127

白油四件

材料：

鷄肫（或鴨肫）	四個	酒	一湯匙	醃肫肝用料
鷄肝（或鴨肝）	四個	鹽	一茶匙	
筍（或小黃瓜萵筍）	一支	太白粉	一湯匙	
乾木耳	二湯匙	胡椒粉	少許	
葱	二支	醬油	一湯匙	綜合調味料
薑	五片	酒	半湯匙	
大蒜	五片	糖	一茶匙	
花生油	三杯	太白粉	一茶匙	
		麻油	少許	
		花椒粉	少許	

做法：

1. 鷄肫剔除白筋後切片，鷄肝也切片全部裝碗中用酒，鹽，太白粉，胡椒粉（即醃料）拌和醃十分鐘左右。

2. 筍去皮煮十五分鐘取出後，待冷切片。木耳用溫水泡軟摘洗乾淨留用。葱切半寸長段。

3. 將綜合調味料在一只小碗內調妥備用。

4. 炒鍋內燒熱花生油後，倒下肫肝用大火炸五秒鐘隨即撈起，鍋中之油全部倒出。

5. 再將炒鍋燒熱用兩湯匙油爆香葱、薑及蒜片然後放下筍片、木耳同炒，再將炸過之肫肝與綜合調味料相繼落鍋急炒數下拌勻，裝入盤中之後撒下炒過之花椒粉即可。

128

Sauteed Giblets and Livers

Ingredients:

6 Chicken gizzards

6 Chicken livers

1 Bamboo shoot or 8 water
   chestnuts

2 T. Dry agaric (fungus)

12 Green Onions (1/2 long)

5 slices Ginger

3 C. Peanut Oil

1 T. Wine   (to marinate giblets)

1 t. Salt   "

1 T Cornstarch   "

1/4 t. Black Pepper "

1 T. Soysauce   (seasoning sauce)

1/2 T. Wine   "

1 t. Sugar   "

1 t. Cornstarch   "

1/2 t. Sesame oil   "

1/2 t. Brown
   Peppercorn Powder   "

Procedure:

1. Remove the membrane from gizzards and livers, then slice into pieces, put in a bowl, add wine, cornstarch, salt, black pepper. Soak about 10 minutes and set aside.

2. Peel and boil whole bamboo shoot about 15 minutes. Cool it and slice, soak agaric in warm water, remove stem and slice.

3. Prepare seasoning sauce in small bowl.

4. Deep fry gizzards and liver in very hot oil for five seconds, remove and drain off oil from frying pan.

5. Heat 2 T. peanut oil, add green onion, ginger and garlic. Stir fry briskly, add bamboo shoot slices and agaric, stir well, add cooked giblets, seasoning sauce. Stir briskly again. Place on plate and sprinkle with brown peppercorn powder and serve.

紅 燜 肉

材料：

猪肉（後腿肉或五花肉）	一斤半	酒	半杯
葱	八支	冰糖（或砂糖）	三兩
八角	二顆	清水	二杯
醬油	一杯		

做法：

1. 選購無雜毛而皮較潔白之上好猪肉，整塊洗淨後，連皮切成一寸半大小之四方塊。

2. 用一只平底鍋子，在鍋底先舖放葱支，葱支上面再放肉塊，然後加入八角，冰糖、酒、醬油等調味料及二杯清水，蓋上鍋蓋。

3. 將鍋子放置火爐上，先用大火煮滾，然後改用小火繼續燒煮，煮約一小時以後，再用中火使汁變稠，唯在燒煮之過程中，不可揭開鍋蓋探看，只需將鍋子端起加以搖動數次，（約每隔二十分鐘搖動一次），以免燒焦和粘住鍋底。

4. 將葱支檢出放在菜盤內作墊底之用，再將已燒好之肉塊盛入盤內卽可上桌供食。

註： 此種紅燜（卽紅燒）之肉類，必需連同肉皮一起燒煮才會使其汁黏稠明亮，否則不够美觀味道也差。

※請參考照片第30號（A）

130

Stewed Pork in Brown Sauce

Ingredients:

2 lbs. Pork (butt or bacon)

8 Green onions

2 Star anise

1 C. Soysauce

1/2 C. Wine

2/3 C. Sugar

2 C. Water

1/4 lb. Pork Rind

Procedure:

1. Cut the pork into 1 ½ inch squares (Add pork rind in a large piece and remove before serving.)

2. Using a deep pot, lay whole green onions on bottom add pork squares and rind piece. Add star anise, soysauce, wine, sugar, water and cover. Bring to boil over high heat. reduce heat to about half, stew for 1 hour, unitl the sauce is reduced to 1/2 cup and is rather thick.

3. To serve, lay onion on bottom of platter, add pork and sauce.

NOTE:

Don't remove the cover, but do shake the pot about every 20 minutes.

_____

* Refer to picture 30 (A).

紅燒牛肉

材料：

牛肉（肋條或腱子肉）	二斤	醬油	一杯
大蒜	五粒	酒	二湯匙
葱	五支	鹽	一湯匙
薑	五大片	猪油或花生油	半杯
八角	三顆	辣豆瓣醬	三湯匙
花椒	一湯匙		

做法：

1. 牛肉切成一寸四方塊，全部在開水中川燙一下（需用大火約三十秒鐘）隨卽將肉撈出，水倒棄，再放肉回原鍋中，並加入開水（高出肉面約兩寸），放下葱薑，八角蓋上鍋蓋置爐上用中小火燒煮（約二小時）。

2. 另在炒菜鍋內，燒熱半杯油後，先爆香大蒜粒，並加入花椒同炒，再放下辣豆瓣醬煸炒一透，繼續加入醬油、酒用小火煮二分鐘。

3. 將第二項之佐料，全部用一只漏勺瀝入牛肉鍋內，再繼續同燴（已調味過之牛肉）直至汁濃而肉已酥爛時爲止，（約需一小時許）便可供食。

註：如不喜辣味可將辣豆瓣醬改爲豆瓣醬，此種紅燒牛肉可做爲紅燒牛肉麵之澆頭，係純四川口味。

Beef Stew Sze-Chuan Style

Ingredients:

2-1/2 lbs. Beef (chuck or flank)   1 C. Soysauce
5 Garlic buds   2 T. Wine
5 Green onions   1 T. Salt
5 slices   1/2 C. Lard (or peanut oil)
3 Star anise   3 T. Hot bean paste
1 T. Brown Peppercorns

Procedure:

1. Cut the beef into 1½ inch squares and cook for half a minute in boiling water, remove beef, drain off the boiling water, return beef and add fresh boiling water to about 2" above beef. Add anise, green onion, and ginger. Use low-heat, stew covered about 2 hours.

2. Heat 1/2 cup oil in frying pan, when hot add the garlic and peppercorns and stir fry. Then add hot bean paste, soysauce and wine. Bring to a boil and cook for 2 minutes.

3. Strain # 2 into the beef pot and mix. Stew another hour or until beef is tender. (about 1 hour).

NOTE:

If you don't like to eat hot pepper, you should use only bean paste or more soysauce.

魚 香 肉 絲

材料：

瘦猪肉	半斤	葱屑	一湯匙
荸薺（或筍一支）	六個	醬油	一湯匙
乾木耳	二湯匙	鎮江醋	一湯匙
薑屑	二茶匙	辣豆瓣醬	一湯匙
蒜屑	一茶匙	酒	半湯匙
醬油	一湯匙	糖	一茶匙
太白粉	二茶匙	鹽	半茶匙
花生油	三杯	太白粉	一茶匙
		麻油	一茶匙
		胡椒粉	少許

（醬油、太白粉、花生油）醃肉絲用

（葱屑～胡椒粉）綜合調味料

做法：

1. 將猪肉全部切成細絲，用醬油及太白粉拌醃一下（時間不拘）。
2. 木耳用溫水浸泡十五分鐘後摘去根蒂洗淨切成粗絲，荸薺去皮洗淨也切絲。
3. 將花生油在炒菜鍋內燒至微熱（如用生油需先燒滾，待冷却至八成熱），傾入拌醃過之猪肉絲炒泡迅速撥散，隨即見肉變色已熟即行撈起，餘油倒出。
4. 另在炒菜鍋內燒熱三湯匙油，先爆炒薑屑及蒜屑後，續放下荸薺絲，木耳絲同炒，然後將猪肉絲合入拌炒數下，並倒下綜合調味料迅速鏟拌均勻至變貼稠，便裝盤趁熱供食。

※請參考照片第31號。

134

Stir Fried Pork String with Hot Sauce

Ingredients:

10 oz Pork Tenderloin

6 Water chestnuts

2 T. Dry Agaric (fungus)

1 t. Chopped Garlic

1 T. Soysauce (to marinate pork)

2 t. Cornstarck   "

3 C. Pearut oil

1 T. Shredded
Green onion (seasoning sauce)

1 T. Soysance   "

1 T. Brown vinegar   "

1 T. Hot Bean paste   "

1/2 T. Wine   "

1 t. Sugar   "

1/2 t. Salt   "

1 t. Cornstarch   "

1 t. Sesame oil   "

1/4 t. Black pepper   "

Procedure:

1. Cut pork in string style, marinate with soysauce and cornstarch about 15 minutes.

2. Soak dry agaric in warm water about 15 minutes then discarding stems, slice them when expanded. Also slice the water chestnuts very fine.

3. Heat peanut oil in frying pan add pork strings, and just stir for 1/2 minute, then remove and put aside. Drain off oil from pan.

4. Heat another 3 T. oil to stir fry garlic and ginger, then add water chestnut, agaric, and pork strings, stir throughly. Last add the ready prepared seasoning sauce, stir evenly and serve.

* Refer to picture No. 31.

粉 蒸 牛 肉

材料：

牛肉	十兩	醬油	三湯匙
蒸肉粉(即五香米粉，做法列後)	三包	酒	一湯匙
葱	二支	糖	一茶匙
薑	三片	鹽	二茶匙
八角	一顆	辣豆瓣醬	一湯匙
		猪油(或熟花生油)	三湯匙

做法：

1. 選購全瘦而無筋之上好牛肉，用刀切成一寸半四方，約一分厚之片狀（需用利刀橫紋切片），放在盆裏加入葱段（拍碎）薑片，八角（切碎），醬油、酒、辣豆瓣醬、鹽及糖等各種調味料拌勻，醃約三十分鐘。

2. 再加入油和蒸肉粉，仔細拌和需將每片肉均沾上蒸肉粉，再逐片攤擺在特製之小蒸籠中（或用鋁盆，淺盤亦可），上鍋用大火蒸熟，（如用小蒸籠十五分鐘便熟，否則需二十餘分鐘）。

註：1. 如將甜薯或馬鈴薯切成小塊墊底同蒸則十分香甜可口。

2. 蒸肉粉係將梗米用小火乾炒（需加入花椒數粒，及八角一、二顆同炒）至米顏色變黃後傾出，待冷却後研磨成粉狀便是。

※請參考照片第35號（A）。

Steamed Beef with Spicy Rice Powder

Ingredients:

3/4 lb. Beef

3 pkg. Rice powder (about 1 C.)

2 Green onions

3 slices Ginger

1 Star anise

3 T. Soysauce

1 T. Wine

1 t. Sugar

2 t. Salt

1 T. Hot bean paste

3 T. peanut oil

Procedure:

1. Cut the beef into small slices about 1 ½″ square and 1/6″ thick; and marinate in onion, ginger, star anise, soysauce, wine, hot bean paste, sugar, salt, and oil for about 30 minutes.

2. After soaking, dredge each slice of beef with the rice powder. Then steam it in a shallow bowl over high heat for 20 minutes (if you use the special small steamer the time will be 15 minutes.)

NOTE:

Go prepare rice power yourself-Place 1 cup of uncooked rice in dry frying pan with 2 star anise and 1 t. brown peppercorn and stir over low heat, for 5 minutes until rice gets a little brown. Remove and let cool. Roll to about the size of bread crumbs.

---

* Refer to Picture No. 35. (A).

乾煸牛肉絲

材料‥

牛肉（腿肉）	十二兩	醬油	四湯匙
芹菜	六兩	酒	一湯匙
胡蘿蔔	半支	糖	一茶匙
紅辣椒	三支	薑汁	一茶匙
鹽	一茶匙	麻油	一茶匙
花生油	八湯匙	熟花椒粉	半茶匙

（醬油、酒、糖、薑汁為醃肉用料）

做法：

1. 將牛肉先切成一分厚之片狀，再順紋切成絲條（不必太細）全部切好後裝入盆內加進醃肉用料（即醬油、酒、糖、薑汁）拌勻醃漬一小時左右，並需時常加予調拌。

2. 芹菜去根並摘去葉子後，批開，（如很細可不必批），切成一寸長之段留用。

3. 胡蘿蔔去皮切成細絲（約一寸長），紅辣椒先除籽也切細絲備用。

4. 在炒菜鍋內燒熱五湯匙油後，倒下全部已醃過之牛肉絲用大火拌炒，見牛肉滲出湯汁時仍繼續用大火煸炒，約五分鐘後，始改為中小火候鏟炒，直至牛肉絲變褐黃而堅硬為止（約需時十二分鐘）由鍋中盛出。

5. 另在鍋內燒熱三湯匙油，先爆紅辣椒絲及胡蘿蔔絲再加入芹菜同炒並放鹽一茶匙調味，隨即將已炒好之牛肉絲合入拌勻並淋下麻油即裝盤撒下花椒粉便可。

註：1.此菜也可將牛肉絲用多量熱油（約六杯）大火炸乾則僅需三、四分鐘便可。

　　2.如喜食辣味，可酌加辣椒醬（或辣椒油）若無芹菜則改用萵筍代替也可。

※請參考照片第32號（A）。

138

Dry Shredded Beef

Ingredients:

1 lb. Beef (round steak)
8 oz. Celery (about 2 C.)
1 Carrot (about 2/3 C.)
3 Red hot peppers
1 t. Salt
1 t. Sesame oil

4 T. Soysauce   (to marinate beef)
1 T. Wine   "
1 t. Sugar   "
1 t. Ginger juice   "
8 T. Peanut oil

Procedure:

1. After cutting the beef into string shape, put in a big bowl and marinate with soysauce, wine sugar and ginger juice for 30 minutes at least, but not over 2 hours.

2. Remove the leaves and roots of celery and cut in one inch long pieces (if very large, cut stalks in half or in fourths).

3. Peel carrots, remove seeds from red pepper, cut both into string shape.

4. Heat 5 T. oil in frying pan, stir-fry the beef about 12 minutes (for first 5 minutes fry over very hot heat, reduce heat to half for 7 minutes and don't stop stirring). When beef is very dark and dry remove to a bowl. (If you need quickly, deep fry beef strings in very hot oil until beef is dark and dry about 4 minutes).

5. With another 3 T. oil fry the red pepper, then add carrots, after 1/2 minute add the celery and salt. Add the beef, stirring until mixed. Sprinkle in sesame oil before serving.

NOTE:

1. For a moist and soft beef dish, see Cantonese "Beef with Oyster Sauce" recipe.

2. Hot sauce or hot oil may be added to this.

---

* Refer to Picture No. 32 (A).

紅油腰片

材料：

猪腰	二個（約十兩）	芝麻醬	二湯匙
小黃瓜	二條（約四兩）	醬油（淡色）	二湯匙
粉皮	十張	鎮江醋	一湯匙
蒜泥	半湯匙	糖	一茶匙
薑屑	半湯匙	鹽	一茶匙
花椒粉	一茶匙	麻油	一湯匙
		味精	一湯匙
		辣椒油	少許

（芝麻醬以下為綜合調味料）

做法：

1. 選購粉黃色而呈有花紋之猪腰，每只由橫面剖開，剔除內部之白筋，在正面（即光滑面）直刀劃切條紋（約五，六條）再橫刀斜切成大薄片，全部切好後將之浸泡在冷水中。

2. 小黃瓜不必削皮，切成半圓形之斜薄片，用半茶匙鹽拌和，醃約半小時左右，再將鹽水擠乾，舖在菜盤內。

3. 另將粉皮（新鮮品）用冷開水冲過切成寬條瀝乾，拌入少許麻油及半茶匙鹽，舖在黃瓜片上。

4. 在一只小碗內將綜合調味料及蒜泥、薑屑、花椒粉調勻備用。（先用冷開水少許將芝麻醬調稀，然後加進各種調味料，辣椒油可留待最後淋下）。

5. 燒一鍋開水（約五杯）將猪腰片投入，用大火燙約十秒鐘即行撈出，再冲一次冷開水後瀝乾並拌入少許鹽及麻油，即整齊排列在盤中粉皮上，上桌時將小碗之綜合佐料澆上拌食即成。

※請參考照片第32號（B）。

140

Kidney with Hot Sauce

Ingredients:

2 Whole pork kidneys (about 12 oz)

2 Small cucumbers (about 4 oz)

10 Small green beans sheets (optional)

1/2 T. Chopped garlic

1/2 T. Chopped ginger

1 t. Brown peppercorn powder

2 T. Sesame seed paste (seasoning sauce)

2 T. Soysauce   "

1 T. Brown vinegar   "

1 t. Sugar   "

1 t. Salt   "

1 T. Sesame oil   "

a little M.S.G.   "

1 t. Red hot pepper oil   "

Procedure:

1. Choose a pink and yellowy kidney with a spongy feel. Cut in half horizontally, and remove the white membrane. Score the outside in 5 or 6 cuts from end to end only 1/3 the thickness of the kidney half. Lay knife almost flat to slice in large thin pieces across the grain. Soak slices in cold water.

2. Slice unpeeled cucumbers in 2″ lengths and sprinkle with 1/2 t. salt. Let sit 1 hour. Squeeze out salt water. Lay on platter.

3. Cut bean sheets into strips and mix with 1/2 t. salt and a little sesame oil. Place on top of cucumber.

4. In a small bowl prepare seasoning sauce, adding garlic, ginger and brown peppercorn powder. Mix the sesame seed paste with 2 T. cold water throughly then add other condiments.

5. To 5 cups of boiling water add kidney slices. Boil for 10 seconds. Remove kidneys and discard water. Wash kidney slices in cold water then squeeze dry. Place in pretty layers on the platter. Serve this with seasoning sauce poured over it. Mix well just before serving.

* Refer to picture No. 32 (B).

辣豆瓣魚

材料：

活鯉魚（或鯽魚）一條（約一斤重）		鹽	一茶匙
葱屑	二湯匙	糖	一茶匙
薑屑	一湯匙	鎮江醋	半湯匙
蒜屑	一湯匙	太白粉	半湯匙
辣豆瓣醬	二湯匙	麻油	一茶匙
醬油	二湯匙	清水	一杯
酒	一湯匙	猪油或花生油半杯	

做法：

1. 活鯉魚需在臨烹調時才將之殺剖，除淨內臟（需小心處理不可弄破苦膽）然後在魚身（兩面）斜切三、四條淺紋。

2. 將炒菜鍋燒熱後放下油再燒熱油，便將魚落鍋兩面煎透，然後將魚推在鍋邊。

3. 用鍋中所剩餘之油，爆炒薑屑與蒜屑並放辣豆瓣醬（或辣椒醬）同炒，再淋下酒與醬油並放糖、鹽調味注入清水便可將魚移入其中同煮，約三分鐘，需將汁向魚面上多澆淋以使之入味。

4. 見鍋中之湯汁只剩一半時，用調水之太白粉鈎芡不可太稠（應提起鍋子轉動）並淋下醋及麻油撒下葱屑便可裝盤。（需小心鏟入以免弄碎）。

142

Carp with Hot Bean Sauce

Ingredients:

1 Live Carp (about 1 lb)   1 t. Salt
2 T. Green onion chopped   1 t. Sugar
1 T. Ginger Chopped   1/2 T. Brown Vinegar
1 t. Garlic Chopped   1/2 T. Cornstarch (make paste)
2 T. Hot bean paste (or 1 T.   1/2 T. Cold water   "
  hot sauce)   1 t. Sesame oil
2 T. Soy sauce   1 C. Cold water
1 T. Wine   1/2 C. Lard or Peanut oil

Procedure:

1. Kill fish by striking a blow to the head (do not remove head or tail). Scale and clean. Cut 3 or 4 diagonal slashes 1/4" deep on each side.

2. Heat fry pan very hot, add oil. When oil is hot, add the fish and fry both side (each side a half minute.) Push aside in the pan.

3. Add the chopped ginger, garilc, hot bean paste or hot sauce in the same frying pan and stir thoroughly, then add wine, soysauce, salt, sugar and cold water place fish into sauce and cook 3 minutes.

4. When the sauce is reduced to half, add cornstarch paste. Stir until sauce has thickened. Sprinkle vinegar, sesame oil and chopped green onion on top and serve.

紙 包 魚

材料：

鱠魚（或其他種白色魚肉）	一斤	薑汁	一茶匙	醃
洋火腿（二寸四方薄片）	四片	鹽	一茶匙	魚
香荽葉	十四枚	酒	一湯匙	用
玻璃紙（5″×5″）	十四張	味精	半茶匙	料
花生油	六杯	麻油	二湯匙	

做法：

1. 在一只碗裏將鹽、酒、味精、與薑汁調勻成為醃魚料。

2. 將魚皮及骨刺剔除乾淨後，切成兩寸半長，一寸寬1/4寸厚之片狀（需橫面切），放入醃魚料中拌醃，約十分鐘（需常加翻動）。

3. 火腿先切成二寸四方大小之薄片，然後再斜角對切二刀，使成為三角形，（共需十四片）。

4. 將玻璃紙一張，尖角相對着放好，在中間部位塗上少許麻油（或其他熱油也可），然後先放一片火腿在中間略偏左部位，再放一枚香荽葉在右邊，然後將醃過之魚片一片擺在中間，折好四邊紙角　包裹成同魚片一樣大小之紙包。

5. 將油燒熱（約八成熱），投下紙包魚用慢火炸約　分鐘左右（正面向下投入）炸至魚片汎白而熟透即可撈出，瀝淨油後裝盤（盤邊可將魚頭、魚尾炸黃擺出裝飾，或用蕃茄片，綠色蔬荽點綴）。

※請參考照片第34號。

144

Paper-Wrapped Fried Fish

Ingredients:

1-1/4 lb. Pomfret (or any kind of white meat fish)	1 t. Ginger juice (to marinate fish)
4 slices Cooked ham (2"x2")	1 t. Salt "
14 pcs. Parsley leaves	1 T. Wine "
14 Cellophane paper (5"x5")	1/2 t. M.S.G. "
6 C. Peanut oil	2 T. Sesame oil "

Procedure:

1. After removing the skin and bones, cut the fish diagonally into 14 slices-2 $\frac{1}{2}$" long, 1 $\frac{1}{2}$" wide and 1/6" thick. Place in a large bowl and add marinade. Soak for 10 minutes, turning carefully several times.

2. Slice ham into 1" squares then cut to make 16 triangles.

3. Brush paper with sesame oil (or peanut oil). With one corner facing you, place one slice of ham to center left and 1 pc. parsley face down on center right. Lay a fish slice on top. Fold up the corner of the paper nearest you. Make a tight package by folding over the left then right corners. Keep corners square. Now tuck in the top corner firmly to close the package.

4. Heat oil to 300° and add packages. Fry about 3 minutes. The fish slice should turn white. Remove from oil and gently press excess oil from the package. Place attractively on a platter and garnish with colorful fresh vegetables or the fish head and tail.

* Refer to picture No 34.

乾 炒 蝦 仁

材料：

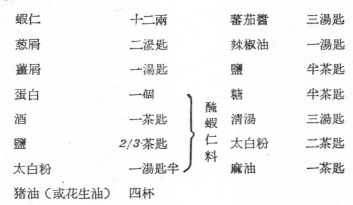

蝦仁	十二兩	蕃茄醬	三湯匙
葱屑	二湯匙	辣椒油	一湯匙
薑屑	一湯匙	鹽	半茶匙
蛋白	一個	糖	半茶匙
酒	一茶匙	清湯	三湯匙
鹽	2/3茶匙	太白粉	二茶匙
太白粉	一湯匙半	麻油	一茶匙
豬油（或花生油）	四杯		

（醃蝦仁料）

做法：

1.蝦仁冲洗乾淨後，瀝乾水份再用乾布包裹吸淨水份，全部放入盆內，加入蛋白、酒、鹽、太白粉（即醃蝦仁料）調拌，醃約半小時以上（時間久長較好）。

2.將油倒在鍋內燒至八成熱後（如用生花生油則需先燒滾一次再使之冷却），傾入醃過之蝦仁用大火迅速泡炸，至蝦仁變成白色後瀝出，油也需全部倒出。

3.另在原鍋內燒熱兩湯匙油，放進葱屑、薑屑爆炒，並加入蕃茄醬拌炒合入清湯、鹽、糖同煮，再用調過水之太白粉鈎茨，使汁呈濃稠狀，迅卽將蝦仁落鍋，並淋上辣椒油、麻油拌合鏟勻，卽可裝盤上桌。

Sauteed Shrimp with Hot Sauce

Ingredients:

1 lb. Peeled fresh shrimp
2 T. Chopped green onion
1 T. Chopped ginger
1 Egg white (to marinate shrimp)
1 t. Wine   "
2/3 t. Salt   "
1-1/2 T. Cornstarch   "
4 C. Peanut oil

3 T. Tomato catsup
1 T. Hot pepper oil
1/2 t. Salt
1/2 t. Sugar
3 T. Soup stock
2 t. Cornstarch
1 t. Sesame oil

Procedure:

1. Clean and dry shrimp, then marinate in egg white, wine, salt and cornstarch mixture. Let stand for at least half hour (longer is better).

2. Deep fry shrimp in oil (not too hot, about 300°). When the shrimp turns white, about 90% done, remove and drain off oil from pan.

3. Put back 2 T. oil in pan, and stir fry chopped green onion and ginger, add tomato catsup, stir quickly. Then add soup stock, salt and sugar. Boil for only a few seconds then add cornstarch paste, stir, add shrimp hot pepper oil and sesame oil. Pour on a plate. Serve.

蝦仁鍋巴

材料：

蝦仁	六兩	醬油（淡色）	半湯匙	醃肉絲用
瘦猪肉	四兩	濕太白粉	一湯匙	
香菇	五個	蕃茄醬	四湯匙	
青豆	二湯匙	醬油（淡色）	一湯匙	
鍋巴（二寸四方大）	十片	糖	一湯匙	
清湯	三杯	醋	一湯匙	
鹽	半茶匙	太白粉	三湯匙	醃蝦仁用
濕太白粉	一茶匙	鹽	一茶匙半	
花生油	六杯	麻油	少許	

做法：

1. 蝦仁洗淨後拭乾水份，用一茶匙濕太白粉（即太白粉加水調溶後所沈澱碗底之凝固者），及半茶匙鹽拌勻。

2. 瘦猪肉切成細絲後，也用一茶匙濕太白粉及半湯匙醬油調拌，醃置片刻。

3. 冬菇用溫水泡漲後，去蒂切成細絲備用。

4. 在炒鍋內燒熱六湯匙花生油，（八成熱即可）先炒熟猪肉絲，隨即鏟出放在盤中，再燒熱鍋中餘剩之油，傾落蝦仁大火炒熟盛在肉絲一起。

5. 放下香菇絲在炒鍋內，並注入清湯煮滾，然後加入蕃茄醬、醬油、糖、醋、鹽調味，待再滾沸後，即用調過水之濕太白粉鈎芡，使汁黏稠，再將炒過之猪肉絲與蝦仁及熟青豆等加入拌勻，改用小火繼續使其保暖（不可太滾以免湯汁變乾），最後淋下少許麻油。

6. 將花生油在另一只鍋內燒得極熱之後，投下鍋巴用大火炸膨至顏色變黃而酥脆時撈出（油不要瀝得太乾）裝在深盤（或大碗）內，同蝦仁料（盛在另一只碗中）一起迅速端上桌面，澆下蝦仁料到鍋巴上，當時必呈油爆之聲，即可迅速供食。

※請參考照片第33號。

148

Popped Rice with Shrimp

Ingredients:

6 oz. Small shrimp

4 oz. Pork tenderloin

5 Dry Black Mushrooms

2 T. Green peas (canned)

10 pcs. Crispy rice

3 C. Soup stock

1/2 t. Salt (to marinate shrimp)

1 t. Cornstarch   "

6 C. Peanut oil.

1/2 T. Soysauce (to marinate pork

1 t. Cornstarch   "

4 T. Tomato catsup

1 T. Soysauce

1 T. Brown vinegar

1 P. Sugar

3 T. Cornstarch   (make paste)

3 T. Cold water   "

1½ t. Salt

2 t. Sesame oil

Procedure:

1. Clean the shrimp, mix evenly with 1 t. of cornstarch and 1/2 t. of salt.

2. Shred pork tenderloin, mix evenly with 1/2 T. of soysauce and 1 t. of cornstarch paste.

3. Soak mushrooms in warm water 15 minutes. Remove stems. Cut tops in shreds.

4. Use 6 T. of peanut oil to fry shredded pork and put it aside. Use the remaining oil to fry shrimp until well done, and remove to bowl with pork.

5. Add shredded mushrooms and soup stock in same fry pan, boil, then add tomato catsup, soysauce, sugar, vinegar and salt. When boiling again add cornstarch paste, cook until starchy, then add pork, shrimp and green peas. Keep this warm over low heat Add sesame oil later.

6. Deep fry crispy rice in very hot oil until brown. Lay on the platter, quickly take rice to table, and pour the hot shrimp mix over it. Listen to it snap and pop.

* Refer to Picture No. 33.

麻婆豆腐

材料：

嫩豆腐（〃2×2〃）八小塊		鹽	一茶匙
絞猪肉（或牛肉） 三兩		太白粉	二茶匙
大蒜屑	一茶匙	花椒粉	一茶匙
葱屑	一湯匙	清湯	2/3杯
辣豆瓣醬	一湯匙	麻油	二茶匙
醬油	三湯匙	花生油	四杯

做法：

1. 豆腐先切除硬邊再切丁（約半吋四方），全部用燒滾之油炸約半分鐘，（也可用滾水川燙），撈出後將油瀝乾，鍋中之油全部倒出，再將原鍋燒熱。

2. 放三湯匙油在鍋內，先爆炒猪肉（絞碎或剁碎皆可），並加入蒜屑及辣豆瓣醬，繼續放下醬油、鹽等調味料，並將豆腐落鍋，輕輕同拌，即可注入清湯，燜煮三分鐘左右。

3. 將太白粉用同量之清水調溶，慢慢淋入鍋中，並輕輕拌鏟均勻，即將葱屑撒下，再淋下麻油（如喜辣味者可酌加辣椒油若干）裝入盤內，然後將已炒過之花椒粉撒落豆腐上便成。

註：此菜必需做得麻辣，且又燙又鹹，才合原則，係一道經濟可口之家常小吃菜。

※請參考照片第30號（B）。

Ma-Po's Bean Curd

Ingredients:

8 cubes Bean curd (2" × 2")

4 oz. Ground pork (or beef)

1 t. Garlic chopped

1 T. Green onion chopped

1 T. Hot bean paste

1 t. Brown peppercorn powder

2 T. Soysauce

1 t. Salt

2 t. Cornstarch   (make paste)

2 t. Cold water   "

2/3 C. Soup stock

1 t. Sesame oil

3 c. Peanut oil

Procedure:

1. Cut the bean curd into 1/2 inch cubes and deep fry in hot peanut oil for about 1/2 minute, (or boil in water).

2. Remove all oil except 3 T. reheat and fry the ground pork well, then add garlic, hot bean paste, soysauce, salt, soup stock and bean curd. Boil for 3 minutes.

3. Thicken with cornstarch paste, then sprinkle with onion and sesame oil. Place in bowl and sprinkle with brown peppercorn powder and serve.

NOTE:

Hot red pepper oil may be added to this last, if you like it hoter.

---

* Refer to picture No. 30. (B).

紹 子 烘 蛋

材料：

雞蛋	六個	鹽	半茶匙	蛋汁調味料
絞豬肉（或牛肉）	二兩	豬油（或熟油）	二湯匙	
芹菜屑	二湯匙	濕太白粉	一湯匙	
葱屑	二湯匙	醬油	二湯匙	
薑屑	二茶匙	鹽	半茶匙	
蒜屑	二茶匙	糖	一茶匙	
清湯	2/3杯	鎮江醋	一茶匙	
酒	一湯匙	太白粉	一湯匙	
花生油	一杯	麻油	半湯匙	

做法：

1. 將雞蛋在大碗內打散後，加入鹽和豬油及濕太白粉用力打鬆，至十分發泡爲止。

2. 在平底鍋內燒熱半杯花生油後，將打鬆之蛋汁倒下，抖轉鍋子使蛋汁攤勻用慢火煎熟，然後再翻轉一面續煎（翻面後需由鍋邊淋下兩湯匙熟油），待內部蛋汁均已凝固而熟透之後，即可盛出，放在乾淨菜板上用利刀切成二寸長方塊，然後裝進菜盤內

3. 另在炒鍋中燒熱三湯匙油炒熟絞豬肉，並加入蒜屑與薑屑，淋下酒與醬油，注入清湯加鹽糖調味，待煮滾後用太白粉（加入同量之冷水調溶）鈎芡，並淋下醋和麻油撒下葱屑及芹菜屑便全部澆到盤中蛋上即可。

註：川菜中烘蛋種類繁多，如白油烘蛋、魚香烘蛋、火腿烘蛋，蝦仁烘蛋……等而烘蛋之做法相同，祇是澆頭變換材料與調味而已。

152

Minced Pork on Egg Omelet

Ingredients:

8 Eggs	1/2 t. Salt	(mix in eggs)
3 oz Ground pork	2 T. Cooked oil	"
2 T. Chopped celery	1 T. Cornstarch	"
2 T. Chopped green onion	1 T. Cold water	"
2 t. Chopped ginger	2 T. Soysauce	
2 t. Chopped garlic	1/2 t. Salt	
2/3 Soup stock	1 t. Sugar	
1 T. Wine	1 t. Brown vinegar	
1 c. Peanut oil	1/2 T. Sesame oil	
	1 T. Cornstarch	(make paste)
	1 T. Cold water	"

Procedure:

1. Beat the eggs well in a bowl, add 1 t. salt, 2 T. oil, 1 T. cornstarch paste. Beat until very smooth and thick.

2. Heat 1/2 cup of peanut oil in fry pan, pour in eggs and fry until golden on the bottom. Then turn over. Splash 2 T. oil around side of pan, when the eggs get firm take out. Lay on warm plate and cut in small pieces.

3. In a frying pan, heat 3 T. oil, stir fry pork. Add ginger and garlic, splash in the wine, soysauce, soup stock, salt and sugar. When it has boiled, add cornstarch paste boil until thickened, and lastly add the vinegar, sesame oil, and sprinkle with chopped green onion and celery. Then pour the sauce over top of eggs and serve quickly.

魚香茄子

料材：

茄子	四支（約十兩）	糖	一茶匙
葱屑	一湯匙	鹽	一茶匙
薑屑	半湯匙	清湯	半杯
蒜屑	一茶匙	鎮江醋	半湯匙
辣豆瓣醬	一湯匙	麻油	半湯匙
醬油	一湯匙	花生油	六湯匙

做法：

1. 選購鮮紫而較挺硬之茄子，去蒂後洗淨切成兩寸長如拇指般粗細之條狀，（最好用手指撕剖）。

2. 在炒菜鍋內燒熱花生油後將全部茄子落鍋煸炒（用小火），炒到茄子變軟無硬心後，用鏟子撳壓將吸進之油擠出，即全部茄子鏟入盤內（或推在鍋邊）。

3. 用鍋內所剩下之油爆炒蒜屑薑屑，並放辣豆瓣醬同炒，再加入醬油、糖、鹽、及清湯煮滾，隨後將茄子倒回鍋內大火拌炒並燒乾。

4. 淋下醋及麻油將葱屑也落鍋鏟拌均勻即可起鍋裝盤。

154

Eggplant Sze-Chuan Style

Ingredients:

4 Eggplant (about 12 oz.)
1 T. Chopped green onion
1/2 T. Chopped ginger
1 t. Chopped garlic
1 T. Hot bean paste
2 T. Soysauce
1/2 T. Brown vinegar

1 t. Sugar
1 t. Salt
1/2 C. Soup stock
1/2 T. Sesame oil
6 T. Peanut oil

Procedure:

1. Choose firm purple egg plant, remove stalk and without peeling, cut into thumb size pieces.

2. Heat oil in fry pan until very hot. Put eggplant in, turn heat to low, stir fry until it's soft about 3 minutes. Then press eggplant, to squeeze out the excess oil. Remove egg plant from pan and set aside.

3. Into the frying pan add chopped garlic, ginger and hot bean paste, stir a few seconds, add soysauce, sugar salt, and soup stock and bring to a boil. Add egg plant, cook about 1 minute until sauce is gone.

4. Add vinegar, and sesame oil. Stir until heated through. Sprinkle with chopped green onion. Mix carefully and serve.

糖 醋 白 菜

材料：

大白菜（或包心菜）	一斤半	糖	二湯匙
乾辣椒	六支	鹽	二茶匙
花椒	半湯匙	麻油	二湯匙
醬油	二湯匙	花生油	五湯匙
鎮江醋	二湯匙		

做法：

1. 將白菜一片片剝下冲洗乾淨後，用手撕裂成半張紙牌大小（菜梗部份較硬需撕得小塊一點）瀝乾水份備用。

2. 乾辣椒拭抹乾淨後切成一寸長之段狀，內部之辣椒籽需抖出不用。

3. 在炒菜鍋內燒熱花生油，先落下辣椒段爆香，至呈黑色之後，再將花椒放入略炒，旋即將白菜下鍋，用大火拌炒，約炒三分鐘，見菜已變軟時，可加入鹽、糖及醬油等調味料，再繼續拌炒數下至菜已相當入味。

4. 最後淋醋及麻油入鍋，略一拌合即行起鍋裝盤。

註：白菜之軟硬程度可隨各人之喜好。此菜很適宜冷吃。

Sweet and Sour Cabbage

Ingredients:

2 lbs. Round cabbage
    or Chinese cabbage
6 Dried red peppers
1/2 T. Brown peppercorns
3 T. Soysauce
2 T. Brown vinegar

2 T. Sugar
2 t. Salt
2 T. Sesame oil
5 T. Peanut oil

Procedure:

1. Carefully remove clean-tear cabbage leaves into small pieces about 2″ long-
   1 ½ ″ wide, cut spine of leaf into smaller pieces.

2. Wipe clean and cut dry red peppers into 1 inch long strips, remove seeds.

3. Heat oil in fry pan, fry red pepper first, when the pepper gets dark add
   pepper corns and cabbage stirring quickly over very high heat for 3 minutes.
   When the cabbage is soft add salt, sugar and soysauce, stir one more minute.

4. Add vinegar and sesame oil, stir until thoroughly mixed. Serve on a platter.

NOTE:

This dish tastes better when eaten cold.

四川泡菜

材料：

花椒	二湯匙	紅辣椒	五支
鹽	三湯匙	白蘿蔔	一個
開水	八杯	胡蘿蔔	半個
高粱酒	二湯匙	小黃瓜	三條
薑	五片	包心菜	半斤

做法：

1. 將一只寬口大瓶子或磁鉢，瓦罐（最好用特製之泡菜罎子）洗淨拭乾水份，放進花椒與鹽，再將開水冲入，放置至水十分冷透，便加進酒、薑片、與用刀切過裂縫之紅辣椒（或斜切小段也可）將之拌勻，即成為泡菜滷。

2. 將白蘿蔔、胡蘿蔔及小黃瓜皆連皮洗淨，拭乾水份，切成如小拇指般大小之細條狀，全部放入上項泡菜滷子中。

3. 包心菜洗淨，用手撕裂成一寸四方大之小塊（或用刀切小也可），裝在大托盤中（用竹籮最佳），略為曬去水份，也裝進泡菜滷中並同其他材料拌勻，蓋嚴蓋子，泡約三天，便可取食。

4. 待已泡過之菜料全部食完之後，再重新泡製，那時只需再加二茶匙鹽與二湯匙酒便可，但次數太多之後（約五、六次）便應重做一份相同之新滷，加人混合而用。

註：挾取泡菜時所用之筷子，湯匙之類，務必要保持清潔，不可沾有油漬，和生水以免滷汁發霉變味。

※請參考照片第35號（B）。

Sze-Chuan Pickle

Ingredients:

2 T. Brown Peppercorn

3 T. Salt

8 C. Boiling water

2 T. Wine (Kao-Lian wine is better)

5 slices Ginger

5 Hot red pepper

1 Turnip

1/2 Carrot (about 1 lb.)

1/2 lb. Cabbage

3 smalls Cucumbers

Procedure:

1. Clean and wipe dry a large mouth bottle or crock. Place pepper corn and salt in bottle, pour in boiling water, let cool. Add wine, ginger, and hot pepper (cut into small pieces or just slash lengthwise but do not cut small pieces). Mix well. This will be the brine of Sze-Chuan Pickle.

2. Cut the turnip, carrot, and cucumber into small pieces the size of a little finger. Don't peel. Add to the brine.

3. Tear the cabbage leaves with fingers into small pieces, wipe dry or place in sun shine a few minutes, then add to the brine. Mix with the other vegetables, and cover with close fitting lid, soak about 3 days.

4. This brine may be used many times, but as new vegetables are used add 2 t. salt and 2 T. wine each time.

NOTE:

It is important that clean and dry forks or chopsticks be used to prevent a scum from forming in the crock.

---

* Refer to picture No. 35 (B).

麻 辣 黃 瓜

材料··

小黃瓜	一斤（約七條）	鹽	二茶匙
大蒜片	十五片	糖	二茶匙
花椒粒	一茶匙	鎮江醋	一湯匙
辣豆瓣醬	一茶匙	麻油	二湯匙
辣椒油	二湯匙	味精	少許

做法：

1. 小黃瓜購顏色鮮綠而形狀直勻者，先用水洗淨，擦乾，稍微切除兩端後，直切兩刀使成爲四長條，再去除瓜籽，橫切成兩寸長之小段，（也可切成滾刀塊）切好後全部裝入盆內，撒下鹽一湯匙拌勻，醃漬，約兩、三小時。

2. 將冷開水倒入盆裏，冲洗一下醃過之小黃瓜，然後撈出並擠乾水份（或瀝乾），再放入大碗裏。

3. 將大蒜片，花椒粒及辣豆瓣醬、辣椒油、糖、醋、麻油等調味料，全部放進大碗中，同小黃瓜條拌勻，再放置醃上四小時左右，便可取食。（約可保存三、四天之久）。

註：此係四川小菜之一種，同泡菜，炸花生米，拌干絲等均可在正菜之前擺上桌去供食。

※請參考照片第35（C）。

160

Sze-Chuan Cucumber Relish

Ingredients:

1-1/4 lbs. Cucumbers (about 7 pcs)   2 t. Salt
15 slices Garlic   2 t. Sugar
1 t. Brown pepper corn   1 T. Brown vinegar
1 t. Hot bean paste   2 T. Sesame oil
2 T. Hot oil (red pepper oil)   1/2 t. M.S.G.

Procedure:

1. Cut off and discard both tips of cucumber, then cut length-wise in 4 strips, remove seeds. Cut 2 inches long. Let stand in bowl, sprinkle with salt and soak two or three hours.

3. Wash the cucumber with cold water and let dry. Put back in bowl.

3. Add garlic slices, brown pepper corns, hot bean paste, hot oil, sugar, vinegar and sesame oil. Mix and soak about 3 hours.

NOTE:

This may be kept for 1 week in refrigerator, covered.

* Refer to picture No. 35 (C).

161

乾 煸 四 季 豆

材料：

四季豆	一斤	糖	一湯匙
乾蝦米	二湯匙	醋（鎮江醋）	一湯匙
榨菜	一兩	鹽	二茶匙
葱屑	二湯匙	麻油	一湯匙
薑屑	二茶匙	清湯（或水）	二湯匙
花生油	五杯	味精	少許

做法：

1. 選購較短扁而翠綠之嫩四季豆、摘去兩端及兩旁之硬筋，全部洗淨瀝乾備用。

2. 乾蝦米用溫水泡軟（約十分鐘）摘去頭、脚等，再切碎，榨菜需冲洗一下切成小粒（屑狀）留用。

3. 在炒菜鍋內注入五杯花生油，燒熱至沸滾程度，將四季豆全部傾入，用大火炸軟，至豆面呈縐縮狀，（約炸三、四分鐘），即可撈出瀝乾，餘油全部倒出。

4. 再將炒菜鍋燒熱放下二湯匙油，先落薑屑爆香，再放蝦米、榨菜拌炒，隨後加入鹽、糖、味精及清湯（或水），並將四季豆合入同拌，煸炒至湯汁全部收乾為止。

5. 淋下醋及麻油，撒下葱屑再略加拌勻，便可裝盤。

註：此菜宜冷吃，也可留存較多時日，尤為佐粥之佳肴。

※請參考照片第30號（C）。

162

Dry Cooked String Beans

Ingredients:

1-1/4 lbs. String beans

2 oz. Ground pork (optional)

2 T. Dry shrimp

2 oz. Salted vegetable or salted
cucumber

2 T. Chopped green onion

2 t. Chopped ginger

5 C. Peanut oil

1 T. Sugar

1/2 T. Brown vinegar

2 t. Salt

1 T. Sesame oil

2 T. Soup stock (or water)

1/2 t. M.S.G.

Procedure:

1. Choose young, tender and short green beans remove tips and strings but do not cut smaller.

2. Soak dry shrimp in warm water about 10 minutes. Remove head and feet, chop into small pieces. Cut salted vegetables into small pieces.

3. Heat oil very hot, deep fry string beans until they are wrinkled (about 3 minutes.) Remove beans and drain off oil from frying pan.

4. Put back only 2 T. oil in pan and fry the pork, chopped ginger, dry shrimp and salted vegetable, add salt, sugar, MSG, and soup stock (or water). Then add the string beans to fry pan, stir well over heigh heat until the sauce is gone.

5. Add vinegar and sesame oil and sprinkle in chopped green onion, stir well.

NOTE:

This dish will keep a few days, and taste better eaten cold.

---

* Refer to picture No. 30 (C).

著者擔任製作與主持電視烹飪節目
已四百餘次，極受觀眾歡迎。

Miss Fu Taiwan's popular
T.T.V.'s chef, is also prod-
ucer and director. She has
prepared over 400 different
recipes from 1964 to the present.

右圖係著者應邀在港某烹飪學校作
特別示範

The autoor demonstrating
special Chinese cuisine at
Hong kong mobil cooking
school.

著者應邀赴日為東京婦人會及料理學校表演中國名菜
The author demonstrating Chinese cuisine by specil invitation of the Tokyo
wonen's clu b and cooking college in 1963.

北 部 菜

Dishes of **Nothern** China

第卅六圖（左）
糖醋全魚
（做法參照第196頁）

(Picture No. 36
**Fried Whole
Fish with
Sweet Sour
Sauce**
(See Recipe Page
197)

第卅七圖（左） **雪花鷄**
（做法參照第168頁）
Picture No. 37 (left)
Flowered Chicken Soup
(See Recipe Page 169)

第卅八圖（右） **鷄茸鮑魚羹**
（做法參照第206頁）

Picture No. 38
Minced Chicken with Abalone Potage
(See RecipPe Page 207)

第卅九圖

涮羊肉
Ⓐ 調味
Ⓑ 涮肉
（參照第192頁）

Picture No. 39
**Rinsed Mutton
in Chefing Pot**
(A) **MiX Seasoning
Sauce**
(B) **Rinseing Mutton
in Pot**
(See Recipe Page 193)

第四十圖 **蒙古烤肉** （做法參照第194頁）

Ⓐ各種肉類　Ⓑ各種蔬菜類

Ⓒ各種調味料　Ⓓ烤肉方法

肉羊　肉鹿　肉猪

Picture No. 40
Mongolian Bar-B-Q
(See Recipe Page 195)
(A) **Meat Part**
(B) **Vegetable Part**
(C) **Condiments Part**
(D) **Stir on Grill**

第四十一圖（左）
紅燒排翅
（做法參照第204頁）

Picture No. 41(right)
Shark's Fan in Brown Sauce
(See Recipe Page 205

第四十二圖（下）　四色蔬菜
（做法參照第212頁）
Picture No. 42 **4 Kinds of Braised Vegetable**
(See Recipe Page 213)

第四十三圖（上）　涼拌三絲
（做法參照第210頁）
Picture No. 43 **ChiCKen and cucumber Salad**　(See Recipe Page 211)

Contents of Northern

北部菜目錄：

Page

165

燻　鷄

材料：

嫩鷄	一隻（約兩斤）	桂皮	一小塊
花椒	二湯匙	醬油	一杯
鹽	二湯匙	糖	半杯
葱	一支	麵粉	半杯
薑	三片	茶葉	半杯
八角	二顆	麻油或鷄油	一湯匙

做法：

1. 將鷄洗淨拭乾水份後用已在乾鍋中炒黃之花椒與鹽抹擦鷄身裏外，醃約五小時左右。清除花椒粒後用滷汁滷熟，如無滷汁可採用下面方法。

2. 在鍋內放八杯淸水，加入葱、薑、八角、桂皮與醬油煮十分鐘。然後將已醃過之鷄放下用文火煮熟（約十分鐘，中間需翻一次面）。取出已煮熟之鷄俟稍冷却以使皮乾爽。

3. 將糖、麵粉、茶葉放進一只舊鍋內（亦可加入葱、薑、八角各少許）再在上面架放一枚鐵絲網，（塗抹少許油在網上），將鷄整隻平擺在網上，覆蓋鍋蓋用文火燻約八分鐘揭開鍋蓋翻轉一面鷄身，再續燻約五分鐘，將火熄去後過五分鐘見鷄身呈深黃色時即取出。

4. 將鷄用刷子刷上少許鷄油或麻油潤亮鷄皮，再斬切成小塊排列在菜盤中上桌。

註： 1. 按燻鷄宜冷吃，也可保存數日不壞。

2. 煮過鷄之湯即可當做滷汁而保存留着滷製其他滷菜所用，（放在冰箱中每隔三天煮滾一次）。

166

Smoked Chicken Peiping Style

Ingredients:

1 *Young chicken (about 2-1/2 lbs.)*	1 *pc. Cinnamon stick (1/2" long)*
2 *T. Brown Peppercorns*	1 *C. Soysauce*
2 *T. Salt*	1/2 *C. Sugar*
1 *Green onion*	1/2 *C. Flour*
3 *slices Ginger*	1/2 *C. Black tea leaves*
2 *Star anise*	1 *T. Sesame oil or chicken grease.*

Procedure:

1. Clean and wipe the chicken, rub with fried brown peppercorns and salt which have been fried over low heat in dry frying pan about 1 minute. Soak about 5 hours.

2. Boil 8 C. water in a large pot. Add green onion, ginger, star anise, cinnamon, and soysauce, cook for 10 minutes. Add the chicken continuing to cook 10 more minutes over low heat. (Turn over once). Remove and let cool.

3. Place the sugar, flour, and tea leaves in heavy iron pan. Add a rack over this and place the chicken on its side on the rack. Cover, smoke this about 8 minutes over low heat. Turn the chicken and smoke for 5 minutes more, until chicken turns brown.

4. Remove the chicken from pan and brush with sesame oil or chicken grease. Cut in 1" wide 2" long pieces, lay on plate in a chicken shape.

NOTE:

1. The soup from No. 2 may be stored in refrigerator, covered. It may be used in other dishes.

2. This may be prepared 1 or 2 days ahead of time and served cold.

167

雪 花 鷄

材料：

鷄胸	一個（約十兩）	蛋白	三個
鹽	半茶匙 ⎫ 醃	太白粉	一湯匙
酒	一茶匙 ⎬ 鷄料	清湯	五杯
蝦仁	四兩	鹽	二茶匙半
肥肉	一兩	熟冬菇	一個
蛋白	一 個 ⎫ 拌	熟火腿	少許
鹽	半茶匙 ⎬ 蝦料	香荽	少許
太白粉	二茶匙 ⎭		

做法：

1. 鷄胸剔除骨頭後將肉較厚部份片切移置較薄處使整塊鷄胸成爲平均厚度，再用刀輕輕敲劃一遍洒下鹽與酒醃十數分鐘。
2. 蝦仁與肥肉分別剁爛成爲泥狀，盛在大碗內加入蛋白，鹽與太白粉，仔細攪拌至呈膠狀爲止。
3. 用一只平荼盤將鷄胸平舖其上（鷄皮向下），並洒下太白粉，然後將第二項之蝦肉平均攤放在上面，並需抹光表面放入蒸籠內用大火蒸熟（約八分鐘左右）。
4. 將已蒸熟之鷄胸，趁熱改切成爲小塊（菱角形）放進大湯碗中，注入已沸滾並加過鹽之清湯。
5. 在另一只平盤內將三個蛋白打硬如雪堆狀，再用火腿片冬菇絲及香荽等舖砌成美麗圖案，放進蒸籠內用大火蒸三分鐘，端出後推進大湯碗之湯面上便可。（食時用湯勺切開，同鷄塊與湯分裝小湯碗內供食。

※請參考照片第37號

168

Flowered Chicken Soup

Ingredients:

1 Whole chicken breast (about 1 lb.)
1/2 t. Salt   (for chicken)
1 t. Wine   "
3/4 C. Shrimp, (shelled and minced)
1/4 C. Pork fat (minced)
1 egg white   (marinate shrimp)
1/2 t. salt   "
2 t. Cornstarch   "

3 Egg white
1 T. Cornstarch
5 C. Soup stock
1-1/2 t. Salt
1 Dried black mushroom
   (soaked and cooked)
10 slices Cooked ham (1/2" square)
5 Pcs. Chinese parsley

Procedure:

1. Remove the bone from whole chicken breast and score the meat lengthwise and crosswise. Splash with salt and wine and let stand about 10 minutes.

2. Place the minced shrimp and pork fat in same bowl, add egg whites, salt and cornstarch. Mix thoroughly.

3. Place the whole chicken breast on a flat plate (skin face down), and sprinkle whole top with cornstarch, then cover with all of the shrimp mixture, flatten and smooth the top. Place plate in steamer and steam about 8 minutes over high heat.

4. Remove the chicken meat and cut into small diamond shaped pieces. Place all in a soup bowl, add boiling soup stock (seasoned with 2¼ t. salt.)

5. Beat 3 egg white very dry place on the oiled flat plate and decorate with mushroom; ham, and parsley to resemble flowers and grass. Place plate in steamer, steam about 3 minutes over high heat, Carefully slip the decorated egg white on top of hot soup. serve.

6. Before eating use a serving spoon to separate the egg topping, making sure each portion of soup contains some of the egg and one piece of chicken in small soup bowl.

* Refer to picture No. 37.

169

紅燒栗子鷄

材料：

光鷄一隻	（約一斤半）	酒	一湯匙
乾栗子	三兩（或新鮮栗子半斤）	糖	二湯匙
葱	三支	花生油	五杯
薑	二片	太白粉	二茶匙
醬油	五湯匙	香菜	少許

做法

1. 乾栗子需用溫水浸泡半天，待已全部泡軟而縐紋也漲開時摘洗乾淨留用（如用新鮮栗子僅剝除外殼及澀衣便可，無須浸泡）。

2. 將鷄斬剁成二寸長一寸寬之長方塊放在大碗內加入醬油及葱支，薑片拌醃十分鐘，再投入已燒熱之油中炸黃（可分爲兩次炸，以免一次太多火力不夠而炸不上顏色），炸黃之鷄塊全部撈起，將鍋中之油倒出後，再重放回鍋內。

3. 將泡鷄塊之醬油料傾入鍋內，並加酒、糖、與三杯清水，先用大火煮滾，再改用小火燜燒，約二十分鐘之後加入栗子，繼續燒煮至湯汁收乾僅剩半杯爲止。

4. 淋下調水太白粉，將鍋中之湯汁鈎芡成黏稠狀，再淋下一湯匙熱油便可裝盤，面上飾以香菜便成。

170

Stewed Chicken with Chestnuts

Ingredients:

1 Chicken (about 2 lbs.)

4 oz. Chestnuts (dry)

    (or 1/2 lb. fresh)

3 Green onions

2 slices Ginger

5 T. Soysauce

1 T. Wine

2 T. Sugar

5 C. Peanut oil

2 t. Cornstarch   (make paste)

2 t. Cold water   "

5 Parsley leaves

Procedure:

1. Soak the dry chestnuts in warm water about 1/2 day. When the chestnuts are smooth clean them. If you use fresh chestnuts, don't soak just remove brown shell and skin.

2. Cut the chiken into 1″ wide 2″ long shapes, place in a bowl. Soak with green onion, ginger and soysauce about 10 minutes. Deep fry half of this in heated oil a few minutes until it's brown. Remove cooked chicken, reheat oil and repeat with remaining half. Drain off oil, return all the chicken to pan.

3. Add soysauce (in which chicken has been soaked), wine, sugar and 4 C. water, bring to a boil, and reduce heat rather low, stew for 20 minutes then add chestnuts, continuing to stew 20 more minutes until the sauce is reduced to 2/3 cup. Remove onions and ginger.

4. Add cornstarch paste and stir the sauce until it has thickened. Splash on 1 T. heated oil. Remove to platter. Decorate with parsley leaves and serve.

炸 八 塊

Stewed Chicken with Chestnuts

材料：

嫩子鷄	一隻（約一斤）		麻油	一茶匙
葱	一支		花生油	六杯
薑	三片	醃	花椒鹽	二茶匙
八角	一顆	鷄		
醬油	四湯匙	用		
酒	一湯匙	料		
蛋白	半個			
太白粉	一湯匙			

做法：

1. 將鷄洗淨擦乾水份，先由頸旁沿脊背剖開成兩大塊後，再每大塊分切做四塊，共可得八塊鷄塊，肉厚部份可用刀尖刺揷數下，全部置放在大碗內，加入葱（拍碎），薑、八角（切小）與醬油、酒、蛋白、太白粉等拌醃（約半小時左右）。

2. 在鍋內燒熱六杯花生油後，投下拌醃過之八塊鷄，用大火炸熟，先炸三分鐘後撈出一次，將油再重燒至滾熱。

3. 重將鷄塊落鍋中熱油內，續炸一分鐘，卽行全部瀝出，裝盤後淋下麻油並搖動鷄塊使其沾染麻油香味。

4. 在菜盤兩邊各置花椒鹽一茶匙，卽可上桌蘸而食之，香嫩可口。

註：花椒鹽係將花椒一湯匙在乾鍋內用慢火煏炒二分鐘左右，至出香味後倒出研磨成粉狀再合入同量之細鹽續加炒黃卽成。

172

Deep Fried Spiced Chicken

Ingredients:

[1 Young chicken (about 1-1/4 lbs.)

1 Green onion   To marinate
                   chicken

3 slices Ginger   "

1 Star anise   "

4 T. Soysauce   "

1 T. Wine   "

1/2 Egg white   "

1 T. Cornstarch   "

1 t. Sesame oil

6 C. Peanut oil

2 t. Flavored peppercorn salt.

Procedure:

1. Clean the chicken and cut in half, then cut each half into 4 pieces. Place in a bowl and marinate with green onion, ginger, star anise, soysauce, wine, egg white and cornstarch for 1/2 hour.

2. Heat peanut oil in frying pan and drop in chicken to deep fry 3 minutes. Take out, heat oil again until very hot, then fry once more about 1 minute until brown. Remove chicken and drain off oil from frying pan.

3. Place on plate and splash sesame oil over the chicken (shaking the plate). Serve immediately with peppercorn salt.

How to make the flavored peppercorn salt:

1 T. brown peppercorn. 1 T. salt-fry over low heat in a dry fry pan about 1 minute. When salt is brown and perppercorn is dark and smells good, let cool then grind very fine and powdery. Sift until very fine Serve. (This keeps well in a tightly covered bottle and is used in fried and roasted dishes).

173

香　酥　鴨

材料：

光鴨	一隻（約三斤）	酒	一湯匙
花椒	二湯匙	醬油	三湯匙
鹽	二湯匙	麵粉	半杯
葱段	二支	花生油	八杯
薑片	三片	花椒粉	二茶匙

做法：

1. 將花椒放在一只乾鍋中，用小火煸炒約兩分鐘後見花椒轉成深黃而透出香味時加入鹽再同炒一分鐘，盛入盆內待冷却後加葱段（拍碎）薑片與酒拌合。

2. 將鴨洗淨，擦乾水份後，用上項綜合料在鴨身及鴨腹各處擦抹，並放置醃約六小時以上（一天以內）。

3. 將已醃過之鴨連盆置入蒸鍋中（需待鍋中水沸滾之後）用大火蒸至鴨肉爛透（約三小時左右）。

4. 由蒸鍋中端出已蒸爛之鴨，並稍晾乾水份後，塗抹三湯匙醬油在鴨皮上並敷上滿身麵粉，旋即投入已燒成滾熱之油中以大火炸成金黃色（需炸兩次，共五分鐘左右）。

5. 將已炸得酥而香脆之整鴨裝在大盤中間（腹部朝上破口處置香荽數支遮蓋），在盤之兩端各置花椒鹽一茶匙即可送席。

註：如製做些活頁小饅頭同時上桌，以便夾食鴨肉則更為理想可口。也可用單餅或吐司麵包代替小饅頭供食。

174

Crispy Duck Home Style

Ingredients:

1 Duck (about 4 lbs.)	1 T. Wine
2 T. Brown peppercorn	3 T. Soysauce
2 T. Salt	1/2 C. Flour
2 Green onions	8 C. Peanut oil
3 slices Ginger	2 t. Flavored peppercorn salt

Procedure:

1. Fry the brown peppercorn over low heat in dry frying pan for 2 minutes, when it is brown and smells good add salt, fry 1 more minute. Place in a bowl and let cool.

2. Clean and wipe the duck. Rub the outside and inside of duck with fried peppercorn and salt (No. 1). Let stand for 6 hours or overnight.

3. Place the duck in its bowl in boiling steamer to steam over high heat for 3 hours, until very tender.

4. Remove the duck from steamer, let cool a few minutes, brush soysauce all over the duck, powder with flour, deep fry in heated oil over high heat about 3 minutes, until brown and crispy. (Much better to fry twice).

5. Lay the fried duck on platter breast side up. Put 1 t. each peppercorn salt on side of platter and serve with the steamed flower-shape bun. (Sliced bread or spring roll skin may be supstituted). Sedarate the duck with chopsticks and place duck meat inside of bun. Tastes alicious.

NOTE:

The receipe of steamed flower-shape bun on page. 233.

北 平 烤 鴨

材料：

活填鴨	一隻（約五斤）	甜麵醬	三湯匙
麥芽糖	三湯匙	麻油	一湯匙
酒	二湯匙	糖	兩湯匙
醋	一湯匙	大葱白	二十支（約二寸長）
溫水	一杯	薄餅	二十張

做法：

1. 將活填鴨（即經人工强制飼餵成長之肥子鴨），割殺後，排出鴨血，燙毛、褪毛、打理乾淨（不可剖腹挖除內臟）。

2. 將一支竹筒（或機器打氣機）插入割殺之刀口處（鴨皮與肉中間）打入空氣使鴨全身能鼓起漲滿為止。

3. 在鴨翅下隔肢處割開一小洞挖出鴨腸、鴨腎、肝、心等五臟，並由該洞插進一支竹片撑住鴨脯與脊背部，並灌入清水冲洗鴨腹內部最後淋淨鴨身外皮，再拭乾水份。

4. 在一只小盆內將麥芽糖（或蜂蜜）、酒、醋和溫水調勻，向鴨身各處燒淋多遍，（必需每一地方都淋到），再用兩小片竹片支撑起兩支鴨翅膀，用一鐵鈎掛住鴨頸懸吊在通風處吹至鴨皮十分乾爽為止（約六小時以上）。

5. 在烤爐內（特製之爐，稱為掛煸爐）燃置木炭火，待爐已相當熱時將吹乾了皮之鴨移進爐內吊掛在爐中之鐵桿上，先用大火烘烤約二十分鐘後改用小火再烤二十分鐘以至完全烤熟，唯需時時加以轉動以使鴨身烤成後顏色均勻。

6. 當鴨皮已烤成金黃色而酥脆，鴨肉也已熟透時由爐中取出，趁熱用利刀先將鴨皮一塊一塊批切下來排列大盤中，再切鴨肉部份（盛在另一盤中）同甜麵醬（需加麻油、糖及半杯水熬煮一分鐘裝碟），薄餅，（作法見本書點心類）及大葱段（切兩寸長直剖兩刀裝碟）一起上桌。食時取薄餅一張夾一支葱段蘸沾甜麵醬塗到餅上並挾取鴨皮或鴨肉一、二片置於餅中，捲成筒狀食用。

註：烤鴨是京菜中最著名之一種，中外聞名，因其皮脆而肉嫩，味香又不膩，唯烤製過程非常不易，不但需選用特殊人工填飼之肥鴨並需使用掛爐（不適平烤），而且批切方法亦具獨特之技術，此係中國菜之代表。

176

Roast Peiping Duck

Ingredients:

1 Duck (specially fed, fat, about 5 lbs.)

3 T. Honey (or maltose)   (syrup mixture)

2 T. Wine   "

1 T. Vinegar   "

1 C. Hot water   "

3 T. Sweet bean paste   Bean paste
(tien mein jam)   sauce

1 T. Sesame oil   "

2 T. Sugar   "

1/2 C. Water   "

20 Scallions (2" long)

20 Flour wheat tortilla
(or thin plain flour pancakes)

Procedure:

1. Clean the outside of a fresh, specially fed, fat duck complete with neck and head.

2. Pump air between the skin and meat at neck opening until the whole duck becomes puffed to the limit.

3. To dress the inside of the duck, cut a slit under a wing and remove all the internal organs. Use a stick to brace the back and the breast. Rinse the inside until the water comes out clean. Pat dry.

4. In a big bowl, baste the duck thoroughly with the warm syrup mixture. Use two small sticks to brace the wings away from the body. Tie a string around the neck and hang the duck in a drafty place. Let wind dry for about 6 hours. Roast in a rotisserie for about 30-40 minutes.

5. A charcoal type oven may be used. Hang it up for even roasting. Roast at high heat for about 20 minutes and then at low heat for another 20 minutes. Turn frequently, the skin will be golden brown and crisp.

6. Slice all of the duck skin into thin pieces, then slice meat part. Serve with bean paste sauce (bring the mixture to a boil for 1 minute), toritllasor pancake, and green onion strips. Put some bean paste sauce and 1 green onion on pancake then add crisp duck one or two pieces on the center. Roll up and eat with fingers.

NOTE:

Peiping duck is a well known popular Chinese dish. The tender, crisp delicious flavor is irresistable. The duck should be a specially fed and fat one which is a result of a particular feeding process. Roasting in a charcoal rotisserie givers better results. The slicing requires special skill.

葱 爆 羊 肉

材料：

羊肉（腿肉）	六兩	大蒜	三粒	
大葱	六兩	醬油	一湯匙	
醬油	一湯匙	鎭江醋	一湯匙	綜合調味料
鹽	半茶匙	蔴油	一湯匙	
酒	一湯匙	味精	半茶匙	
花椒粉	半茶匙	豬油（或花生油）	六湯匙	
熟花生油	二湯匙			

（醃肉用料：醬油、鹽、酒、花椒粉、熟花生油）

做法：

1. 羊肉需選購瘦多肥少之部份，橫切成大薄片（先冰凍之後再切比較易切），放進醃肉料中（需預先在碗內調妥），拌勻醃置十五分鐘以上。

2. 大葱先對剖，再斜切成絲狀，大蒜切薄片備用。

3. 將油在鍋內燒得極熱，先爆炒蒜片，隨後傾下肉片用大火急速翻炒，約十秒鐘後將大葱絲也落鍋並即刻將預先調合妥當之綜合調味料淋下炒拌均勻，約五秒鐘，見大葱稍微脫生即速裝盤供食。（亦可酌加香荽提味）。

註：1. 如不喜食羊肉可改用牛肉片。

2. 烹炒此菜關鍵在於火候必需强旺，而動作應迅速可使肉嫩味美。

178

Saut.eed Sliced Lamb with Green Onion

Ingredients:

1/2 lb. Lean lamb (sliced)

1/2 lb. Young green onion

2 T. Peanut oil (To marinate lamb.)

1 T. Soysauce   "

1/2 t. Salt   "

1 T. Wine   "

1/2 t. Brown   "
     peppercorn powder

3 Garlic buds

1 T. Soysauce   (Seasoning sauce)

1 T. Brown vinegar   "

1 T. Sesame oil   "

1/2 t. M.S.G.   "

6 T. Lard or peanut oil

Procedure:

1. Choose lean lamb and slice it very thin. It slices more easily when partially frozen. Place in bowl, marinate with soysauce, salt, wine, peppercorn powder and oil. Soak 15 minutes at least.

2. Cut onion lengthwise first, then slice diagonally. Slice each garlic bud into 4 or 5 slices.

3. Mix together soysauce, brown vinegar, sesame oil and M.S.G. in a small bowl. This is the seasoning sauce.

4. Heat oil in frying pan very hot, add sliced garlic first then add the lamb, stir fry quickly over high heat for 10 seconds. Add onion and seasoning sauce continuing to stir fry until thoroughly heated. Serve immediately.

NOTE:

1. Lean beef may be substituted for lamb.

2. The secret of this dish is to use the highest fire and cook quickly. This makes meat juicy and tender.

回鍋肉

材料：

豬肉（後腿肉）	六兩	甜麵醬	一湯匙半
青辣椒	二個	醬油	二湯匙
紅辣椒	三支	辣豆瓣醬	一湯匙
大蒜	三粒	糖	二茶匙
花生油	三湯匙		

做法：

1. 豬肉洗淨，整塊放入冷水中用大火煮二十分鐘左右（可在水中加少許酒和葱薑等同煮），見肉已熟透即可撈出，待冷後，橫紋切薄片（用推刀法切愈薄愈好）。

2. 將青紅辣椒去籽切成滾刀塊或一寸四方塊。

3. 大蒜切薄片，如有青蒜季節可用青蒜一支切成斜絲，代用更好。

4. 將甜麵醬同辣豆瓣醬、醬油、糖在一只小碗內預先調和妥當備用。

5. 在炒菜鍋內燒熱三湯匙油，先爆炒肉片，至肥肉收縮，油已滲出為止，再放下大蒜片同炒，並加入青、紅辣椒拌炒數秒鐘即行盛出（或全部推撥在鍋沿）。再利用鍋中所餘之油炒香甜麵醬料，然後將肉片辣椒等倒回鍋內拌炒均勻即成。

註：如用青蒜，可在最後起鍋之前加入略拌即可。

180

Double Cooked Pork Slice

Ingredients:

1/2 lb Pork (boneless)
1 Green onion
2 slices Ginger
2 Green peppers
3 Red peppers
3 Garlic buds

1 ¼ T. Sweet soybean paste
1 T. Hot bean paste
2 T. Soysauce
2 t. Sugar
3 T. Peanut oil

Procedure:

1. Stew the whole pork with a little wine, ginger and green onion for about 20 minutes, then slice it.

2. Cut the green and red pepper into 1″ squares (remove seeds first).

3. Slice the garlic lengthwise.

4. Mix in small bowl the sweet soy bean paste with soysauce, sugar and hot bean paste.

5. Fry the pork slices in 3 T. peanut oil for one minute. Then add garlic, green and red pepper, stir 1 more minute. Remove from pan. In the remaining oil fry the sweet soy bean paste 10 seconds. Return pork mixture, stir well and serve.

181

醋溜丸子

材料：

絞猪肉（前腿或肥大排骨肉）	十二兩		糖	四湯匙	
葱屑	半湯匙	拌肉料	鎮江醋	四湯匙	綜合調味料
薑屑	一茶匙		清水	半杯	
醬油	一湯匙		醬油	一湯匙	
酒	半湯匙		鹽	半茶匙	
鹽	半茶匙		味精	半茶匙	
太白粉	一湯匙		太白粉	三茶匙	
鷄蛋	一個		麻油	一茶匙	
葱絲	三湯匙		花生油	六杯	

做法：

1. 將絞猪肉置砧板上（即切菜板）並加入冷水二湯匙，用刀重行斬剁一分鐘，然後裝在大碗內，放入葱屑、薑屑、醬油、酒、鹽、太白粉與鷄蛋仔細拌擾至肉生黏性而極勻滑爲止。

2. 將油在鍋內燒熱後，用左手抓住一把上項肉料，撥動拇指並由指縫擠出圓形肉丸，右手執湯匙（沾點冷水）刮下肉丸投入油中，採同樣動作迅速將肉料全部做成肉丸投下油中用慢火炸熟，（約三分鐘）。

3. 用漏勺將肉丸全部撈出，將油重行燒至滾熱，然後再續炸肉丸一次（約半分鐘）。倒出油到容器中。

4. 將已倒出油之炒鍋重行燒熱，僅用一湯匙油落下葱絲拌炒，隨後將預先調在小碗中之綜合調味料倒下用大火煮滾，見汁已變成黏稠後即將肉丸落鍋拌合急速裝盤。

182

Meat Balls with Sour Sauce

Ingredients:

1 lb. Ground pork	4 T. Sugar (Seasoning sauce)
(To mix with pork)	1/2 C. Water "
1/2 T. Chopped	4 T. Vinegar "
green onion "	1 T. Soysauce "
1 t. Chopped ginger "	1/2 t. Salt "
1 T. Soysauce "	1/2 t. M.S.G. "
1/2 T. Wine "	3 t. Cornstarch "
1/2 t. Salt "	1 t. Sesame oil "
1 T. Cornstarch "	3 T. Shredded green onion
1 Egg "	6 C. Peanut oil

Procedure:

1. Chop the pork with 2 T. cold water about 1 minute, place in a bowl, add green onion, ginger, soysauce, wine, salt, egg and cornstarch. Mix well.

2. Heat oil in frying pan. Wet left hand and place 2 or 3 T. pork mixture in palm of hand, close fingers. An amount about the size of a walnut will spurt from the top of the fist, with a wet spoon (right hand) remove the ball and drop in hot oil. Separate the balls as they rise to the top and become crispy and golden. Keep oil at 340° and fry about 2 minutes.

3. Remove the balls, then heat oil again until very hot. Add balls and fry 1/2 more minute. Remove them and drain off oil from frying pan.

4. Use 1 T. oil to stir fry the shredded green onion. Add seasoning sauce. As soon as the sauce is boiling and thickened, add the balls, mix well. Pour in a deep plate. Serve.

183

南 炒 豬 肝

材料：

豬肝	半斤	醬油	二湯匙	⎫
乾木耳	二湯匙	酒	半湯匙	
筍	一支	太白粉	一茶匙	
豌豆夾	十個	糖	半茶匙	⎬ 醃豬肝用料
葱段（一寸長）	十支	味精	半茶匙	
薑	六小片	胡椒粉	1/4茶匙	
鹽	半茶匙	鹽	半茶匙	⎭
清湯	三湯匙	花生油	六湯匙	

做法：

1. 選購微黃而乾爽之粉豬肝，略冲洗一下，用利刀切成薄片，全部投入開水中川燙一次（約十秒鐘），撈出後瀝乾水份，放入碗內拌入醬油、酒、太白粉、糖、味精、胡椒粉等醃豬肝用料拌漬片刻。
2. 乾木耳用溫水泡軟，摘去蒂後洗淨，筍煮熟後切片狀留用。
3. 用三湯匙油炒筍片、豌豆夾、木耳、並加入清湯及鹽、味精拌炒至豆夾已熟即可全部盛入盤中。
4. 另燒熱三湯匙油在鍋內先爆炒葱段及薑片，隨後將豬肝落鍋用大火速炒，約十秒鐘即行起鍋，盛在前項材料上，即可供食。

註：此菜也可將醃豬肝用料當做綜合調味料，拌炒在豬肝中也可，又可將豌豆夾改為青菜心，或黃瓜片，萵苣筍等（需先煮過）。

184

Stir Fried Pork Livers

Ingredients:

10 oz. Pork liver	2 T. Soysa e (To marinate liver)
2 T. Dry agaric	1/2 T. Wi: "
1 Bamboo shoot (cooked or canned)	1/2 T. Cornstarch "
10 Snow Pea Pods	1/2 t. Sugar "
10 Green onions (1" long)	1/2 t. M.S.G. "
6 slices Ginger	1/4 t. Black pepper "
6 T. Peanut oil	1/2 t. Salt
	3 T. Soup stock

Procidure:

1. Chose a pink and yellowy liver, slice into small pieces about 1/6" thick. Boil in boiling water only 10 seconds. Remove, using a strainer, and let drain dry. Marinate with soysauce, wine, cornstarch, sugar, and pepper a few minutes.

2. Soak the dry agaric with warm water and remove stem. Slice the bamboo shoot the same size as the liver.

3. Heat 3 T oil to stir fry bamboo shoot, snow peas, and agaric. Add soup stock, salt, until the peapods are done (about 1 minute). Place on a plate.

4. Heat another 3 T. oil. Add green onion and ginger, fry a few seconds and add pork liver, stirring quickly. Lay liver on top of the vegetables attractively.

NOTE:

A variation of this No. 1 procedure would be to use the marinade sauce only at end of procedure 4. In this case it is called a seasoning sauce.

火 爆 腰 花

材料：

猪腰	二個（約一斤）	醬油	二湯匙
筍（或萵苣筍）	一支（或荸薺八個）	酒	一湯匙
乾木耳（或小多菇六個）	二湯匙	糖	半茶匙
葱屑	一湯匙	鹽	半茶匙
薑屑	一茶匙	太白粉	一茶匙
		麻油	一茶匙
花生油	四杯	味精	半茶匙
		胡椒粉	1/4茶匙

（右側花括號標示：綜合調味料）

做法：

1. 將猪腰每個由橫面切開，剔除內部白筋洗淨，在表面（即光滑面）切入交叉細粒花刀，再分切成六或八小塊，裝入大碗裏，並加冷水浸泡。

2. 筍去皮煮熟後切成薄片，乾木耳先泡軟摘去蒂根洗淨備用。

3. 將綜合調味料在一只小碗內調備妥當。

4. 在炒鍋內將花生油燒至極熱，傾下已在冷水中泡過而瀝出之腰花，炸五秒鐘，隨即撈起，油也迅速倒出，僅餘下二湯匙油重再燒熱。

5. 先落葱屑及一薑屑入鍋，並加進筍片與木耳同炒，續將已炸過之腰花落鍋並淋下綜合調味料，大火速加翻炒拌勻即行裝盤供食。

註：此菜中之腰花也可改用開水川燙過後即行烹炒，而不必用油炸過。

186

Sauteed Pork Kidney

Ingredients:

3 Pork kidneys (about 1-1/2 lbs.)

1 Cooked bamboo shoot

  (or 8 water chestnuts)

2 T. Dry agaric

  (or 6 dry mushrooms)

1 T. Shredded green onion

1 t. Shredded ginger

2 T. Soysauce   (seasoning sauce)

1 T. Wine   "

1/2 T. Sugar   "

1/2 t. Salt   "

1 t. Cornstarch   "

1 t. Sesame oil   "

1/4 t. Blackpepper   "

1/2 t. M.S.G.   "

4 C. Peanut oil   "

Procedure:

1. Cut the pork kidney in half horizontally, and remove the white membrane. Score outside lengthwise and crosswise each 1/8″ deep. Then cut into 6 or 8 pieces, put in bowl and soak with cold water
2. Slice the cooked bamboo shoot (or canned), into 1″ square. Soak dry agaric in warm water and remove stems.
3. Prepare the seasoning sauce in a bowl.
4. Heat oil very hot, fry the kidney 5 seconds, remove kidney and drain off oil from pan.
5. Put back 2 T. oil and stir fry shredded green onion and ginger, add bamboo shoot and agaric, continue stirring for half minute. Add kidney and seasoning sauce quickly, stir until thickened, then heat thoroughly and serve.

NOTE:

1. Once the kidney is cooked, it should be served immediately as it toughens upon standing.

黃燜牛肉

材料：

牛肉（肋條或前後肘部份）一斤		醬油	2/3杯
葱	三支	酒	二湯匙
薑	五片	糖	二湯匙
八角	三顆	豬油（或花生油）四湯匙	

做法：

1. 將牛肉洗淨瀝乾水份，切成一寸寬一寸半長，半寸厚之塊狀，投入八杯已沸滾之水中川燙三分鐘後，將鍋離火，撈出鍋中之全部牛肉塊，再將糖加入該燙過牛肉之水中拌攪溶化，放置十分鐘使鍋中之渣質全部沈下，變為清徹留用。

2. 另在炒鍋內燒熱四湯匙油，然後先落下葱段及薑片爆香隨後加入醬油、酒、八角與牛肉塊以大火拌炒，再將上項在另外鍋中已沈澱過之湯汁慢慢全部傾入，用大火燒開，再改用小火，燜燒（蓋合鍋蓋）。

3. 見牛肉已燒至十分軟爛，而湯汁僅剩下半杯時，便好（約需時三小時左右）。

註：此菜所用之牛肉應選購筋多有脂肪部份為宜。帶

188

Braised Beef with Brown Sauce

Ingredients:

1-1/4 lbs. Beef brisquet or hind
        shank
3 Green onions
5 slices Ginger
3 Star anise

2/3 C. Soysauce
2 T. Wine
2 T. Sugar
4 T. Lard or peanut oil

Procedure:

1. Cut the beef into 1″ wide, 1¼″ long, 1/2″ thick pieces. Add to 8 cups boiling water to cook 3 minutes, lift the pan from fire. Remove the beef. Add sugar to the pan and let stand. This causes the soup to clear, the impurities will sink and should be discarded.

2. Heat oil in frying pan, fry the green onion, ginger, add soysauce, wine, star anise and beef. Stir fry a few minutes. Add the soup stock from No. 1. Bring to a boil, reduce the heat, cover, and stew about 2 or 3 hours.

3. When the beef is very soft and juice is reduced to 1/2 cup and is rather thick, remove to plate with juice and serve.

羊 羔

材料：

羊肉（後腿肉連皮）一斤		八角	二顆
猪肉皮（或膠粉一包）四兩		花椒	一茶匙
白蘿蔔	半只	醬油	四湯匙
葱	五支	酒	二湯匙
薑	三片	糖	三茶匙（或冰茶一兩）
大蒜	三粒	醬色	一茶匙
桂皮	一小塊	清湯	七杯

做法：

1. 用一只深底鍋，放進整塊洗淨之羊肉及猪肉皮加入清水（以蓋過肉塊半寸爲度），用大火羹約十分鐘，取出羊肉和肉皮另換清湯（或開水），重放下羊肉及肉皮，並加葱、薑、大蒜、桂皮、八角、花椒及糖、酒與切成大坛之白蘿蔔，用文火燒羹一小時。捞出猪肉皮，加入醬油及醬色再繼續小火燒煮十分鐘。

2. 將整塊羊肉取出揭下肉皮，鋪在平底方模型（或飯盒）中，羊肉則撕成小塊略爲整齊的排在肉皮上。

3. 將白蘿蔔由鍋中取出，再放回剁成細碎之猪肉皮重行燒煮十分鐘，至湯僅剩下一杯時，用紗布或篩子過濾一次，濾出之湯汁澆在模型內羊肉中。待稍凉後放進冰箱內冷凍（約需一小時以上至凝固成堅硬塊爲止）。

4. 取出凍過之羊羔，切成長約二寸，厚約三分之片狀排置盤內，另在盤邊附上嫩薑絲及甜麵醬各少許以便蘸食。

註：如用膠粉代替猪肉皮可將一包膠粉用半杯清水溶解後加入（在白蘿蔔取出之後），與湯同煮至剩下一杯爲止，再過濾到羊肉中便可。

190

Jellied Stewed Mutton

Ingredients:

1-1/4 lbs. Mutton or lamb

4 oz. Pork skin (or 1 envelope unfla ored gelatin)

1/2 lb. Turnip

5 Green onions

3 slices Ginger

3 Garlic buds

1 pc. Cinnamon stick (1" long)

2 Star anise

1 T. Brown peppercorn

4 T. Soysauce

2 T. Wine

2 t. Sugar

1 t. Kitchen Bouquet for color.

7 C. Soup stock

Procedure:

1. Place the whole mutton and pork skin in a deep pot, add cold water to cover 1/2" above meat. Boil about 10 minutes. Remove mutton and pork skin. Discard the water, Add soup stock to pot, bring to boil over high heat. Return mutton and skin, add onion, ginger, garlic, cinnamon, star anise, peppercorn, sugar, wine and turnip which should be cut into large pieces. Stew about 1 hour over low heat. Remove skin from pan, add soysauce and food color continuing to stew 10 more minutes.
2. Remove mutton and tear with fingers into shreds, lay in a mold (square is better).
3. Remove the turnip and discard. Add the chopped pork skin to the pot, stew again about 10 minutes. When the soup is reduced to 1 cup, strain into the mutton mold. Place in refrigerator for at least 1 hour or until firm.
4. Remove from mold and slice 1/4" thick. Serve with some sweet bean paste and shredded young ginger.

NOTE:

If you use the unflavored gelatine (1 envelope) change step 3 to: Remove turnip and discard. Dissolve gelatin in 1/2 C. water and add to stew pot, cooking 10 more minutes. When soup is reduced to 1 cup, strain into mutton mold. Place in refrigerator for at least 1 hour or until firm.

191

涮 羊 肉

材料：

羊肉（胸肉或腿肉）	葱　花	半湯匙
羊肝	香菜末	一茶匙
羊肚	芝麻醬	半湯匙
黃芽白菜	花椒油	一湯匙
菠菜	醬　油	半湯匙
同蒿菜	蝦　油	半湯匙
粉絲	麻　油	一茶匙
凍豆腐	辣　油	一茶匙
	酒	半茶匙
	糖	半茶匙
	紅豆腐乳滷	半湯匙
	韭菜花	少許

調味料（一人份之大約量）

做法：

1. 羊肉需切成寬一寸半，長三寸許之大薄片（愈薄愈好），攤放在平底碟中，碟之大小可隨意，唯需一片一片平排擺放較好。
2. 羊肝切片，羊肚切成寬條狀分別裝進碟中。（此兩種也可不用）。
3. 白菜切大塊，菠菜切長段，同蒿菜可除去老葉撕開洗淨裝盤中，粉絲泡軟，凍豆腐切成拇指般大小塊裝盤上桌。
4. 將各種調味料分別用小瓷缽或大杯裝好全部用一只大形托盤端到桌上，由食者分別自行取配若干於各自所用之小湯碗內，調合均勻備用。（上項所列十二種並非全部必用，可按喜愛口味調配之）。
5. 在火鍋內盛裝沸清湯或開水，（應先放進蝦米少許）由食者自行夾取羊肉片放在其中燙熟（筷子需夾住肉片，不可擲入）然後蘸沾小碗中之調味料進食。其他蔬菜，粉絲，凍豆腐等可稍待遲緩時加入需經較長時間滾煮至熟或軟始可取食之。（最後可利用剩湯煮麵條而食，鮮美異常）。

※請參考照片第39號。

192

Rinsed Mutton In Chafing Pot

Ingredients:

(about 6 servings)
2 lb. Mutton (tenderloin lamb)
1/2 lb. Mutton liver (optional)
1/2 lb. Mutton tripe (optional)
2 C. Chinese cabbage
2 C. Spinach
1-1/2 C. Bean noodle (softed)
2 C. Frozen beancurd

1/2 T. Green onion   (sauce for each
1 t. Parsley leaves   person some kinds
1 T. Sesame seed Paste   is optional)
1/2 t. peppercorn oil   "
1/2 T. Soysauce·   "
1/2 T. Shrimp oil   "
1/2 T. Sesame oil   "
1/2 t. Hot pepper oil   "
1/2 t. Leek flower paste   "
1/2 t. Salted beancurd paste   "
1/2 t. Wine   "
1 t. Sngar   "

Procedure:

1. Slice the mutton into 1½" wide, 3" long paper thin pieces. Arrange the slices in one layer on platters.
2. Slice the liver. Cut the tripe into strips.
3. Cut cabbage, spinach into big pieces. Bean curd into 1" square pieces.
4. Put the vegetables, bean noodles and remaining ingredients including seasonings in individual serving containers. Each individual prepares his own seasoning mixture to suit his taste.
5. Into a chafing pot full of boiling soup or water, dip mutton slices until just done, immediately dip into the sauce mixture and eat. After several dippings of meat start putting other ingredients such as cabbage, spinach, bean moodle or bean curd into the chafing pot. Let each individual help himself when cooked. The soup in the pot gets tastier and tastier as the cooking progresses. The soup or water must boil continuously. It make a delicious noodle soup.

NOTE:

1. The quantity of seasoning condiments is optional.
2. If you don't like to eat mutton, the beef will be used.

---

* Refer to picture No. 39.

蒙 古 烤 肉

材料：

牛肉（裏脊或前腿肉）	醬油
羊肉（前腿肉或後腿肉）	酒
鷄肉	糖水
猪肉（全瘦肉）	清水（加入檸檬片若干）
葱絲	薑水
香菜絲	辣油
青辣椒絲	麻油
洋葱絲	蝦油
生菜絲（或包心菜絲）	紅辣椒屑

做法：

1. 將肉類逆絲切成大薄片（約一寸寬兩寸半長）分別裝盤。其他各種蔬菜也分別裝盤置於桌上。

2. 各種調味料分別用玻璃罐或瓷缸之類容器盛裝置於肉類，蔬菜類之旁。

3. 食者用一只大碗（或深盤）前往自行挾取若干肉類，再取喜愛之蔬菜如葱絲（或洋葱絲），香菜屑，青椒絲（或生菜絲）於碗中，並加入各種調味料各若干（按各人口味調配）。

4. 將一具特製之烤肉鐵鍋燒熱後，倒下前項裝在碗中之材料（與調味料）使用一雙長竹筷迅速在鍋上平面撥動，炒煎，約兩三分鐘，見肉已轉熟即可盛入原碗內端往桌上食之。

註：烤肉之老嫩，可隨意，只將在鍋上撥炒之時間增減便可。

194

Mongolian Bar-B-Q

Ingredients:

(about 6 servings)

1-1/2 lb. Beef tender loin or sirloin

1 lb. Mutton (lean)

1 lb. Chicken

1 lb. Pork (lean)

6 Green onions or onion (shredded) (quantity optional to personal preference)

1 C. Chinese parsley personal

1 C. Green pepper "

1 C. Cabbage "

2 C. Lettuce "

1 T. Soysauce

1/2 T. Wine

1/2 T. Shrimp oil

1/2 T. Sugar water (4 T. sugar in 1 C. water)

1 T. Cold water (or add some limon slices)

1/2 T. Ginger water (10 slices ginger soaked in 4 C. water)

1/2 t. Hot pepper oil (optional)

1 T. Sesame oil

Red hot pepper chopped (optional)

Procedure:

1. Slice the meat into 1½″ wide, 3″ long thin pieces. Arrange the meat slices on separate platters. Place on serving or dining table.
2. Put all the other ingredients in individual serving containers. Place on the table.
3. With an individual bowl, each person helps himself to various ingredients to suit his own taste. (Take the meat part first, then vegetable, condiments at last).
4. On a charcoal heated Mongolian Bar-B-Q grill pour the mixture all at once. Use long chopsticks to stir 1-2 minutes. Tastes delicious when piping hot. Shao-Bing usually is served with the Bar-B-Q. (Shao-Bing can also be opened at one side and the Bar-B-Que put inside.)

NOTE:

1. This is do-it-yourself meal. The seasoning and the length of cooking time should be flexible to suit the individual.
2. Shao-Bing is one special Chinese baked roll, like the small Hamburger bun.

* Refer to picture No. 40.

糖 醋 全 魚

料材

新鮮黃魚（或鯉魚）一條（約1½斤）

葱	一支	醃魚料	糖	五湯匙	綜合調味料
薑	三片		鎮江醋	五湯匙	
鹽	二茶匙		清水	五湯匙	
酒	二湯匙		蕃茄醬	三湯匙	
太白粉	半杯		太白粉	一湯匙	
葱絲	1/3杯		鹽	一茶匙半	
薑絲	1/3杯		麻油	一茶匙	
多菇絲	1/4杯		花生油	八 杯	
紅辣椒絲	1/6杯				

做法：

1. 將魚刮洗乾淨後拉下背鰭並斬棄一牛尾鰭，然後再在兩面魚身用刀割切深而薄，並可翹起之刀紋（刀深需觸及大骨），放在盤中，用葱（拍碎）薑（拍碎）及鹽酒之混合料抹擦（需將每一切開之魚片縫均擦到），醃置半小時左右。

2. 將半杯太白粉盛在盤內，用着沾裹魚全身各處需仔細敷緊，然後提着魚尾慢慢投入已燒熱之油中然後提出兩三次至魚片完全開放後始可全部落入油中，炸至酥脆（約五分鐘左右），撈出魚後將油全部倒出。

3. 另在鍋內燒熱三湯匙油炒多菇絲、薑絲、葱絲及紅辣椒絲，並將綜合調味料傾入以大火炒煮，至沸滾而汁黏稠後再淋下一湯匙熱油迅即澆到已裝在盤中之魚上（應使其直立），即可上桌供食。

註：1. 炸魚時如嫌魚太長而操作不便，可將魚切成兩截同時下鍋炸，炸好之後在盤中接連成一條原魚狀即成。

  2. 如果喜食較多糖醋汁可將綜合調味料加倍或酌量增加。

※請參考照片第36號。

196

Fried Whole Fish with Sweet Sour Sauce

Ingredients:

1 Whole fish, fresh lean
  (about 15" long, 1-1/2 lbs.)
1 Green onion (To marinate fish)
3 slices Ginger   "
3 t. Salt   "
2 T. Wine   "
1/2 C. Shredded green onion
1/3 C. Shredded ginger
1/4 C. Shredded dry black
       mushrooms (soaked)

1/6 C. Shredded red hot pepper
1/2 C. Cornstarch
5 T. Sugar   Seasoning sauce
5 T. Brown vinegar   "
5 T. Cold water   "
3 T. Catsup   "
1 T. Cornstarch   "
1½ t. Salt   "
1 t. Sesame oil   "
8 C. Peanut oil

Procedure:

1. Clean the fish and make several diagonal cuts almost touching the bone on both sides of it. Trim off 1/2 the tail fin. Marinate the fish for 15 to 30 minutes.
2. Use 1/2 C. cornstarch to powder the whole fish and put it into the hot oil. Fry about 5 minutes, basting constantly until it looks golden on both sides and crispy. Drain off oil. Place fish in swimming position on an oblong platter.
3. Heat another 3 T. oil to fry mushrooms, ginger, green onion and red pepper over high heat, then add the seasoning sauce. Stir the sauce until it turns thick then pour it on the fried fish.

NOTE:

1. If the fish is too big to fry cut into halves, and arrange them into the shape of a whole fish on the platter after fried.
2. Double the seasoning sauce, if you like. It is so good.

_____

* Refer to picture No. 36.

醋溜瓦塊魚

材料：

青魚（或鯉魚）中段一斤		糖	四湯匙
薑屑	半湯匙	鎮江醋	三湯匙
蒜屑	半湯匙	清水	三湯匙
雞蛋	二 個	醬油	一湯匙
麵粉	五湯匙	酒	一湯匙
太白粉	三湯匙	太白粉	二茶匙
鹽	半茶匙	鹽	半茶匙
清水	酌量	麻油	一茶匙
		花生油	五杯

麵糊料（麵粉、太白粉、鹽、清水）

綜合調味料（糖、鎮江醋、清水、醬油、酒、太白粉、鹽、麻油）

做法：

1. 將魚段刮洗乾淨後，由背部下刀切開，除去中間大骨，再直着片切成大斜片（如瓦片狀），全部撒上鹽（半茶匙）拌醃片刻。

2. 在一只碗內打散雞蛋，加入麵粉及太白粉調拌，並合入少量清水攪拌成適當之糊狀留用。

3. 將糖，醋，清水，醬油，酒，太白粉，鹽與麻油在一只碗內調勻成為綜合調味料備用。

4. 將油在鍋內燒熱，再將魚片每片先在麵糊中沾滿，迅速投入油中用大火炸熟，約三分鐘即行撈出，再重燒滾鍋中之油，（至冒烟程度）落下魚片續炸一分鐘（大火）便可撈起濾淨油漬。

5. 另在鍋內僅燒熱二湯匙油，爆炒薑屑及蒜屑，隨後將綜合調味料倒下以大火炒羹，見已變黏稠時，迅將魚片落鍋略行拌勻即可盛入盤內，趁熱上桌。

註：此菜因魚片所切之形狀像瓦狀而得名，係京菜中頗為著名之菜式。

198

Crispy Fish Slices with Sweet Sour Sauce

Ingredients:

1-1/4 lbs. Fish meat (any firm
                white meat
1/2 T. Chopped garlic
1/2 T. Chopped ginger
2 Eggs   (flour batter)
5 T. Flour   "
3 T. Cornstarch   "
1/2 t. Salt

4 T. Sugar   (Seasoning sauce)
3 T. Brown vinegar   "
3 T. Cold water   "
1 T. Soysauce   "
1 T. Wine   "
3 t. Cornstarch   "
1/2 t. Salt   "
1 t. Sesame oil   "
5 C. Peanut oil

Procedure:

1. Clean the fish and remove the large bone. Lay knife almost flat to slice in thin pieces like a tile. Put in a bowl and soak with 1/2 t. salt a few minutes.

2. Beat eggs in small bowl, add flour, cornstarch and some cold water to make a flour batter similar to a normal pancake batter.

3. In another bowl mix the sugar, water, wine, soysauce, cornstarch, salt and sesame oil for seasoning sauce.

4. Coat each piece of fish with flour batter and deep fry about 3 minutes until golden brown. Take out all fish, heat oil again very hot and fry 1 more minute, remove fish and drain off oil from frying pan.

5. Put back into frying pan 2 T. of oil, stir fry shredded garlic and ginger, add the seasoning sauce, stir until starchy over high heat. Turn off heat, add the fish immediately and mix carefully until fish is well coated. Serve.

199

炸 蝦 托

材料：

蝦仁	六兩	吐司麵包	六片
肥猪肉	一兩半	黑芝蔴	二茶匙
蛋白	一個	火腿屑	一湯匙
薑汁	半茶匙	花生油	七杯
鹽	一茶匙	生荼葉	五枚
酒	半湯匙	花椒鹽	一茶匙
太白粉	一湯匙		

（薑汁、鹽、酒、太白粉：拌蝦用料）

做法：

1. 蝦仁抽淨砂筋，冲洗一次，瀝乾水份後全部剁碎使成泥狀置入大碗內，另將肥猪肉也剁爛成泥狀同蝦仁共盛一碗中，加入鹽，酒，薑汁攪勻，再放蛋白與太白粉調勻成爲蝦泥餡。（需仔細攪拌至有黏性爲止）。

2. 將六片麵包切除四週硬邊後，每片分切成四小塊，或修切成一寸半直徑之圓片（共廿四片），將上項調好之蝦泥餡塗抹在每小片麵包上成爲凸起之半圓形，再將黑芝蔴與火腿屑撒在蝦仁餡上各少許做爲裝飾。

3. 在鍋內燒熱花生油後將上項做成之蝦托，逐個放下油中用小火炸熟（有蝦仁餡之面先向下入油中），約兩分鐘後便需翻過一面續炸一分鐘。

4. 將生荼葉洗淨擦乾水份舖在盤底，上面排列已炸熟之蝦托趁熱上桌，食時可蘸花椒鹽。

註：如將麵包切成圓片則稱爲金錢蝦托。

200

Deep Fried Shrimp Cake

Ingredients:

1/2 lb. Shrimp (without shell)
2 oz. Pork fat
1 Egg white   mix with shrimp
1 t. Ginger juice   "
1 t. Salt   "
1/2 T. Wine   "
1 T. Cornstarch   "

6 slices White bread
2 t. Black sesame seeds
1 T. Ham (chopped)
5 Lettuce leaves
7 C. Peanut oil

Procedure:

1. Clean and chop the shrimp and pork very fine, put in a bowl, add salt, wine, ginger juice, mix well. Add egg white and cornstarch. Mix thoroughly.

2. Remove the crust from sliced bread, cut each slice into 4 pieces (or 4 round). Put about 1 T. shrimp mixture on each piece bread and spread evenly to edges. Sprinkle some black sesame seeds and chopped ham on top for decoration.

3. Heat peanut oil in pan, deep fry shrimp cake (No. 2), face the shrimp side down first. Fry about 2 minutes, turn over and fry another 1 minute.

4. Decorate the plate with lettuce leaves, lay the fried shrimp cake attractively on the lettuce and serve.

清 炒 明 蝦 片

材料：

明蝦（或大型砂蝦）	八隻（約一斤）	清湯（或水）	四湯匙	
大洋菇	八個	太白粉	一茶匙	
小黃瓜	二條	麻油	一茶匙	綜合調味料
熟火腿	一兩	鹽	半茶匙	
蛋白	半個	味精	半茶匙	
鹽	半茶匙	猪油（或花生油）	三杯	
酒	半湯匙			
太白粉	一湯匙			

（蛋白至太白粉：醃蝦用）

做法：

1. 明蝦摘除蝦頭並剝去外皮抽出砂腸後略洗，拭乾水份將每隻橫切成四片，由背部下刀先切成兩大片再每大片切開為兩薄片，全部放在大碗內，加入蛋白，鹽，酒及太白粉拌勻，醃置半小時左右。

2. 小黃瓜削去皮後切成一寸半長之薄片，用開水燙半分鐘撈出冲過冷水後留用。洋菇每個切除蒂後橫刀切成三片，火腿也切薄片（如同黃瓜片大小）備用。

3. 在一只小碗內調備所有綜合調味料留用。

4. 將油在鍋內燒至八成熱度，便速傾入蝦片，用大火泡熟（約十秒鐘）見蝦片呈白色夠九成熟時即行全部瀝出。油也倒回容器中

5. 另在鍋內燒熱三湯匙油，炒洋菇片，黃瓜片及火腿片，並加入綜合調味料炒勻，至變黏稠時即將蝦片落鍋迅速拌合便成。

202

Sauteed Sliced Prawns

Ingredients:

8 Green prawns (about 1/2 lb.)
  or large shrimp
8 button Mushrooms (canned)
2 Small cucumbers
1 oz. Cooked ham
1 Egg white (To marinate prawns)
1/2 t. Salt   "
1/2 T. Wine   "
1 T. Cornstarch   "

4 T. Soup stock   (Seasoning
  (or water)   Sauce)
1 t. Cornstarch   "
1 t. Sesame oil   "
1/2 t. Salt   "
1/2 t. M.S.G.   "
3 C. Lard or peanut oil

Procedure:

1. Clean, de-vein and shell the prawns or shrimp. Slice each prawn into 4 slices lengthwise, set in a bowl and mix with egg white, salt, wine, cornstarch and marinate at least one half hour.

2. Peel and slice the cucumber into 2″ long pieces, boil in boiling water about 1/2 minute, then plunge into cold water immediately. Slice each mushroom crosswise in half. Slice ham same size as cucumber.

3. Prepare seasoning sauce in a bowl.

4. Heat oil to 280°, add prawns and fry about 10 seconds. When they turn white and are 90% done, remove prawns and drain off oil from frying pan.

5. Put back only 3 T. oil in pan. Stir fry the sliced mushrooms, cucumbers and ham. Add the seasoning sauce, stir until thickened. Add the prawns and heat thoroughly. Serve in a shallow oval platter.

紅燒排翅

材料：

水發大排翅	兩塊（約一斤半）	豬油	四湯匙
火腿	六兩	麵粉	三湯匙
五花豬肉	六兩	醬油	三湯匙
葱	三支	濕太白粉	一湯匙
薑	五片	雞油	一湯匙半
酒	一湯匙	香菜	數支
雞湯	四杯		

做法：

1. 將已發透而摘洗乾淨之排翅以翅根相對排列在小淺盆中成為圓餅狀，放進葱支與薑片並加酒及兩杯雞湯上鍋中蒸燉，約半小時即行端出。

2. 將小盆中之湯汁泌出不要，並揀棄葱，薑再放進已在開水中燙煮過三分鐘之豬肉塊與火腿塊，並加入另外兩杯雞湯再上鍋蒸燉至魚翅相當軟滑為止（約一小時左右）。

3. 由蒸鍋內端出已蒸軟之魚翅，取出其中之豬肉與火腿（可留作他用），並將湯汁泌出在另只碗內留用。

4. 在炒鍋內將豬油溶化，加入麵粉焗炒均勻（小火）並將留出之湯汁（第三項）傾入攪勻（用小火），再加醬油味精調味淋下濕太白粉鈎芡並淋入雞油便可離火。

5. 將魚翅小心覆扣在大菜盤內，揭除蒸盆，澆下第四項之湯汁並綴上香菜數支即可上桌。（此菜也可將白菜心或青菜心炒熟之後墊在下面，以增加分量）。

註：水發魚翅之方法係將乾魚翅用冷水浸泡一天，刷洗乾淨後置入大鍋內加多量清水燒煮．約一兩小時（小火）然後熄去爐火待鍋中之水冷却後始行揭開鍋蓋，取出魚翅另換清水，再煮一兩小時再待水冷後換水浸泡，如視魚翅已夠軟而易散開時，便改置入大碗中（或小盆）加水及葱支，薑片與酒蒸燉一兩小時，棄去蒸汁便可。（按各魚翅之大小，種類均不相同故其煮泡時間長短無法一定）。

※請參考照片第41號。

204

Shark's Fins in Brown Sauce

Ingredients:

2 lbs. Shark's fins soaked

    (2 or 3 large pieces,)

1/2 lb. Ham

1/2 lb. Pork (half lean, half fat)

3 Green onions

5 slices Ginger

1 T. Wine

4 C. Chicken soup

4 T. Lard (or Peanut oil)

3 T. Flour

3 T. Soysauce

1/2 t. M.S.G.

1 T. Cornstarch   (make paste)

1 T. Coold water   "

1/2 T. Chicken grease (optional)

8 Parsley leaves

Procedure:

1. Lay the soaked shark's fins in a bowl, place root (or base) sections in center. Add green onion, ginger, wine and 2 c. of chicken soup, steam for about 1/2 hour. Remove.

2. Discard the soup, onion and ginger. Add the boiled ham and pork into this bowl with shark's fins. Pour in 2 c. chicken soup to steam another 1 hour, until fins are tender.

3. Remove the bowl (shark's fins) pour the soup out (save it), remove the ham and pork and reserve for another dish.

4. Heat oil in frying pan not too hot over low heat. Add flour and mix until smooth. Add the saved soup and soysauce, M.S.G. Bring to a boil. Thicken with cornstarch paste and add the chicken grease.

5. Place a serving platter up side down over the bowl with fins. Turn the whole thing over so that the fins are on the serving platter. Pour the cooked soup (gravy) over the fins. Saute' green vegetable, season to taste, arrange along the rim of the fins platter, or bottom of the fins.

---

* Refer to picture No. 41.

鷄絨鮑魚羹

材料：

罐頭鮑魚	2/3罐（或1/2罐）	豬油	五湯匙
鷄胸肉（淨肉）四兩		酒	半湯匙
鷄蛋白	四個	鹽	二茶匙半
熟火腿屑	一湯匙	清湯	五杯
麵粉	四湯匙	鷄油	一湯匙

做法：

1. 將鷄肉剔除鷄皮與筋後仔細斬剁，使成細茸狀（全無粒塊程度），放進大碗內加入酒半湯匙及鹽半茶匙拌攪均勻，然後將鷄蛋白加入一個再拌攪（需向同一方向攪）見鷄茸勻細後加入第二個蛋白再加拌攪，如此將四個蛋白全部陸續加進拌勻為止。

2. 鮑魚由罐中取出切成薄片（一寸寬兩寸長為標準），罐中之湯汁倒出留用（約一杯）。

3. 將鍋燒熱，放入豬油，待油微熱時加進麵粉用小火拌炒至勻滑後傾下清湯及鮑魚汁調拌均勻，用大火煮滾，放下鮑魚片並加鹽二茶匙，待再煮滾時將第一項之鷄茸慢慢傾入並加速拌攪調合，隨卽離火以免鷄絨變老硬。

4. 將煮成之鷄茸鮑魚倒進細瓷大湯碗內或深底榮盤中，淋下鷄油在面上再撒下熟火腿屑卽可上桌分食。

※請參考照片第38號。

Minced Chicken with Abalone Potage

Ingredients:

1 can Abalone (or 10 oz. fresh)	5 T. Lard (or peanut oil)
2/3 C. Minced chicken meat	1/2 T. Wine
4 Egg white	2-1/2 t. Salt
1 T. Shredded ham (cooked)	5 C. Soup stock
4 T. Flour	1 T. Chicken grease

Procedure:

1. Put the minced chicken meat in a bowl, add wine and 1/2 t. salt. Mix it well, then add 1 egg white in bowl at time, mix well between additions.

2. Remove the abalone from can and slice it very thin, about 1″ wide 2″ long. Reserve the abalone juice from can in another bowl.

3. Heat lard in frying pan (about 260°), add flour and fry a few seconds, add soup stock and reserved abalone juice. Mix thoroughly and bring to a boil. Add the sliced abalone and 2 t. salt. When it boils again, add the minced chicken meat. Stir fry briskly until thoroughly mixed. Turn off fire immediately.

4. Pour the abalone potage into a soup bowl, splash in chicken grease and sprinkle shredded ham on top. Serve.

---

* Refer to Picture No. 38.

紅燒海參

材料：

黑刺參（水發）	一斤半	鹽	一茶匙
葱	五支	糖	半茶匙
薑	五片	味精	一茶匙
醬油	五湯匙	太白粉	一湯匙
酒	二湯匙	清湯	三杯半
猪油	六湯匙	麻油	半湯匙

做法：

1. 將已發透之海參洗淨腹壁後放入鍋內，加入葱一支薑三片酒一湯匙及清水三杯，用小火煑二十餘分鐘以除腥氣。

2. 將海參撈出，倒棄鍋中之水等，另放回海參加入清湯三杯再煑十分鐘左右（小火）。

3. 撈出海參橫切成大片全部用二湯匙燒熱之猪油爆炒並加入醬油兩湯匙煨煑兩分鐘左右然後撈出，湯汁倒棄（因有腥味）。

4. 將猪油三湯匙在炒鍋內燒熱，放入葱三支及薑二片爆香，隨後將海參落鍋並淋下酒一湯匙，加入醬油三湯匙、鹽，糖味精與清湯半杯，用大火燒煑二分鐘然後淋下濕太白粉鈎茨拌勻，再澆上一湯匙熱猪油及麻油便可裝盤。

註：乾海參之發泡方法係將海參先用冷水浸泡半天，再置火上煑半小時，離火後待鍋中水冷却始取出，另換清水再泡再煑再待水冷揭蓋取出海參，剪開腹部挖除腸筋及砂質洗淨，再浸泡一天便可使用，唯浸與煑時不可用有油漬之鍋，以免海參溶化縮小。

208

Seacucumber in Brown Sauce

Ingredients:

2 lbs. Seacucumber (soaked)

5 Green onioni

5 slices Ginger

6 T. Soysauce

2 T. Wine

6 T. Lard or peanut oil

1 t. Salt

1/2 t. Sugar

1 t. M.S.G.

1 T. Cornstarch   (make paste)

1 T. Cold water   "

3-1/2 C. Soup stock

1/2 T. Sesame oil

Procedure:

1. Clean the soaked seacucumber, cook with 1 green onion, 3 slices ginger, 1 T. wine and 3 c. cold water about 20 minutes over low heat.

2. Discard the water, ginger and onion. To the seacucumber add 3 c. soup stock and cook 10 minutes over low heat again.

3. Remove and discard stock. Slice each seacucumber into 3 or 4 large pieces. Heat 2 T. oil and fry seacucumber. Add 2 T. soysauce and cook about 2 minutes. Remove and discard this sauce.

4. Heat 4 T. oil in frying pan, fry 3 green onions, 2 slices ginger and then add seacucumber. Splash 1 T. wine and 4 T. soysauce, 1 t. salt, 1/2 t. sugar and 1/2 C. soup stock cook about 3 minutes. Thicken with cornstarch paste, add sesame oil. Pour in platter. Serve.

涼 拌 三 絲

材料：

乾洋菜絲	2/3兩		
黃瓜絲	2/3杯	鎮江醋	一湯匙半
熟鷄絲	半杯	芝麻醬	二湯匙
熟火腿絲	二湯匙	鹽	一茶匙
芥末醬	一湯匙	麻油	一湯匙
醬油	二湯匙	味精	半茶匙

做法：

1. 洋菜買回後剪成一寸長放在溫水中浸泡十數分鐘，擠去水份放在盤內墊底。再將切妥之小黃瓜絲排在上面，然後撒下熟鷄絲，最頂面飾以火腿絲，放置冰箱中冰冷（時間不拘）。

2. 在一只小碗內將芝麻醬用醬油慢慢調溶，再加入醋，麻油，鹽，味精拌合留用。

3. 芥末醬係用一湯匙乾芥末粉加入少量溫水調合成醬狀，放置片刻至有辣味透出後便可使用。

4. 將菜上桌後即淋下第二，第三兩種佐料仔細拌合即可供食。

註：如無洋菜絲可改用粉皮或粉絲，鷄肉也可改用豬肉絲，其他材料也不限制，可酌量增減無妨。

※請參考照片第43號。

Chicken and Cucumber Salad

Ingredients:

2/3 C. Dried Agar Agar
    (or Vermicelli)
2/3 C. Cucumber shredded
1/2 C. Cooked chicken shredded
2 T. Cooked ham shredded
1 T. Mustard (Paste)

2 T. Sesame seed paste (seasoning
                                sauce)
2 T. Soysauce   "
1-1/2 T. Vinegar   "
1 t. Salt   "
1 T. Sesame oil   "
1/2 t. M.S.G.   "

Procedure:

1. Cut agar agar in 1″ long pieces. Soak in warm water about 15 minutes. Squeeze dry and lay on plate. Arrange the shredded cucumber on top of agar agar, then place the chicken shreds on top of cucumber. Sprinkle ham shreds on top, place in refrigerator to keep cool.

2. Mix the sesame seed paste with soysauce, then add vinegar, salt, sesame oil, and M.S.G. in a small bowl for seasoning sauce.

3. Pour seasoning sauce and mustard over salad. Mix all ingredients thoroughly before eating.

NOTE:

1. Other kinds of meat and vegetable may be used too.
2. Bean Vermicelli may be subtituted for the agar agar. In this case it should be soak in hot water longer.

---

* Refer to picture No. 43.

四 色 蔬 菜

材料：

蘆筍	一罐	鹽	一茶匙半
小多菇	十五個	味精	一茶匙半
（或草菇	一罐）	清湯	四杯
蕃茄	四個	太白粉	四茶匙
小青梗菜	三十棵	猪油	三湯匙
醬油	一湯匙半	鷄油	一湯匙

做法：

1. 蘆筍由罐中倒在大碗裏（連湯）上鍋用大火蒸熱（約十五分鐘）。

2. 青梗菜修切整齊（每支約二寸半長）放在開水內燙熟（大火兩分鐘）撈出用冷水冲涼並擠乾。

3. 蕃茄購買紅而較生硬又圓形者，先剝去皮後切成五大片（先切片再燙去皮也可）小多菇泡軟去蒂留用。

4. 在鍋內燒滾二杯清湯，放進青梗菜並加鹽一茶匙，味精半茶匙，猪油一湯匙煑約一分鐘，撈出瀝乾水份整齊排成兩個倒三角形（鍋內湯汁仍留用）。

5. 將蕃茄片傾進鍋內用煑過菜之湯汁煮半分鐘，隨後瀝出也排入菜盤中如青梗菜。另外排列蘆筍在其他兩處空位（湯汁不再用）。

6. 燒熱二湯油炒多菇，並加入泡多菇之湯半杯及醬油一湯匙半味精少許煑約兩分鐘，淋下太白粉一茶匙鈎茨堆置在菜盤中間處。

7. 將清湯一杯在鍋內煮滾，加鹽半茶匙，味精半茶匙調味後淋下濕太白粉二茶匙鈎茨，再滴入鷄油，便澆到多菇以外之三種蔬菜上即可。

※請參考照片第42號。

212

4 Kinds of Braised Vegetables

Ingredients:

1 can White asparagus
    (or 16 fresh green tips)
15 Small dry black mushrooms
    (or canned button mushrooms)
4 Medium fresh tomatoes
30 Green vegetable heart (2 turnips
    or 1 small cauliflower)

1 T. Soysauce
1-1/2 t. Salt
1-1/2 t. MSG
1-1/2 T. Cornstarch   (make paste)
1-1/2 T. Cold water   "
4 T. Peanut oil
1 T. Chicken grease (optional)

Procedure:

1. Place canned asparagus (with juice) into bowl, steam 15 minutes until hot.
2. Cut the green vegetable heart to $2\frac{1}{2}$ " long, cook in boiling water about 2 minutes. Plunge into cold water and immediately squeeze dry.
3. Peel and cut each tomato into 5 slices (4 from outside and 1 from tip). Soak mushrooms in warm water and remove the stem. (Reserve   is water).
4. Cook the green vegetable (or white vegetable) with 3 C. boiling soup stock, add 1 t. salt, 1/2 t. M.S.G. and 3 T. oil. Remove after 3 minutes using a strainer, let drain dry. Lay attractively on large round platter in 2 sections. Reserve the soup in frying pan.
5. Add tomato into the same soup (# 4), cook about 1/2 minute. Remove and lay on platter in 2 sections near green vegetable and discard the soup. Lay drained asparagus in remaining section of the platter.
6. Heat *2* T. oil, fry the mushrooms, add 2/3 C. of reserved mushroom water (or soup stock), add 1 T. soysauce, 1/2 t. M.S.G., cook about 3 minutes. Thicken with 1/2 T. cornstarch paste, pour in the center of the platter.
7. Boil 1 c. soup stock, season with 1/2 t. salt 1/2 t. M.S.G., Add *2 t.* cornstarch paste and cook until thickened. Sprinkle in 1 T. chicken grease, pour on the three kinds vegetable parts, not over the mushrooms.

NOTE:

    The beauty of this dish is its color. When using green asparagus, choose white vegetables for contrast (turnip, cauliflower). This should look like a wheel with the mushrooms as the hub, so a round platter is suggested.

* Refer to Picture No. 42.

北平辣白菜

材料：

洋白菜（即包心菜）或大白菜	一斤半	鹽	一湯匙半
紅辣椒絲	1/3杯	糖	五湯匙
薑絲	一湯匙	白醋	五湯匙
花椒	半湯匙	麻油	五湯匙

做法：

1. 將菜洗淨瀝乾水份後切成一寸多長之細絲，全部放在盆中撒下鹽拌勻，醃約四小時左右，再擠去鹽水放回乾淨盆中（或大碗），上面撒放切成細絲之紅辣椒及薑絲。

2. 將麻油在鍋中燒熱，先放入花椒炸香，再加入糖及白醋煮滾，待糖全部溶化後澆到盆中之菜面上，並迅速拌勻，蓋上蓋子，放置約四小時便可取食。

註：此菜如放置冰箱中可保存一星期，也可將菜切成較大之寬條製做則更形脆爽。

Sweet Sour Cabbage Salad Pei-Ping Style

Ingredients:

2 lbs. Round cabbage or   5 t. Salt
       Chinese cabbage   5 T. Sugar
3 Red hot peppers shredded   5 T. Vinegar
1 T. Ginger shredded   4 T. Sesame oil
1/2 T. Brown peppercorn   1/2 t. M.S.G.

Procedure:

1. Clean and cut cabbage into 1¼" long shreds. Put in bowl and sprinkle with salt, mix and soak about 4 hours.

2. Squeeze out the brine and discard it. Place cabbage in bowl, add the shredded hot peppers and ginger to the cabbage.

3. Heat sesame oil in frying pan, add brown peppercorn, fry until dark and good smelling. Add sugar and vinegar and bring to a boil. Pour this sauce over cabbage immediately and mix well. Cover with lid, soak about 4 hours.

NOTE:

This may be kept for 1 week in refrigerator.

著者在自設之烹飪班爲中外婦女授課情形（班址在臺北和平東路三段八九巷八號）。

The author instructing Chinese, American and Japanese ladies on Chinese Cooking in her home. She can explain with English, Japanese. and many Chinese dialects. (The address of her class is No. 8, Lane 89. Sec. 3 Ho-Ping East Rd. Taipei).

點　心　類

Snack and Desserts

第四十五圖（左）
Ⓐ豆沙鍋餅
Ⓑ四色燒賣
（做法參照第248
252頁）

Picture No. 45
(A) Sweet
Bean Paste
Pan Cake
(B) Four Color
Sho-My
(See Recipe Page
249,253)

第四十四圖（右）
ⒶⒷ餛飩
做法參照第218頁）
Ⓒ鍋貼
做法參照第224頁）

Picture No. 44(right)
(A)(B)Hun-Tung
in Soup
(See Recipe Page 219)
(C)Fried Dump
lings
(See Recipe Page 225)

第四十六圖　Ⓐ銀絲捲（做法參照第240頁）
　　　　　　Ⓑ蒸　餃（做法參照第228頁）

Picture No. 46　(A) Steamed Shredded Rolls　(See Recipe Page 241)
　　　　　　　　(B) Steamed Dumplings (See Recipe Page 229)

第四十七圖
八寶飯
（做法參照第244頁）

Picture No. 47
Eight Treasure Rice Pudding
(See Recipe Page 245)

四十八圖
肉大包
（做法參照第246頁）

ture No. 48
at and Vege-le Pastries
e Recipe Page 247)

Ⓐ **春捲** （做法參照第222頁）
第四十九圖 Ⓑ **什錦炒麵** （做法參照第250頁）
Ⓒ **杏仁豆腐** （做法參照第256頁）

Picture No. 49
(A) Spring Rolls (See Recipe Page 223)
(B) Assorted Chow-Mein Shang-Hai Style (See Recipe Page 251)
(C) Almond Jelly Chinese Style (See Recipe Page 257)

餛 飩

材料：

B（餡）		A（皮）	
鷄肉或瘦猪肉（絞碎）	六兩	麵粉（高筋）	二杯
鷄蛋	一個	鷄蛋	一個
靑梗菜（或白菜）	三兩	鹽	半茶匙
葱屑	一湯匙	清水	半杯
鹽	一茶匙半	太白粉	約半杯
醬油	一湯匙		
猪油	一湯匙		
麻油	一湯匙		

做法：

1. 在一只盆內將麵粉、鹽與清水調合，並揉搓至十分光滑，覆蓋上一塊乾淨白布，放置十數分鐘。
2. 在麵板上撒下太白粉，取出麵糰用趕麵杖推壓撚趕，使成大而極薄之餅皮狀爲止，再用刀分切成三寸左右之方塊，卽成爲餛飩皮。
3. 將絞碎之鷄肉或猪肉置大碗中，加入葱屑、鹽、醬油、猪油、麻油調拌均勻。
4. 靑梗菜或大白菜，剝下葉子用開水燙熟（約兩分鐘）撈出後切成碎屑，擠乾水份加入上項之肉餡中拌合均勻。
5. 將肉餡放進約一茶匙量在每一張餛飩皮中間，然後折覆手邊之麵皮，扭合另兩端，用力使其黏合，便成爲有兩尖角之餛飩。（約可包成五十多個）。
6. 在一個中型碗內放小半湯匙醬油，⅓茶匙鹽及數滴麻油或猪油，冲下一杯鷄湯（或以清湯加少許味清代之亦可）然後放進六個或八個羹熟之餛飩（餛飩之羹法係待水沸滾之後，將餛飩放入，蓋上鍋蓋，用大火羹，待水再滾時，淋下半杯冷水，再待其沸滾時便可撈出），將熟火腿絲，及蛋皮絲或榨菜絲各少許，撒在餛飩之湯面上，便可。

註：1. 餛飩之內餡可改用全肉，不必加菜，湯汁也可隨各人之喜好而加添其他材料。
　　2. 包成之餛飩也可用油炸熟，澆上糖醋汁拌食，（糖醋汁之份量，可參照粵菜中之菠蘿肶球）。

※參考照片第44號（A）、（B）。

218

Hun-Tung in Soup

Ingredients:

A. (For wrapping)
2 C. Hard Flour
1 Egg
3/4 C. Cold water
1/2 t. Salt
1/2 C. Cornstarch (for rolling)

B. (For filling)
1/2 lb. Chicken meat or pork
1 Egg
1 T. Green onion (chopped)
1-1/2 t. Salt
1 T. Soy sauce
2 T. Lard or peanut oil

Procedure:

1. Mix the A ingredients (flour, egg, salt and water) in a large bowl and knead until very smooth. Let stand about 10 minutes.

2. Remove the No. 1 dough to a board which has been sprinkled with cornstarch. Use rolling pin to roll dough again and again, turning dough 1/4 each time until very thin. Cut into 3" squares, to make Hun-Tung skins.

3. Place minced meat in bowl, add egg, green onion, salt, soysauce, lard and sesame oil, mix well. This is the "Hun-Tung" filling.

4. Place 1 t. filling in center of each square Hun-Tung skin, fold corner to corner to make a triangle, Pinch together the widest 2 outer corners so that the filled Hun-Tung folds up to resemble a childs paper hat.

5. Drop Hun-Tung into deep pot of boiling water, cover with lid cook several seconds over high heat when water boils again, add ½ cup of cold water, let boil up one more time. Remove with a slotted spoon.

6. In one medium size soup bowl, place 1/3T. soysauce 1/2t. salt and 1/2t. sesame oil, then add 1 C. boiling soupstock, place 6 or 8 pieces of cooked Hun-Tung decorate with 1/2 shredded ham and egg sheet on top of Hun-Tung. Serve.

NOTE:

1. A variation of this is to deep-fry the Hun-Tung and serve with sweet-sour sauce. Refer to Cantonese section, sweet and sour sauce dishes.

* Refer to picture No. 44. (A) and (B).

水　餃

材料：

麵粉（高筋）	兩杯半	薑屑	一茶匙
鹽	1/4茶匙	醬油	二湯匙
冷水	一杯	鹽	一茶匙
猪肉（前腿部份）	半斤	猪油	二湯匙
大白菜（或韭菜四兩）	半斤	麻油	一湯匙
葱屑	二湯匙		

做法：

1. 將麵粉盛在盆內，慢慢加進放了鹽之冷水，並用右手輕輕拌合，至水全部加完，便用力揉合全部麵粉使其成爲一糰，覆上一塊潮濕白布，放置十五分鐘以上使麵糰光潤。

2. 將猪肉剁碎（也可絞碎）放在盆內，加入葱薑及各種調味料拌勻，最後再將白菜剁碎成爲細屑狀，撒下少許鹽拌合並擠去大部份水份，也放進盆內再仔細攪拌至有黏性爲止。

3. 將麵糰移到麵板上再加以揉搓至十分光滑時，平均分成四十小塊，先搓弄成圓球狀，再用手掌壓扁並用趕麵杖趕成二寸半直徑中心稍厚之餅皮，將肉餡放進約半湯匙在中心部位，然後由手邊折合上半邊麵皮，再用雙手之大拇指與二拇指同時向中間擠合用力揑緊便可成爲一個水餃，（也可按包蒸餃方式製做）。

4. 在一只深底鍋中用大火燒滾十杯開水，然後將已包妥之水餃一個個迅速擲入（每次可擲二十個）用湯勺略加轉動一下即蓋上鍋蓋用大火煑至再度沸滾。

5. 淋下約2/3杯冷水下鍋後再加蓋合，重又煑滾並再加過一次冷水，待又滾沸時水餃便已够熟，即刻用漏勺撈出裝在盤內，趁熱上桌，食時可蘸用少許醬油、醋或辣芥醬，或大蒜泥等所調合之味料。

註：水餃之餡，可按各人喜好採用牛肉，魚肉或加入蝦仁，冬菇，海参等物。

220

Boiled Meat Dumplings

Ingredients:

2-1/2 C. Hard flour

1-1/4 t. Salt

1 C. Cold water

3/4 lb. Pork or beef (ground)

3/4 lb. Chinese cabbage
    (or spinach)

2 T. Chopped green onion

1 t. Chopped ginger

2 T. Soysauce

1 t. Salt

2 T. Lard.

Procedure:

1. Place flour in bowl. Add salt and water (slowly) mix with fingers and knead to form a soft dough, cover with damp cloth. Let stand for at least 15 minutes.

2. Mix meat, green onion, ginger, soysauce, salt, lard and sesame oil in a bowl thoroughly, then add chopped cabbage (sprinkle a little salt on chopped cabbage first, then squeeze dry). Mix thoroughly to make filling.

3. Remove the No. 1 dough to lightly floured board, knead again until very smooth. Divide the dough into 45 pieces. Flatten each piece with hand and roll into a round thin pancake (about $2\frac{1}{2}''$ diameter, the center should be thicker than edges). Place 1/2 T. of filling in center, fold over and pinch in center first. Hold in hand, grasp edges between thumb and index finger to seal, repeat other half with other hand press up slightly toward center, the shape is just like a paper boat.

4. Boil 8 C. water in deep pan, drop dumplings one by one into boiling water (each time drop about 20 dumplings). Stir carefully with large spoon to prevent sticking to bottom of pan and cover with lid. Cook about 1/2 minute until water boils up again.

5. Add 2/3 C. cold water in pan, cover and let come to a boil one more time. Add another 2/3 C. cold water, when it again boils the dumplings will be done. Remove the dumplings with a slotted spoon to plate. Serve hot. In small individual bowls place some soysauce, vinegar, red pepper oil or mashed garlic, dip the dumpling into the mixture and eat.

春　捲

材料：

瘦猪肉（或叉燒，火腿）	四兩	鹽	半茶匙 ⎱ 醃蝦仁料
蝦仁	三兩	太白粉	一茶匙
白菜	半斤	醬油	一湯匙
綠豆芽	四兩	鹽	一茶匙
韭黃	二兩	清湯	半杯
春捲皮	二十張	太白粉	一湯匙
醬油	半湯匙 ⎱ 醃肉料	麵粉	一湯匙
太白粉	一茶匙	花生油	六杯

做法：

1. 猪肉切成細絲用醬油、太白粉拌醃，蝦仁用鹽及太白粉拌勻，將白菜橫紋切成一寸半長之細絲，韭黃切成寸長留用。

2. 將五湯匙油在炒鍋內燒熱後先放下猪肉絲炒熟，隨後盛出，另用剩下之油炒熟蝦仁，也盛出放在肉絲中，將白菜絲下鍋拌炒並加清湯半杯羹兩分鐘，倒下豆芽用大火拌炒半分鐘後，淋下濕太白粉使汁乾稠便加入韭黃及肉絲、蝦仁拌勻盛入碗內。

3. 在每一張春捲皮中（光面向下）放入一湯匙半餡料，然後由手邊捲裹，捲到一半時將左右兩端折向中間，再捲成筒狀，封口處用麵粉糊黏住，排在盤內（封口向下）。

4. 將油燒熱，投下春捲炸黃（一次只可放下十個）大約三分鐘便可炸黃，供食時可蘸醬油。

註：春捲餡之材料亦可按季節或各人喜好變換與增減。與香醋，十分鬆脆可口。

※請參考照片第49（A）。

222

Spring Rolls

Ingredients:

6 oz. Lean Pork (or ham or roast pork)	1/2 T. Soysauce (to marinate Pork)
4 oz. Shrimp (shelld)	1 t. Cornstarch "
1/2 lb. Cabbage	1/2 t. Salt (to marinate shrimp)
6 oz. Bean sprouts	1 t. Cornstarch "
2 oz. Spring Onion (shredded)	1 T. Soysauce
20 pc. Spring roll skins	1 t. Salt
6 C. Peanut oil	1/2 C. Cold water
	1 T. Cornstarch (make paste)
	1 T. Cold water "
	1 T. Flour

Procedure:

1. After cutting the pork into string shapes, marinate with soysauce and cornstarch. In another bowl marinate shrimp with salt and cornstarch. Shred cabbage into string shapes about 1 ½ " long.

2. Heat 5 T. oil in frying pan, stir fry the pork about 1/2 minute, drain and put it aside. Use the same oil to fry shrimp until well done. Remove to bowl with pork. Add the shredded cabbage to the frying pan, stir fry a moment, add soysauce, salt and water, cover with lid, cook about 2 minutes. Add the bean sprouts, stir fry another 1/2 minute over high heat, stir in the cornstarch paste until thickened Then add spring onions, pork and shrimp. and remove to a bowl.

3. Place 2 T. filling on the spring roll skin, about 1 " from the edge that is toward you, roll once or twice, then fold right side toward center, then left side toward center, continue rolling into a tight roll. Stick outer edge of skin to roll with flour paste (to 1 T. flour add 1 ½ T. of water) Place with this side face down to hold tightly and to keep its shape until time for frying.

4. Heat the oil in pan, deep fry spring rolls 10 at a time. Use high heat, fry about 3 minutes or until golden. Serve with some soysauce and brown vinegar.

* Refer to picture No. 49. (A).

鍋　貼

材料：

麵粉	兩杯半	葱屑	一湯匙
開水	2/3杯	薑屑	一茶匙
冷水	1/3杯	醬油	兩湯匙
豬肉（瘦多肥少）	十兩	鹽	二茶匙
蝦仁	三兩	豬油或麻油	二湯匙
冬菇	三個	花生油	三湯匙
青梗菜（或菠菜或白菜）	半斤		

做法：

1. 將麵粉盛在盆內（或大碗），冲入開水，同時用筷子攪拌均勻，待兩三分鐘之後，加入冷水並用手調合揉成一團，放置十五分鐘以上，（如放置較長久時間則應蓋上一塊微濕之白布）。

2. 將豬肉剁爛（或絞軋也可），蝦仁切成小粒，冬菇用溫水泡軟之後也切成小丁，全部放在一只大碗中，並加入葱屑，薑屑與醬油，鹽，麻油，仔細調拌均勻，至有黏性爲止。

3. 青梗菜（或菠菜、白菜）不用切碎即投入開水中燙煮，約兩分鐘（菠菜可僅燙半分鐘）即撈出，瀝乾水份（需用冷水冲涼），全部切碎再略加擠除多餘水份便可加入上項肉料中同拌。

4. 將第一項之燙麵放在案板上加以揉搓並平均分爲四十小粒，每粒用趕麵杖趕成橢圓形皮子（約兩寸半直徑），放進第三項之肉餡一湯匙半，折合並捏緊半圓邊，使其成爲較長之餃子狀。

5. 將平底鍋在爐上燒熱，淋下兩湯匙油，待油熱後，將已包好之鍋貼順沿鍋之形狀排列進去（如用8寸直徑之平底鍋可排列二十個），用大火煎烤一下底面至結黃鍋巴爲止約一分鐘，便加入2/3杯熱水，（水中放一茶匙麻油及醋）蓋上鍋蓋用大火燒煮至鍋中水份完全收乾爲止（約三分鐘）。

6. 由鍋四週沿淋下一湯匙熱油再乾煎半分鐘，蓋上一個平底菜盤後先傾斜鍋子泌出鍋中多餘之油，再反轉一下使鍋貼全部落在盤內（鍋貼底面向上）便成。

註：鍋貼之肉餡所用材料不限定，可按季節加以變化時鮮蔬菜如白菜、小白菜、韭菜、葫瓜、四季豆等，肉料也可改用牛肉、羊肉、魚肉等，配料也並不限定用蝦仁和冬菇。

※請參考照片第44（C）。

224

Fried Dumpling

Ingredients:

2 1/2 C. Flour

2/3 C. Boiling water

1/3 C. Cold water

3/4 lb. Ground pork (not too lean)

4 oz. Shrimp shelled

3 Dried black mushrooms

10 oz. Cabbage (or spinach)

1 T. Chopped green onion

1 t. Chopped ginger

2 T. Soysauce

2 t. Salt

2 T. Lard or sesame oil

3 T. Peanut oil

Procedure:

1. Add boiling water to flour, mix with chopsticks, then add cold water, and knead it very well, let stand for at least 15 minutes covered with cloth.
2. Place pork in bowl, add shrimp (cut into small pieces), mushrooms (soaked in warm water first and cut into small pieces), green onion, ginger and soysauce, salt, sesame oil. Mix thoroughly until thickened.
3. Cook the cabbage in boiling water about 2 minutes, plunge into cold water squeeze dry and chopped finely, squeeze dry again, add to No. 2 mixture.
4. Remove the dough to floured board, knead again until smooth. Divide the dough into 40 pieces. Flatten each piece with hand and roll into 2 1/2 " round thin pancake, put 1 T. of filling (No. 3 mixtue) in center then fold over to make a half circle and pinch edges together. Stretch a little longer, carefully.
5. Heat a flat frying pan until very hot, add 2 T. oil, when oil is hot add enough dumplings to cover the bottom of the pan without overlapping (approximately 20 to an 10" pan). Move into an attractive flower shape. Cook until bottom is golden, (about 1 min.) add 2/3 C. water, cover and cook until water has evaporated.
6. Add 1 T. oil to side of pan and fry another half minute. Place a serving plate over the frying pan and invert the pan quickly. Now prepare the remaining portions. These may be kept warm by covering.

NOTE:

Many stuffings can be used (finely chopped beef, lamb, fish or vegetables).

* Refer to picture No. 44 (C).

炒　飯

材料：

小蝦仁	半杯（約三兩）	葱屑	一湯匙
叉燒肉丁（或火腿）	半杯	米飯	四杯
雞蛋	二個	鹽	二茶匙
豌豆仁	二湯匙	花生油	八湯匙
葡萄乾（可免）	一湯匙		

做法：

1 將蛋在小碗內打散，用兩湯匙油在鍋內炒熟，需攪拌散開，使成爲碎小之粒狀，便

　盛出在盤內留用。

2 另在鍋內燒熱三湯匙油，爆炒蝦仁及切成小丁之叉燒，並加入葡萄干（需先泡軟）

　及豌豆仁同炒，共一分鐘便全部盛出。

3.在原炒鍋內再燒熱三湯匙油，先爆香葱屑後，將米飯下鍋拌炒，洒下鹽二茶匙，用

　小火繼續翻覆鏟炒均勻，至十分香透後，加入上項已炒過之各種材料·再行拌炒至

　勻便成。

226

Stir Fried Rice

Ingredients:

1/2 C. Small shrimp
    (cooked or fresh)
1/2 C. Roast Pork or ham (diced)
2 Eggs
2 T. Green Peas
1 T. Raisins (optional)

1 T. Chopped green
4 C. Cooked rice
2 t. Salt
8 T. Peanut oil

Procedure:

1. Heat 2 T. oil in pan. Pour in the beaten egg and stir fry quickly until eggs are in tiny pieces. Remove from pan.

2. Heat another 3 T. oil, stir fry shrimp and pork, add soaked raising (abou 10 minutes) and green peas, fry about 1 minute and remove from pan.

3. Heat anther 3 T. oil in same frying pan, fry the onion and cooked rice, mix well. Add salt. Reduce heat & stir until rice is thoroughly heated then add 1 and No. 2 mixes. Combine well and serve on pretty platter.

蒸　餃

材料：

麵粉	兩杯半	葱屑	一湯匙
開水	2/3杯	薑屑	一茶匙
冷水	1/3杯	醬油	兩湯匙
猪肉	十兩	鹽	二茶匙
蝦仁	三兩	猪油（或麻油）	兩湯匙
冬菇	五個		
筍（或青菜）	兩支		

做法：

1. 將麵粉裝在盆內（或大碗），慢慢將開水淋下，並用筷子拌匀，待稍微冷却之後，加入冷水用手調合搓揉成一團，覆蓋上一塊淨布（微潮濕）放置十五分鐘以上使其醒鬆。

2. 猪肉切成小塊剁爛（絞碎也可），蝦仁切成小粒，冬菇泡軟後也切成小粒，筍煮熟（如用罐頭品可不必煮）也切小粒。將各種材料同放在大碗內，加入葱屑，薑屑與各種調味料（醬油，鹽，猪油），用筷子加以調拌攪匀至十分黏稠為止。

3. 將已醒過之麵糰，放在麵板上揉搓至相當光滑時，平均分成五十小粒。每粒均加以搓圓壓扁，然後趕成兩寸半直徑之圓形薄皮狀，托在左手掌並加入一湯匙餡料在中間，用右手折合並在後面捏成十數個小摺子包成餃子狀。

4. 將做好之餃子全部排列入蒸籠中（需舖上濕布在籠底），放在水已沸滾之鍋上（蓋閣蓋子）用大火蒸約十分鐘便成。揭開蒸籠蓋子，趁熱取出餃子排置在碟中上桌供食。

※請參考照片第46（A）

228

Steamed Dumplings

Ingredients:

2-1/2 C. Flour

2/3 C. Boiling water

1/3 C. Cold water

10 oz. Pork (ground or chopped)

4 oz. Shrimp (shelled)

5 Dried black mushrooms (soaked)

2 Bamboo shoots (or 10 oz.
   cabbage)

1 T. Chopped green onion

1 t. Chopped ginger

2 T. Soysauce

2 T. Salt

1 T. Sesame oil

2 T. Lard (or sesame oil)

Procedure:

1. Place flour in a large bowl, add boiling water and mix well. Add cold water, knead dough with hand until thoroughly mixed. Cover and let sit for at least 15 minutes.

2. Place in bowl ground or chopped pork. Add the shrimp (cut into small cubes) and mushrooms (after soaking, cut into small cubes), bamboo shoot (cooked and cut in small cubes too). Mix well, add green onion, ginger, soysauce, salt, lard, continue to mix a moment.

3. Knead dough on lightly floured pastry board. Cut or pinch off into 1″ pieces (about 40) flatten with hand and roll out thin to about 2½″ round (like a pancake). Place on palm and put 1 T. No. 2 mixture (stuffing) in center of pancake and fold into a half circle. Pinch the edges together forming darts only on the back half of the dumpling.

4. Arrange on cloth in steamer ring and place over boiling water. Cover and steam for 10-15 minutes over high heat. Remove from steamer and arrange attractively on plate to serve.

NOTE:

If steamer is attractive, it may be brought directly to the table for service.

* Refer to picture 46. (B).

單 餅

材料：

麵粉（高筋）	三杯半	冷水	半杯
開水	一杯	麻油（或熟花生油）	一湯匙

做法：

1. 將麵粉三杯量置在盆中，慢慢淋一杯開水，同時右手執竹筷加以拌勻，約候三分鐘之後，加入冷水，並用右手調合揉成一團，至無乾麵粉為止，蓋上一塊乾布，放置十五分鐘，（如需放置半小時以上則應覆蓋微濕之布，始可防止乾裂）。

2. 將麵團取出，放在麵板上，再用雙手搓揉至十分光滑為止。平均分成四十小粒，每粒用手掌壓扁，再兩粒為一組，其中之一粒在一面上塗抹少許麻油（或熟花生油），再兩粒合起用趕麵杖趕壓成五寸直徑之圓形薄餅狀。

3. 將平底鍋在爐子上烘熱後，放下上項趕成之薄餅，用小火烙約半分鐘，將餅反過一面再繼續煎烙半分鐘便熟（不必蓋上鍋蓋）。

4. 將煎烙熟之餅由鍋內倒出，放在盤內，並需馬上用手分揭成為兩張，置入盤中覆上乾淨之白布，以保持溫暖及柔軟。

註：這種單餅可同烤鴨或鴿鬆、金錢肉等上桌，以便捲裹而食。

230

Dan Bings

Ingredients:

    3 C. Flour (hard white wheat
         flour is best)
    1/C. Boiling water
    1/3 C. Cold Water

Procedure:

1. Add 1 C. boiling water to the 3 C. flour and mix well. Add 1/3 C. cold
    water. Knead the dough thoroughly until it is smooth. Cover and let rest
    for 15 minutes. This will have the consistency of yeast bread dough.

2. Working on a lightly floured board, divide dough into 2 parts and roll each
    15″ long and 2″ round; cut or pinch into 1″ pieces (about 40). Flatten each
    piece with hand keeping cut sides on top and bottom. Lightly oil whole top
    surface with sesame or cooking oil. Lay a second pancake on top of oiled
    surface, pat down a little then roll out both layers very thin, to about 6″
    rounds. Oil makes them easier to separate after cooking.

3. Using an unoiled pan heated to medium heat, cook pancake on 1 side until
    bubbles rise (about 20 sec.) turn and cook until light brown. Remove and
    separate quickly by pulling the 2 rounds apart very carefully. This leaves
    you with the 2 original layers.

4. Stack these separated layers in a pile and cover with a dry towel. When
    all are prepared, fold each one into quarters.

NOTE:

1. These Dan-Bings are always served with minced pigeon or roast duck.
    fried chicken slices or roast pork.

2. These may be made in advance, stacked, covered and refrigerated. When
    needed, warm in a steamer until hot then fold into quarters.

荷葉夾

材料：

麵粉	一杯半	發泡粉	二茶匙
豬油	一湯匙	冷水	半杯
糖	一湯匙	麻油（或花生油）	一湯匙

做法：

1. 將麵粉一杯半和發泡粉一起過篩後放置在麵板上，在中間撥一凹穴，加入豬油及糖，再慢慢將冷水淋下，同時用手指撥拌，使麵粉獲得平均潮濕而且與豬油、糖等混合均勻，再用力以手掌搓揉使成爲平滑而柔軟之麵團。

2. 將麵團平均分爲二十小粒，每粒用手掌壓扁，使成爲兩寸多直徑之圓餅狀（中間應略厚些），刷上少許麻油在半圓面，再復上另一半面，使成活頁式之扁饅頭狀。

3. 利用小刀或刮麵用刀片，在活頁饅頭上劃切交叉花紋，並推入兩角使圓邊成爲荷葉形，做好後全部排入蒸籠內，用大火蒸約四、五分鐘至熟便成。

註：此種荷葉饅頭除可夾香酥鴨食用之外也可用做夾金錢雞，焦肉代餅、叉燒肉等用

232

Steamed Flower Shaped Ban

Ingredients:

1-1/2 C. Flour   2 t. Baking Powder
1 T. Lard   1/2 C. Cold water
1 T. Sugar   1 T. Sesame oil (or Peanut oil)

Procedure:

1 Sift flour and baking powder on to a pastry board, spread heap to form a hollow in center, add sugar, baking powder lard and water. Blend all ingredients with fingers then knead the dough thoroughly until it is smooth.

2. Divide dough into 20 pieces (cut or pinch). Flatten one piece with hand (keeping cut sides on top and bottom). Brush oil on one half of top, fold other half over.

3. Use knife to score the top length wise and crosswise. Pinch in slighty the round edge at intervals to form a lotus leaf shape. Place in steamer on a damp cloth and cover with lid. Steam 5 minutes using use high heat.

NOTE:

This bun may be used with crisp duck, roast chicken or roast pork, and served as a sandwich.

蔥 油 餅

材料：

麵粉	三杯	蔥屑	三湯匙
開水	一杯	鹽	三茶匙
冷水	1/3杯	花生油（或豬油）	一杯
豬油	六湯匙		

做法：

1. 將麵粉盛放盆內，慢慢冲下開水，同時需用筷子將麵粉不停攪動，使水與麵粉得以調拌均勻，大約過三分鐘後，再徐徐注入冷水，並需用右手揉搓成為一光滑之麵團（用濕布覆蓋後，放置一些時間使其醒好）。

2. 將麵團分成六塊（也可再多分成數塊），每塊均需用手掌壓扁，再用趕麵杖趕壓成一尺大小之薄餅狀，將一湯匙豬油均勻刷上（或抹上），並撒下半湯匙蔥屑及半茶匙鹽，然後由手邊捲裹成筒子狀，將兩端先捏緊一下（以免油向外溢），再盤旋成螺絲形，並用手加以壓扁，稍加趕平，使成為約三分厚薄之大餅即成。

3. 取用一平底鍋（炒鍋也可）先燒熱兩湯匙油後，放餅入鍋，用慢火煎烙（加蓋鍋蓋）約兩分鐘後翻轉一面，再續煎烙至另一面也呈金黃為止（在煎烙過程中需將鍋時加顛動，以使餅層容易分離而鬆弛）。

註：此餅做成供食時可切開成數小塊裝盤，也可用手撕開而食之，十分香酥鬆脆。

234

Green Onion Pies

Ingredients:

3 C. Flour

1 C. Boiling Water

1/3 C. Cold Water

6 T. Lard or Peanut oil

3 T. Chopped green onion

3 t. Salt

1 C. Peanut oil

Procedure:

1. Place flour in bowl. Add the boiling water and mix with chopsticks immediately. Let cool. After 3 minutes add cold water and knead the dough thoroughly until it is smooth. Cover and let rest a while.

2. Remove dough to floured board, divide dough into 6 even pieces (or more than 6), knead and roll each piece of dough into 10" round as in making pie crust. Rub 1/2 T. lard on dough and sprinkle the whole top with 1/2 t. salt and 1/2 T. chopped green onion. Roll up as for jelly roll making sure the ends are tightly closed. Now form into a round snail shape tucking the final end into the center of the bun, then press down and roll out until 1/4" thick.

3. Heat 2 T. oil in flat frying pan, place the pie in and fry about 2 minutes. Use low heat and cover the pan. Flip over and splash 1 T. oil down pan side. Continue frying until this side is golden and crispy shake and jiggle the pan often while frying as this action makes a flaky pastry.

4. Cut into small pieces to serve.
   These may be kept in a barely warm oven until all are prepared.

馬 拉 糕

材料：

鷄蛋	四個	鹼水	一湯匙
黃砂糖	一杯半	發泡粉	二茶匙
牛奶（罐頭淡奶）	3/4杯	猪油	三湯匙
麵粉	一杯半	花生油	三湯匙

做法．

1. 將鷄蛋在大碗中打鬆（愈鬆泡愈好，但不可打硬）加入糖後再繼續調打至糖全部溶化，將牛奶倒進再輕輕篩入麵粉，順手調拌均勻，放置四小時至六小時以使其鬆醒。

2. 將鹼水一湯匙（係用兩粒花生米大之固體鹼，加一湯匙溫水溶化）及發泡粉（加半湯匙冷水溶化）合入上項麵糊中，並再加入猪油及花生油（需使用已燒過而冷却之乾淨油）拌勻。

3. 將上項材料倒入已放置四方木製模型中（籠底需墊舖一張紙）然後將蒸籠移置在沸滾之水鍋上蓋嚴用大火蒸二十分鐘便可。（如無四方模型可改用圓型鋁製模型或大碗亦可）。

4. 蒸好之馬拉糕由籠中取出，用利刀切成兩寸寬之菱形小塊，裝碟供食之。

註：如加入少許香精（或香草片）在麵糊中同蒸，則可增強芬芳。

Sponge Cake Chinese Style

Ingredients:

4 Eggs.
1-1/2 C. Light brown sugar
3/4 C. Milk
1-1/2 C. Flour, sifted

1/2 t. Baking soda (dissol..e in 1 T. water)
2 t. Baking Power (dissolve in 1/2 T. water)
3 T. Lard or shortening (room temp.)
3 T. Peanut oil or Wesson

Procedure:

1. Beat eggs until very stiff, add sugar and continue to beat until sugar disappears. Add milk mix well. Fold in flour, let stand 4 to 6 hours.

2. Add the dissolved baking soda and dissolved baking powder into No. 1 mixture then add lard and oil, mix well but lightly.

3. Pour the mixture into a greased cake pan 8″ round or 8″x8″x2″ square. Place in steamer to steam about 20 minutes.

4. Remove the cake from the pan while hot and place browned side up. Cut with sharp knife into 2″ squares, diamonds or triangle wedges and serve while warm.

NOTE:

1/2 t. extract of vanilla may be included.

237

叉 燒 包

材料：

麵粉	三杯	叉燒肉	半斤
酵母粉	一湯匙	醬油	三湯匙
溫水	$1\frac{1}{4}$杯	糖	二湯匙
糖	二湯匙	麻油	一湯匙
豬油	二湯匙	麵粉	一湯匙
發泡粉	二茶匙	太白粉	一湯匙
鹼水	一湯匙	水	半杯

做法：

1. 用溫水將酵母粉溶解後倒進用盆或大碗所盛之麵粉中用手揉合使其成為軟度適當之麵糰覆蓋一塊乾淨微濕之白布待其發酵（約二小時左右）。

2. 將已發酵成之麵糰（已澎脹為雙倍以上），在中間撥開一穴加入糖，豬油，發泡粉（加半湯匙水溶化）及鹼水（用半茶匙鹼粉或兩粒花生米大小之固體鹼加溫水一湯匙溶解），用手加以揉搓至光滑為止，平均分成二十小塊。

3. 用一只鍋放進醬油，糖，麻油，麵粉，太白粉及水，慢火煮滾使成糊狀，再將已切成二分四方大小如指甲片狀之叉燒肉放入拌合盛在碗內待冷備用。

4. 在每一小塊麵皮中（可用趕麵杖趕成兩寸長圓形或用手掌壓扁也可），放入一湯匙叉燒肉餡，將週邊捏成小摺在中心收攏便可。

5. 將全部做好之叉燒包在包底墊一張二寸四方之白紙後排入蒸籠中蓋嚴，放到沸水鍋上大火蒸約十五分鐘左右便成。

238

Barbecued Pork Pastries

Ingredients:

3 C. Flour
1 T. Dry yeast
1-1/4 C. Warm water
2 T. Sugar
2 T. Lard
2 t. Baking powder
    (Dissolved in 1/2T. water)
1/2 t. Baking soda
    (Dissolved in 1 T. water)

10 oz. Barbecued Pork
3 T. Soysauce   (seasoning sauce)
2 T. Sugar   "
1 T. Sesame oil   "
1 T. Flour   "
1 T. Cornstarch   "
1/2 C. Cold water   "

Procedure:

1. Dissolve the dry yeast in warm water and add to flour which should be in a large bowl. Knead with hands until very smooth cover with wet cloth, let stand and rise for about 2 hours.

2. Add the sugar, lard, baking powder and baking soda to the risen dough. Remove to a floured board and knead again. Cut dough into 20 small pieces.

3. Cook the seasoning sauce in a pan until thick, add the sliced barbecued pork cut to the size of a little finger nail (about 1/3″ cubes). Mix well for filling. Remove to a bowl, let cool.

4. Flatten each small piece of dough with palm of hand and roll out 2″ in diameter keeping the center thicker. Place 1 T. filling in center of wrapping, pinch pleat dough let all the edges come up to top center and pastry is round.

5. Put each pastry on white paper (the size is 2″ square) then place all of them in steamer and steam for about 15 minutes.

銀 絲 捲

材料：

高筋麵粉	三杯	碱水	一湯匙
酵母粉(一包)	二茶匙	絞肥猪肉（或熟猪油）	一杯
溫水	1⅓杯	白糖	2/3杯
發泡粉	二茶匙	熟火腿屑	二湯匙

做法：

1. 將酵母粉放進溫水中溶解後倒入盛在盆中之麵粉內，用手拌合並揉搓成軟度適當之麵糰，蓋上一塊潮濕白布使其發酵（約需三小時左右）。

2. 待麵糰發好（約有雙倍多時）在中間撥開一穴加入發泡粉及碱水（碱塊如花生米大小用一湯匙溫水溶化而用）再用手揉搓，由盆中取出到麵板上重加揉光並趕成一大片如薄餅狀，然後將絞肥猪肉與糖（需預先攪拌均勻），塗遍在餅皮上（全部）再由手邊慢慢推捲使成為筒狀。

3. 用刀將捲好之筒狀麵糰切成細絲，約每七，八絲做為一束，用雙手向左右拉長，（約一尺長）再將其盤旋成為上尖而底大之塔形，在最尖上放少許火腿屑點綴。

4. 將做成之銀絲捲置入蒸籠中用大火蒸約八分鐘即可趁熱裝盤供食。

註：此係湖南之名點與北方之大銀絲捲不同，冷後亦可再油炸而食。

※請參考照片第46（A）。

240

Steamed Shredded Roll

Ingredients:

3 C. Hard flour

2 t. Dry yeast

1-1/3 C. Warm water

2 t. Baking powder

1 C. Ground pork fat or crisco

2/3 C. Sugar

2 T. Cooked ham, chopped

Procedure:

1. Dissolve the yeast in warm water, add to flour and knead until very smooth to form dough. Cover with damp cloth, let rise about 2-3 hours.

2. When the dough has risen, add the baking powder, knead again. Remove to a lightly floured board, knead a few minutes and roll until very thin about 2 feet square. Spread with fat and sugar mixture which has been previously combined. Roll up tightly as for jelly roll to about 2″ wide and 2' feet long. Gently pat the top of the roll to flatten slightly. Cut the roll crosswise in narrow slices, using about 8 slices for each cake. Press a group of 8 strings together gently and stretch out to about 10″ to 12″, form into snail shape tucking the end in the top firmly. Cover with chopped ham.

3. Place cakes on damp cloth in steamer and steam for about 8 minutes over high heat. Serve hot.

NOTE:

These may be reheated the next day in steamer or deep fried.

* Refer to picture No. 46 (A).

核 桃 酪

材料：

胡桃仁	四兩	太白粉（或玉米粉）	六湯匙
白糖	六兩（約一杯）	花生油	三杯
鹽	1/4茶匙	清水	五杯

做法：

1. 在鍋內燒滾五杯開水，放下桃仁燙煮約半分鐘，即用漏勺撈出，瀝乾水份。（如用帶衣之桃仁，則需燙煮得長久一點，並連開水倒在大碗內，待水冷之後，將桃仁衣用手剝除方可使用）。

2. 將油燒至八分熱後，倒下桃仁，用中火慢炸，並不斷用炒鏟翻攪，約三分鐘，見桃仁呈金黃色時，即行撈出，攤放在紙上吹涼，分三次用臼或鉢搗碎成細粒狀。

3. 在一只深底鍋內燒滾五杯開水，並加入白糖，待糖水再沸滾時，改用小火，倒下已搗碎成細粒之桃仁，並拌攪，同時慢慢淋下太白粉（用六湯匙水溶解）使成為稠糊狀即可。

註：如搗碎桃仁無臼鉢之類，則可改用絞拌機或榨果汁機打拌唯需加一杯水與之同打

Sweet Walnut Soup

Ingredients:

1-1/2 C. Shelled blanched walnut
    halves

1-1/2 C. Sugar

1/4 t. Salt

6 T. Cornstarch   (make paste)

6 T. Cold water   "

3 C. Peanut oil

Procedure:

1. Boil 5 C. water in pan, add walnuts and boil about 1/2 minute, remove and drain dry.

2. Heat oil in frying pan and pour in walnuts. Fry about 3 minutes over medium heat. When golden brown, remove the nuts to a paper towel to drain. When cold crush in blender or mortar bowl very fine.

3. Boil 6 C. water in deep pan, add sugar and salt. When it boils again add walnuts and sugar. Stir well, thicken with cornstarch paste. Serve from pretty tureen at table.

NOTE:

1. To blanch walnuts pour boiling wate over them and allow to stand 5 minutes. Cool nuts and remove skins.

2. If using walnut meats rather than halves, cut the boiling and frying time.

八 寶 飯

材料：

糯米	一杯半	葡萄乾	三十粒
豆沙	半杯	桔餅	一個
糖蓮子	二十粒	猪油	三湯匙
紅棗	十粒	白糖	五湯匙
花生仁	二十粒	太白粉	一湯匙
桂圓肉	二十粒	桂花醬	半茶匙
靑梅	十粒		

做法：

1. 將糯米洗淨用清水浸泡五、六小時後，放進蒸鍋用大火蒸至熟透（或加入一杯半冷水煮成糯米飯也可），裝在大碗內趁熱拌入猪油二湯匙，及白糖二湯匙備用。

2. 取一只大碗，塗抹一大匙猪油後，將上列各種乾菓（大形則切成小塊），隨各人喜好依不同顏色相隔而整齊排列在碗底使成美麗圖案（或可排成福字或壽字）。

3. 鋪入三分之二量糯米飯在有圖案之大碗內，（需壓緊），並在中間做成凹形，以豆沙填滿凹處，再將餘下之糯米飯覆蓋在豆沙上攤平，即可放入蒸鍋內，隔水蒸二小時以上，取出後反扣在大圓盤中。

4. 在鍋中放一杯水及三湯匙糖，待煮開後加入用水調開之太白粉及桂花醬汁再用小火煮滾，使成為稠汁，即可澆在八寶飯上。

註：乾果之種類及份量不限制，唯紅棗需先用溫水泡漲，切片後方可使用之。

※請參考照片第47號。

Eight-Treasure Rice Pudding

Ingredients:

1-1/2 C. Glutinous rice
1/2 C. Sweet red bean paste
20 Candied lotus seeds
10 Red dates
20 Peanuts
20 Longan pulp or white seedless raisins

10 Walnut halves
30 Raisin, brown
4 pcs Squash candy or candied citron
1/4 C. Candied Orange peel
3 T. Lard (or ground suet)
5 T. Sugar
1 T. Cornstarch   (make paste)
1 T. Cold water   ″

Procedure:

1. Wash the rice in water until clean, place in deep pot, add same amount of cold water, use high heat, bring to a boil and cook about 3 minutes until the water is absorbed. Reduce the heat to low, cover pot with lid and cook slowly for another 10 minutes. Remove the rice to bowl, add 2 T. lard and 2 T. sugar, mix well.

2. Using a mold or 6″ bowl, brush the bottom with added oil (lard is better), lay all of the ingredients except rice very attractively in rows or other designs. Squash candy and orange peel must be cut in small pieces first.

3. Place 2/3 of mixed rice in the bowl carefully covering the fruit and nuts then put the sweet red bean paste in center. Cover the bean paste with remaining rice, flatten it. Steam the pudding for at least 2 hours. Unmold on a serving platter.

4. Boil 1C. water in pan, add 3T. sugar, make it sticky with cornstarch paste (1 T. cornstarch dissolved in 1T. cold water). Pour the syrup on pudding- serve immediately.

NOTE:

The kinds and quantity of nuts or fruits is optional, but dry ingredients should be soaked in warm water before using, All large ingredients must be cut in small pieces.

* Refer to Picture No 47.

245

菜 肉 大 包

材料：

麵粉	三杯半	葱屑	一湯匙
溫水	一杯半	醬油	三湯匙
發酵粉	一包（約二茶匙）	鹽	三茶匙
豬肉（前腿部份）	半斤	豬油或麻油	二湯匙
靑梗菜（或大白菜）	十二兩		

做法：

1. 將發酵粉傾入溫水中泡約兩分鐘，攪拌均勻後，倒進麵粉中，並用手調合揉成為軟度適中之麵團，覆蓋上一塊微濕之白布，放置一旁，待其發酵成為雙倍。

2. 豬肉切成如指甲大小之丁粒，放在大碗內，加入葱屑及醬油、豬油拌勻。

3. 靑梗菜（或大白菜）洗淨也切成小丁，全部裝進盆內，撒下鹽二茶匙略拌，放置五分鐘後用兩手握緊，使力擠乾鹽水，將菜加入肉餡中同拌至十分均勻。

4. 將已發酵完成之麵團，放在案板上用力加以揉搓，至十分光滑後平均分成三十小粒，每粒均用手掌壓扁，再趕成三寸直徑之圓餅狀（中間需略厚些），放進大約一湯匙半之菜肉餡，再提起麵皮外沿捏出許多小摺並在最後合攏成一圓包狀放進蒸籠中。

5. 待全部包子做好排入蒸籠後醒發二十分鐘左右，即可移在滾水鍋上用大火蒸約二十分鐘，趁熱裝盤便可供食。

※請參考照片第48。

246

Meat and Vegetable Pastry

Ingredients:

3-1/2 C. Flour
1-1/2 C. Warm water
1 pkg. Dry Yeat
10 oz. Pork
1 lb. Cabbage

1 T. Chopped green onion
3 T. Soysauce
2 t. Salt
2 T. Lard (or cooked oil)
1 T. Sesame oil

Procedure:

1. Place flour in a large bowl Dissolve yeast in warm water (about 95-98°F) thoroughly dissolved. Add to flour and knead about 5 minutes until well mixed. Cover with a wet cloth and let rise until double in bulk.
2. Cut the pork into small cubes (1/4" square), place in bowl add green onion, soysauce, sesame oil and mix well.
3. Cut the cabbage into small cubes too, then sprinkle in salt. Squeeze dry after 5 minutes, add it to pork and mix together.
4. Knead the dough on pastry board then cut into 30 small pieces, flatten each piece with hand and roll out thin about 3" diameter round pancake style, (keeping the center thicker), place 1½ T. filling in center of pancake. Pinch pleat dough so that all the edges come to top center and dumpling is round with a swirl design on top. Make certain this is closed tightly.
5. Let the shaped dumplings rest for 20 minutes. Then place on a wet cloth on steamer rack. Put rack in place over boiling water. Steam about 20 minutes.

NOTE: Many different stuffings may be used.

---

* Refer to picture No. 48.

247

豆沙鍋餅

材料：

鷄蛋	三個	豆沙	六兩
麵粉	一杯半	花生油	六杯
冷水	2/3杯		

做法：

1. 將蛋在大碗內打散合入麵粉加以拌勻，再將冷水慢慢加進仔細拌攪成濃度適宜之糊漿狀。

2. 用一只平底鍋，在爐上先燒熱後刷上少許花生油待油再熱，即將糊漿料傾入六分之一，迅速轉動鍋子，使糊漿流動成8寸直徑大之圓形薄餅狀，再用慢火煎熟（不必翻面），六張全部做好。

3. 將做好之圓形薄餅放在案板（或大盤子）上，再放進各⅙量豆沙在中間，用手指將豆沙攄壓使成為長方形（約二寸寬六寸長），折合四週餅邊包成長方形，用所剩下之糊漿沾黏封住。

4. 將花生油在鍋中燒至極熱，投下已包成長方形之豆沙餅用大火炸至金黃色而酥脆（約兩分鐘）為止。

5. 撈出已炸好之豆沙餅，用利刀切成六，七分寬之條狀，排列在盤內上席供食。

註：此種鍋餅也可將豆沙改為棗泥或肉餡（如三鮮餃子餡）。

※請參考照片第45（**A**）•

Sweet Bean Paste Pan Cake

Ingredients:

2 Eggs

1 C. Flour (hard)

2/3 C. Cold water

1/2 lb. Sweet red bean paste or
ground dates

6 C. Peanut oil

Procedure:

1. Beat the eggs in a bowl, add flour and cold water mix well until just like flour batter.

2. Heat a flat frying pan, rub on little oil, pour in 1/4 of flour batter. Tilt the frying pan quickly to let the flour batter flow to about 6" round very thin pan cake. Use low heat to cook a few seconds, remove from pan but don't flip over.

3. Place the pan cake on a board or large platter uncooked side up and add 1/4 sweet bean paste in the center. Spread paste out to 6" wide 2" long. Fold bottom edge up first, then fold left and right sides toward center making an envelope. Brush outer edge of pan cake with remaining flour batter and fold down, sticking together well.

4. Heat oil very hot, deep fry pan cake until golden and crispy about 2 minutes.

5. Remove from oil and cut into 6 or 7 pieces immediately. Place on plate attractively and serve hot.

NOTE:

Meat filling may be used in the same way.

* Refer to Picture No. 45 (A).

什錦炒麵

材料：

蝦仁	三兩	鹽	半茶匙	醃蝦仁用
鷄肝	一個	太白粉	一茶匙	
鷄肫	一個	醬油	半湯匙	醃猪肉用
猪肉	三兩	太白粉	一茶匙	
冬菇	四個	醬油	二湯匙	
筍	一支	鹽	一茶匙	
菠菜	二兩	清湯	二杯	
葱絲	1/3杯	太白粉	二湯匙	
乾麵（餅狀）	十二兩	花生油	十湯匙	
醬油	一湯匙	麻油	半湯匙	
麻油	一湯匙			拌麵用

做法：

1. 蝦仁加入鹽，太白粉（即醃蝦仁用料）拌醃　猪肉切絲用醬油及太白粉（即醃猪肉用料）拌勻，鷄肫，鷄肝均切絲或長薄片，冬菇用溫水泡軟後切絲，菠菜切成一寸長之段留用。

2. 乾麵放進開水中煮熟（約三分鐘），撈出後用冷開水冲過並瀝乾水份，盛大碗內加入醬油及麻油各一湯匙拌勻，再在炒鍋內燒熱四湯匙油傾下麵條煎酥（約三分鐘，需用炒鏟壓緊），然後翻過一面，並淋下兩湯匙油（從鍋沿）再繼續煎黃另一面，盛放在大盤中。

3. 用四大匙油炒猪肉絲（油不可太熱），至肉絲變熟即先行盛出，再用所剩之油，炒蝦仁至蝦仁轉紅而熟時。加入鷄肝鷄肫，冬菇及筍絲同炒，並放醬油，鹽與清湯煮一滾後即淋下調水之太白粉鈎芡，再將菠菜與葱絲落入鍋內拌合，淋下麻油便全部澆到盤中麵上即成。

※請參考照片第49（B）。

250

Assorted Chow Mein Shang-Hai Style

Ingredients:

4 oz. Small shrimp (shelled)	1/2 T. Salt	(for shrimp)
1 Chicken liver (optional)	1 t. Cornstarch	"
1 Chicken gizzard (optional)	1/2 T. soysauce	(for pork)
4 oz. Pork	1 t. Cornstarch	"
4 Dried black mushrooms	2 T. Soysauce	
2 oz. Spinach	1 t. Salt	
1/3 C. Shredded green onion	2 C. Soupstock	
1 lb. Dry noodle (thin or spaghetti)	2 T. Cornstarch	(make paste)
1 T. Soysauce (to marinate	2 T. Water	"
noodles)	10 T. Peanut oil	
1 T. Sesame oil "	1/2 T. Sesame oil	

Procedure:

1. Clean shrimp, add salt and cornstarch, mix well. Cut the pork into strings and mix with soysauce and cornstarch, slice the chicken liver and gizzard. Cut the soaked mushroom in strings. Cut spinach 1" long.

2. Cook the dry noodles in boiling water about 3 minutes, remove and immediately rinse with cold water. Drain well. Place in bowl, add soysauce and sesame oil, mix well. Heat 4 T. oil in frying pan, Pour all noodles in. Fry about 3 minutes, until the bottom is brown. Turn noodles over, splash in 2 T. oil around the edge of the pan and fry until that side is brown. Remove to large platter.

3. Heat 4T. oil and fry pork strings first. When they turn white remove to a bowl. Using the same oil, stir fry the shrimp. When shrimp turn pink add chicken liver, gizzard, mushrooms, bamboo shoots, soysauce, salt and soup stock. Bring to a boil and thicken with cornstarch paste, add spinach and green onion and fried pork mix well. Splash on the sesame oil, mix and pour over prepared noodles.

* Refer to Picture No 49(B).

四 色 燒 賣

材料：

高筋麵粉	二杯	太白粉	二茶匙
鷄蛋	一個	麻油	一湯匙
開水	半杯	胡椒粉	少許
豬肉	半斤	冬菇屑	一湯匙
筍丁	半杯	火腿屑	一湯匙
醬油	半湯匙	菠菜屑	一湯匙
鹽	一茶匙半	蝦米屑	一湯匙

做法：

1. 將麵粉放置在麵板上（或盆內）冲下開水，並用筷子拌勻再將鷄蛋打下，用手同麵粉加以揉合搓成軟度適中之麵糰。

2. 將豬肉絞碎或剁爛盛大碗內加入筍丁（先整支煑熟再切碎）及調味料（醬油，鹽，麻油，胡椒粉，太白粉）仔細攪拌成餡。

3. 將第一項之麵糰再揉搓一次並分成三十粒小塊，每塊用趕麵杖趕成兩寸直徑之圓形薄餅皮，在中間放進半湯匙許餡料，用大拇指與二拇指將麵餅皮交叉捏緊使餡料被裹在內部而上面呈四個洞孔狀。

4. 將四種不同顏色之屑料分別各裝入少量在每只四個洞孔中，排列蒸籠內上鍋用大火蒸十五分鐘便成。

※請參考照片第43（B）。

Four Color Shon-My

Ingredients:

1-1/2 C. Hard flour
1 Egg.
1/2 C. Boiling water
10 oz. Pork (ground)
1/2 C. Bamboo shoots (chopped)
1/2 T. Soysauce
1/2 t. Salt

2 t. Cornstarch
1 T. Sesame oil
1/4 t. Black Pepper
1 T. Dry black mushroom
    (Soaked and Chopped)
1 T. Cooked ham (chopped)
1 T. Cooked green cabbage
    (or spinach) finely chopped.
1 T. Dry shrimp (soaked and chopped)

Procedure:

1. Place flour in bowl, add the boiling water, mix with chopsticks thoroughly, then add egg, mix again and knead until smooth.

2. Mix the pork, bamboo shoots, soysauce, salt, cornstarch, sesame oil and black pepper in a bowl very thoroughly.

3. Remove the dough to lightly floured board. Knead and divide it into 30 small pieces. Roll each out 2″ in diameter, place 1T. filling (2) in center. Pinch up apposite sides of dough by joining in center only, then pinch up the remaining opposite sides to center forming a square with four holes. which looks like a four leaf clover.

4. Into one hole place a little mushroom, in the 2nd hole put a little ham, in the 3rd stuff in the cabbage and the 4th will contain the dry shrimp.

5. Place in steamer on a damp cloth and steam for about 15 minutes over high heat. Serve hot.

----

* Refer to Picture No. 43 (B).

拔絲香蕉

材料：

香蕉	四支（約一斤）		花生油	一湯匙
蛋	二個		糖	六湯匙
太白粉	四湯匙	做麵糊料	水	二湯匙
麵粉	五湯匙		花生油	六杯
清水	五湯匙			

做法：

1. 將蛋在碗內打散，加入五湯匙麵粉，四湯匙太白粉及五湯匙清水調勻，使成為糊狀備用。

2. 選購較生而直形香蕉，剝去外皮後，每支切成大滾刀塊，先撒上乾麵粉少許，再裹上前項調就之蛋麵糊，隨卽投入已燒熱之六杯花生油中用大火炸黃。

3. 另在炒鍋內，用一大匙油炒溶糖及水（二湯匙），並用小火熬煮使成為糖漿。至能拉出糖絲為止（初學者可以將糖漿少許滴入冷水中，若能凝結不散便可），旋卽放入炸好之香蕉迅速拌合，卽可裝盤供食。（盤內需刷油少許，以便易於洗滌）。

254

Candied Banana Fritters

Ingredients:

4 Bananas		1 T. Peanut oil	
2 Eggs	(make flour batter)	6 T. Sugar	
4 T. Cornstarch	"	2 T. Cold Water	
5 T. Flour	"	6 C. Peanut oil	
6 T. Cold Water	"	1 t. Sesame seeds roasted.	

Procedure:

1. Beat the eggs in a small bowl, add cornstarch, flour and water to make the flour batter.

2. Cut each banana into 5 diagonal pieces after peeling, sprinkle some added flour. Coat pieces with flour batter. Deep fry in hot oil until golden (about 1 minute). Remove the bananas and drain off oil from pan.

3. Heat 1 T. oil in frying pan, add sugar and water, stir fry a while over low heat, when it is like syrup and when poured makes a thread, add the bananas and mix carefully, serve immediately. (The serving plate should be brushed with some sesame oil).

NOTE:

1. Sprinkle sesame seeds roasted on the bananas just before serving.

2. To deep fry the bananas (Procedure # 2) and make the candy (procedure # 3) same time in separate fry pan is better.

杏 仁 豆 腐

材料：

洋菜（或兩包膠粉）	三錢	杏仁露（或杏仁精二茶匙）	四湯匙
冷水	五杯	冷凍糖水	四杯
糖	二湯匙	（四杯開水加三杯糖溶化）	
牛奶水	三湯匙	各種水菓丁	酌量

做法：

1. 洋菜用冷水冲洗乾淨後，置鍋中加入冷水五杯，用中火煮約十五分鐘。

2. 加入二湯匙糖攪勻後，即將鍋離火而過濾一次使全部湯汁濾在一只乾淨大碗或小盆中。

3. 待稍冷却後，加入三湯匙牛奶水及二大匙杏仁露拌勻，並候其完全冷却之後，移進冰箱中（如無冰箱，可放較涼處或多量冷水中）。

4. 約二小時後，見已全部凝固，成白豆腐狀時，即可端出，切成菱形小塊裝進大湯碗中（或分裝在小碗中）。

5. 將各種水菓丁，撒佈或排列在面上，然後倒下已冷凍過之糖水，並淋下另外二湯匙杏仁露，即成。（食時分裝在小碗中）。

※請參考照片第49（C）

256

Almond Jelly Chinese Style

Ingredients:

1/3 oz. Agar Agar

5 C. Cold water

2 T. Sugar

3 T. Milk (Canned unflovared)

4 T. Almond surup

   (or 2 t. almond extract)

4 C. Cold sugar water

   (4 C. cold water 2 C. sugar)

1 C. Diced fresh fruit (Assorted)

   (or canned fruit cocktail)

Procedure:

1. After cleaning the agar agar with water, squeeze and place in a deep pan, cook with 5 C. cold water about 15 minutes over medium heat. If using gelatin, dissolve the powder in 4T. water.

2. Add 2 T. sugar to agar agar or gelatin When the sugar is blended, strain into a big bowl.

3. Add milk and 2 T. almond syrup (or 1 t. almond extract) stir briskly until thoroughly mixed. Let cool and remove to refrigerator for at least 2 hours or until firm.

4. Remove the chilled almond jelly from refrigerator and cut into small pieces, then place in a soup bowl or individual dessert bowls.

5. Place the diced fruit on top of almond jelly pour in the cold sugar water and splash remaining almond syrup or almond extract. Serve.

NOTE:

A little of the canned fruit cocktail syrup may be added.

---

* Refer to picture No. 49. (C).

烹飪用料中英文名稱對照表
English-Chinese List of Foodstuffs

Abalone　鮑魚

Agar-Agar　洋菜

Almond　杏仁

Aniseed　八角

Apple　蘋果

Apricot　杏子

Banking powder　發粉

Bamboo shoot　筍

Banana　香蕉

Bean curd　豆腐

Bean curd, dried　豆腐乾

Bean curd, pickled　豆腐乳

Bean curd, strips　豆腐乾絲

Bean curd sheets　豆腐衣

Bean sprout　豆芽

Beef　牛肉

Beets　紅菜頭

Bird's nest　燕窩

Black mushroom　香菇

Black pepper　黑胡椒

Broccoli　芥菜花

Brown peppercorn　花椒

Brown sugar　黃砂糖

Brown vinegar　鎮江醋

Cabbage round　洋白菜

Catchup　蕃茄醬

Carrot　胡蘿蔔

Cauliflower　菜花

Celery　芹菜

Cherry　櫻桃

Chestnut　栗子

Chicken　鷄

Chineses cabbage　大白菜

Clam　蛤蜊

Coconut　椰子

Cooking wine　料酒

Coriander or Chinese parsley　香菜

Corn　玉蜀黍

Cornstarch　玉蜀黍粉

Crab　蟹

Cube sugar　方糖

Cucumber　黃瓜

Curry　咖哩

Cuttlefish　墨魚

Date red　紅棗

Duck　鴨

Duck's egg　鴨蛋

Duck's egg salted　鹹鴨蛋

258

English-Chinese List of Foodstuffs

Eel 鱔魚
Egg 鷄蛋
Eggplant 茄子

Fermented bean 豆豉
Fish, fresh 河魚
Fish, saltwater 海魚
Fresh mussel 蚌
Fresh soybean 毛豆
Frog 食蛙，田鷄
Fungus or Woodear 木耳

Garlic 大蒜
Ginger 薑
Ginkgo fruit 白果
Gizzard 肫肝
Goose 鵝
Grape 葡萄
Green Cabbage 小青菜
Green garlic 青蒜
Green onion 葱
Green peas 豌豆
Green pepper 青辣椒
Green small bean 綠豆
Green small bean strings 粉絲

Green small bean sheets 粉皮

Ham 火腿
Honey 蜂蜜
Hot bean paste 辣豆瓣醬
Hot pepper oil 辣椒油

Jelly fish 海蜇

Kelp or Sea weed 海帶
Kidney 腰子

Lard 猪油
Leeks 韭菜
Lemon 檸檬
Lettuce 生菜
Lima bean 蠶豆
Line egg or Thousand years egg 皮蛋
Litchi 荔枝
Liver 肝
Lobster 龍蝦
Loquat 枇杷
Lotus seeds 蓮子
Lotus root 蓮藕
Lung-gans 龍眼，桂圓

English-Chinese List of Foodstuffs

Mango 芒果
Moon cake 月餅
M.S.G. or flavor essence 味精
Mushroom 洋菇
Muskmelon 香瓜
Mussel 蚌
Mustard 芥末醬
Mustard green 芥菜
Mutton 羊肉

Noodles 麵條

Oil 油
Octopus 章魚
Onion 洋葱
Orange 橙子
Oyster 蚵；蠔
Oyster sauce 蠔油

Papaya 木瓜
Peanut 花生
Peanut oil 花生油
Peach 梨
Persimmon 柿子
Pigeon 鴿子

Pineapple 鳳梨
Plum 李子
Pomelo 柚子
Pork 猪肉
Potato 馬鈴薯
Prawn 明蝦
Pumpkin 南瓜
Pumpkin seeds 南瓜子
Prume 梅子

Quail 鵪鶉
Quail egg 鵪鶉蛋

Radish 紅蘿蔔
Raisin 葡萄乾
Rape 油菜
Red pepper 紅辣椒
Rice 米
Rice flour noodles 米粉
Rice glutinous 糯米
Rock sugar 冰糖

Salt 鹽
Salted fish 鹹魚
Salted jelly fish 海蜇皮

English-Chinese List of Foodstuffs

Salt peter　硝
Scallion　大葱
Scallop　干貝
Sea slug or Sea cucumber　海參
Sesame seeds　芝麻
Sesame seeds oil　麻油
Sesame paste　芝麻醬
Shark's fin　魚翅
Shark's lips　魚唇
Shrimp　小蝦
Shrimp dried　蝦米
Shrimp oil　蝦油
Small Cabbage sprouts　鷄毛菜
Small red bean　紅豆
Snow peas　豌豆夾
Soy bean　黃豆
Soy been paste　豆瓣醬
Soy sauce　醬油
Spiced bean curd　五香豆腐乾
Spinach　菠菜
Squid, fresh　新鮮魷魚
Squid dried　乾魷魚
Squash　南瓜
Strawberry　洋莓
String bean　四季豆

Sugar　糖
Sugar cane　甘蔗
Sweet poato　蕃薯
Sweet soy bean paste　甜麵醬
Syrup　糖漿

Tangerine　蜜橘
Tea　茶葉
Tomato　蕃茄
Turkey　火鷄
Turnip　白蘿蔔
Turtle　甲魚

Vermicelli　粉絲或乾米粉
Vinegar　醋

Walnut　胡桃
Water chestnuts　荸薺
Watercress　西洋菜
Water melon　西瓜
Water melon seeds　西瓜子
Wheat flour　麵粉，小麥粉
Winter melon　冬瓜
White soysauce　淡色醬油
Yeast　酵母粉

INDEX OF RECIPES

Chicken and Duck:

菜名分類表

鷄鴨類：

262

Pork and Beef: 　　　　　　猪、牛肉類：

Fish and Shrimps:

Other Sea Food:

264

魚蝦類：

乾貨、海鮮類：

Vegetables and Eggs: 蔬菜、蛋類：

湯 類：

(Contents of Snack & Desserts on Page 217)   （點心類目錄在217頁）

培 梅 食 譜
Pei Mei's Chinese CookBook

Writed by:

  Fu. Pei Mei.

Designer:

  Lawrence Lon

General Agency:

  Chinese Cooing Class td.

  (TEL 771700)

編 著 者：傅　　培　　梅

封面設計：龍　　思　　良

發 行 者：傅　　培　　梅

總 經 銷：中國京飪補習班

  （臺北市和平東路三段八九巷八號）

  （電話七七一七〇〇）

本書在臺零售價

新臺幣八十元 (NT$ 80.00)　　　　　美金二元 (U.S.$ 2.00)

港　幣十三元 (H.K.$ 13.00)　　　　國外訂購需加掛號平寄郵費美金五角

中華民國五十八年五月出版

著作權執照

茲據 傅培梅 聲請

註冊 培梅食譜一書 經依法審查

應准註冊合行發給 台內著 字第貳陸陸壹號

執照

計開

著作物 名	培梅食譜	編冊數
著作人 姓名	傅培梅	出生年月日籍貫 十二 山東省福山縣
著作財產人	傅培梅	
發行人	傅培梅	

右給 傅培梅 收執

中華民國 八月 日